Album

Pieces
of
Baltimore

The Ultimate Collection

Pam Bono Designs, Inc.

1

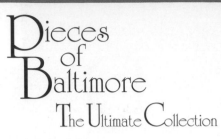

Pieces of Baltimore
The Ultimate Collection

Published by

LEISURE ARTS
5701 Ranch Drive
Little Rock, AR 72212
www.leisurearts.com

Produced by

Pam Bono Designs, Inc.
P.O. Box 659
Pagosa Springs, CO 81147
www.pambonodesigns.com

EDITORIAL STAFF

Editor-in-Chief:
Pam Bono
Editorial Assistants
Susan Clark and Nora Smith
Editors
Robert Bono, Susan Clark, and Tara Coronado
Art Director and Book Design
Pam Bono
Graphic Illustrations
Pam Bono
Photographer For Pam Bono Designs
Christopher Marona
Photographer For Zelda Wisdom
Shane Young
Photo Stylists
Christopher Marona, Pam and Robert Bono and
Susan Clark
Photo Stylists for Zelda Wisdom
Carol Gardner and Shane Young

Made in the United States of America.

Softcover ISBN 1-57486-402-5

10 9 8 7 6 5 4 3 2 1

Dedication:

To our talented team in Pagosa Springs; Susan Clark, Nora Smith, and Tara Coronado. Your hard work and dedication is greatly appreciated. Here's to an ultimate future, and a ton of fun for all of us.

Credits

Designs by Pam and Robert Bono. Apple Blossom Time quilt design by Pam Bono and Susan Clark.
Quilting by Mary Nordeng
Piecing by Susan Clark, Nora Smith, Margaret Ellsworth, Kim Zenk, Joan Lewison, and Tara Coronado.
Binding by: Carolyn Matson

Special Thanks To:

Sandra Case and the art department team at Leisure Arts for being so great to work with.

Sandy Medearis, Manager of the General Palmer House Hotel in Durango, Colorado. Thanks for opening your beautiful rooms to us for photography. Your hospitality is appreciated.

Robert Kaufman Fabrics for helping us to present your lovely collection in this book.

Husqvarna Viking Sewing Machine Company for the loan of our Designer 1 machines.

RJR Fabrics for your supply of beautiful fabrics.

Carol Gardener, Shane Young and the fabulous "Ms. Zelda" for your participation in this book to add joy and laughter.

Our friends Wanda Nelson, and Pat and John Nicholas for your continued friendship and encouragement.

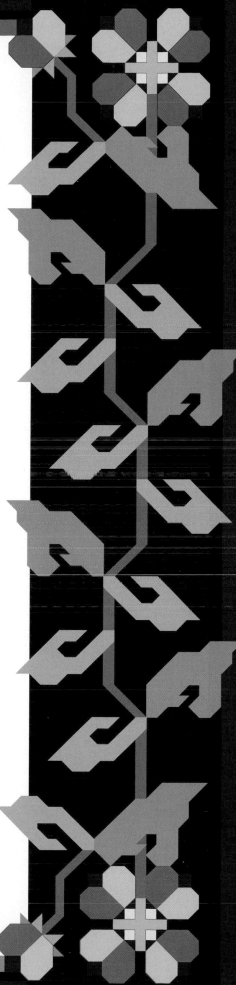

The twenty-four pieced blocks in this collection are all 18" square when finished. If you have made, or if you are planning to make the *Pieces Of Baltimore* Block-Of-The-Month, the blocks in this book are interchangeable.

Blocks can be made with any background that you choose. We chose to make the quilts with a black, and with a muslin background. Therefore all fabric requirements for both black and muslin are designated as "background".

If you are planning to use muslin, or a lighter colored background, we suggest making the *Love Birds*, *Sailing Ship*, and *Freedom* blocks with a dark background so that the white in the blocks does not fade into the background. With the exception of the three blocks mentioned above, all blocks are shown on both backgrounds in the block instructions.

There are two borders to choose from, and as all sashing is 2" wide (finished), the borders are interchangeable as well.

Study and practice our techniques if you are not familiar with them. The techniques that we use give the designs an appliqué look.

Enjoy!

Table of Contents

Learning Our Techniques

**The techniques that are shown on the following pages are used throughout projects in the book. Please refer to these techniques frequently, and practice them with scraps.

STRIP PIECING

Strip piecing anti-directional sewing

Cut strip set into segments.

For some projects, you'll join strips of different fabrics to make what is called a strip set. Project directions not only show illustrations of each strip set, but specify how many strip sets to make, how many segments are to be cut from each strip set, and the specific size of each strip and segment. To sew a strip set, match each pair of strips with right sides facing. Stitch through both layers along one long edge. When sewing multiple strips in a set, practice "anti-directional" stitching to keep strips straight. As you add strips, sew each new seam in the *opposite direction* from the last one. This distributes tension evenly in both directions, and keeps your strip set from getting warped and wobbly.

DIAGONAL CORNERS

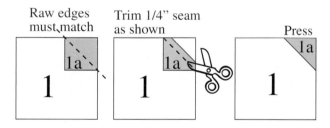

Raw edges must match   Trim 1/4" seam as shown   Press

This technique turns squares into sewn triangles. It is especially helpful if the corner triangle is very small, because it's easier to cut and handle a square than a small triangle. By sewing squares to squares, you don't have to guess where the seam allowance meets, which can be difficult with triangles. Project instructions give the size of the fabric pieces needed. These sizes given in the cutting instructions include seam allowance. The base triangle is either a square or rectangle, but the contrasting corner is <u>always</u> a square.

1. To make a diagonal corner, with right sides facing, match the small square to one corner of the base fabric. It is important that raw edges match perfectly and do not shift during sewing.
2. As a seam guide, you may wish to draw or press a diagonal line from corner to corner. For a quick solution to this time consuming technique, refer to our instructions on the following pages for The Angler 2.

3. Stitch the small square diagonally from corner to corner. Trim seam allowance as shown on the diagonal corner square only, leaving the base fabric untrimmed for stability and keeping the corner square. Press the diagonal corner square over as shown.

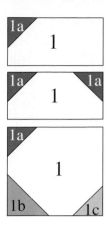

4. Many units in the projects have multiple diagonal corners or ends. When these are the same size, and cut from the same fabric, the identifying unit letter is the same. But, if the unit has multiple diagonal pieces that are different in size and/or color, the unit letters are different. These pieces are joined to the main unit in alphabetical order.
5. Many of our projects utilize diagonal corners on diagonal corners as shown below. In this case, diagonal corners are added in alphabetical order once again. First join diagonal corner, trim and press out; then add the second diago-

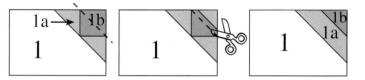

nal corner, trim and press out as shown.
6. Our designs also utilize diagonal corners on joined units such as strip sets. In this case, the joined units will have one unit number in the center of the unit as shown at right, with the diagonal corner having its own unit number.

DIAGONAL ENDS

Diagonal Ends

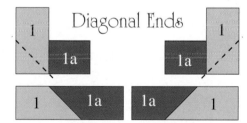

Diagonal End - Left Slant   Diagonal End - Right Slant

1. This method joins two rectangles on the diagonal and eliminates the difficulty of measuring and cutting a trapezoid. It is similar to the diagonal corner technique, but here you work with two rectangles. Our project instructions specify the size of each rectangle.
2. To sew diagonal ends, place rectangles perpendicular to each other with right sides facing, matching corners to be sewn.
3. Before you sew, mark or press the diagonal stitching line, and check the right side to see if the line is angled in the desired direction.
4. Position the rectangles under the needle, leading with the top edge. Sew a diagonal seam to the opposite edge.
5. Check the right side to see that the seam is angled correctly. Then press the seam and trim excess fabric from the seam allowance.
6. As shown, the direction of the seam makes a difference. Make mirror-image units with this in mind, or you can put

different ends on the same strip. This technique is wonderful for making *continuous* binding strips. Please note on illustration below, diagonal ends are made first; then diagonal corners may be added in alphabetical order.

7. Refer to Step 6 in *diagonal corner section*. Diagonal ends may be added to joined units in the same manner as shown below.

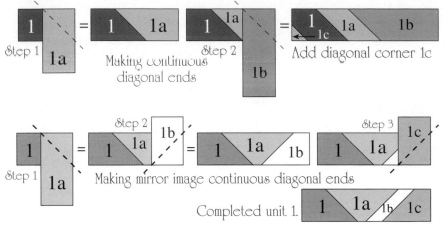

Step 1 — Making continuous diagonal ends — Step 2 — Add diagonal corner 1c

Step 1 — Making mirror image continuous diagonal ends — Step 2 — Step 3

Completed unit 1.

TRIANGLE SQUARES

1. Many patchwork designs are made by joining two contrasting triangles to make a square. Many people use the grid method when dozens of triangles are required in a design. However, for the designs in this book we use a simple way to make one or more triangle-squares. To do so, draw or press a diagonal line from corner to corner on the back of the lightest colored square.

2. As an extra tip, we have found that spraying the fabric with spray starch before cutting the squares to be used keeps them from distorting. A bit more fabric may be used; however, it is a quick and easy technique.

3. Place squares right sides together and stitch on the line. Trim the seam as shown and press.

4. The illustration at right shows how triangle-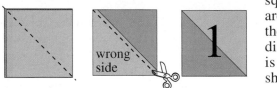square units are marked in the book. A diagonal line is always shown, separating the two fabric colors. The unit number is always shown in the center of the square.

wrong side

MACHINE PIECING

An accurate, consistent 1/4" seam allowance is essential for good piecing. If each seam varies by the tiniest bit, the difference multiplies greatly by the time the block is completed. Before you start a project, be sure your machine is in good working order and that you can sew a precise 1/4" seam allowance. Refer to instructions and illustrations for use of The Angler 2 in this section to aid with accurate seams.

1. Set your sewing machine to 12-14 stitches per inch. Use 100%-cotton or cotton/polyester sewing thread.

2. Match pieces to be sewn with right sides facing. Sew

each seam from cut edge to cut edge of the fabric piece. It is not necessary to backstitch, because most seams will be crossed and held by another seam.

SEWING AN "X"

1. When triangles are pieced with other units, seams should cross in an "X" on the back. If the joining seam goes precisely through the center of the "X", the triangle will have a nice sharp point on the front.

PRESS AND PIN

1. To make neat corners and points, seams must meet precisely. Pressing and pinning can help achieve matched seams.

2. To press, set your iron on cotton. Use an up-and-down motion, lifting the iron from spot to spot. Sliding the iron back and forth can push seams out of shape. First press the seam flat on the wrong side; then open the piece and press the right side.

3. Press patchwork seam allowance to one side, not open as in dressmaking. If possible, press toward the darker fabric to avoid seam allowance showing through light fabric. Press seam allowances in opposite directions from row to row. By offsetting seam allowances at each intersection, you reduce the bulk under the patchwork. This is more important than pressing seam allowances toward dark fabric.

4. Use pins to match seam lines. With right sides facing, align opposing seams, nesting seam allowances. On the top piece, push a pin through the seam line 1/4" from the edge. Then push the pin through the bottom seam and set it. Pin all matching seams; then stitch the joining seams, removing pins as you sew.

EASING FULLNESS

1. Sometimes two units that should be the same size are slightly different. When joining such units, pin-match opposing seams. Sew the seam with the shorter piece on top. As you sew, the feed dogs ease the fullness on the bottom piece. This is called "sewing with a baggy bottom."

2. If units are too dissimilar to ease without puckering, check each one to see if the pieces were correctly cut and that the seams are 1/4" wide. Remake the unit that varies the most from the desired size.

CHAIN PIECING

1. Chain piecing is an efficient way to sew many units in one operation, saving time and thread. Line up several units to be sewn. Sew the first unit as usual, but at the end of the seam do not backstitch, clip the thread, or lift the presser foot. Instead, feed the next unit right on the heels of the first. There will be a little twist of thread between each unit. Sew as many seams as you like on a chain. Keep the chain intact to carry to the ironing board and clip the threads as you press.

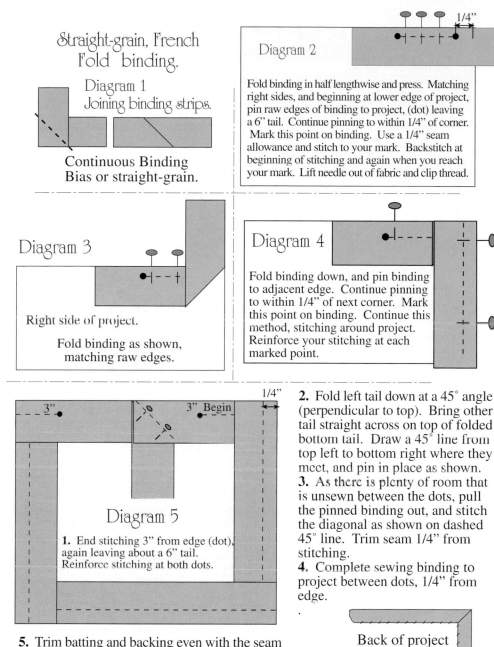

Straight-grain, French Fold binding.

Diagram 1
Joining binding strips.

Continuous Binding
Bias or straight-grain.

Diagram 2

Fold binding in half lengthwise and press. Matching right sides, and beginning at lower edge of project, pin raw edges of binding to project, (dot) leaving a 6" tail. Continue pinning to within 1/4" of corner. Mark this point on binding. Use a 1/4" seam allowance and stitch to your mark. Backstitch at beginning of stitching and again when you reach your mark. Lift needle out of fabric and clip thread.

Diagram 3

Right side of project.

Fold binding as shown, matching raw edges.

Diagram 4

Fold binding down, and pin binding to adjacent edge. Continue pinning to within 1/4" of next corner. Mark this point on binding. Continue this method, stitching around project. Reinforce your stitching at each marked point.

Diagram 5

1. End stitching 3" from edge (dot), again leaving about a 6" tail. Reinforce stitching at both dots.

2. Fold left tail down at a 45° angle (perpendicular to top). Bring other tail straight across on top of folded bottom tail. Draw a 45° line from top left to bottom right where they meet, and pin in place as shown.

3. As there is plenty of room that is unsewn between the dots, pull the pinned binding out, and stitch the diagonal as shown on dashed 45° line. Trim seam 1/4" from stitching.

4. Complete sewing binding to project between dots, 1/4" from edge.

Back of project
Diagram 6

5. Trim batting and backing even with the seam allowance. Fold the binding over the seam allowance to the back. Blind stitch the folded edge to backing fabric. Fold and mitre into the binding at back corners

HOW TO MAKE ONE BLOCK

Cutting instructions are given for making the project as shown. There may be times that you want to make just one block for a project of your own design. All you have to do is count, or divide if preferred.

With each cutting list there is an illustration for the blocks (s). Unit numbers in the cutting list correspond with the units in the illustration. Count how many of each unit are in the block illustration. Instead of cutting the number shown on the cutting list, cut the number you need for one block. Should you wish to make two or more blocks, multiply the number of units X the number of blocks you wish to make.

Using Our Instructions..

The following points explain how the instructions in our book are organized. You will find that all projects are made easier if you read this section thoroughly and follow each tip.

• Yardages are based on 44-45" wide fabric, allowing for up to 4% shrinkage. 100% cotton fabric is recommended for the quilt top and backing.

• At the beginning of each project, we tell you which techniques are used so you can practice them before beginning. Seam allowances *are included* in all stated measurements and cutting.

• The materials list provides you with yardage requirements for the project. We have included the exact number of inches needed to make the project, with yardages given to the nearest 1/8 yard. By doing this, we are giving you the option to purchase extra yardage if you feel you may need more.

• A color key accompanies each materials list, matching each fabric with the color-coded illustrations given with the project directions. We have made an effort to match the colors in the graphics to the actual fabric colors used in the project.

• Cutting instructions are given for each fabric, the first cut, indicated by a •, is usually a specific number of cross grain strips. The second cut, indicated by *, specifies how to cut those strips into smaller pieces, or "segments." The identification of each piece follows in parenthesis, consisting of the block letter and unit number that corresponds to the assembly diagram. For pieces used in more than one unit, several unit numbers are given.

• Every project has one or more block designs. Instructions include block illustrations that show the fabric color, and the numbered units.

• Organize all cut pieces in zip top bags, and label each bag with the appropriate unit numbers. We use masking tape on the bags to label them. This avoids confusion and keeps the pieces stored safely until they are needed. Arrange all fabric colors, in their individual bags with like fabrics together, making it easy to find a specific unit and fabric color.

• In order to conserve fabric, we have carefully calculated the number of units that can be cut from specified strips. In doing this, units may be cut in two or three different places in the cutting instructions, from a variety of strips. So that cut units may be organized efficiently, the units that appear in more than one strip are shown in red on the cutting list. This immediately tells you that there will be more of that specific unit. Additional cuts are not only shown in red, but the words "add to" are shown within the parenthesis so you may keep that zip top bag open, knowing in advance there will be more units to add. "Stack this cut" will appear frequently in the cutting instructions. Refer to the drawing below. We utilize the width of the strip with the first unit to be cut; then other units can be stacked on top of each other to best utilize the strips.

"Stack this cut......."

2"	Cut #1 two 1" x 2"	Cut #2 stacked. four 1" x 3"	Cut #3 two 1 3/4" squares

2" wide strip. Do not cut strips down unless directed.

• Large pieces such as sashing and borders are generally cut first to assure you have enough fabric. To reduce further waste of fabric, you may be instructed to cut some pieces from a first-cut strip, and then cut that strip down to a narrower width to cut additional pieces.

• Cutting and piecing instructions are given in a logical step-by-step progression. Follow this order always to avoid having to rip out in some cases. Although there are many assembly graphics, we strongly suggest reading the written instructions along with looking at the graphics.

• Individual units are assembled first. Use one or more of the "quick piecing" techniques described on pages 6 and 7.

• Strip set illustrations show the size of the segments to be cut from that strip set. The illustration also designates how many strip sets are to be made, and the size of the strips. The strip set segments are then labeled as units within the block illustration. Keep strip set segments in their own labeled zip top bag.

• Each unit in the assembly diagram is numbered. The main part of the unit is indicated with a number only. A diagonal line represents a seam where a diagonal corner or end is attached. Each diagonal piece is numbered with the main unit number plus a letter (example: 1a).

• Many extra illustrations are given throughout the projects for assembly of unusual or multiple units for more clarity.

Robert invented the first Angler between our first and second books for Oxmoor House/Leisure Arts. He watched me drawing diagonal line seam guides that took forever! He said: "There has got to be a quicker way!" He found a quicker way. This little tool is now used by millions of quilters all over the world with results that cut piecing time in half, after a bit of practice. The instructions and illustrations are shown for the new upgrade, allowing you to make up to 7 3/4" squares. It can be purchased where ever sewing notions are sold.

DIAGONAL CORNERS & FLYING GEESE

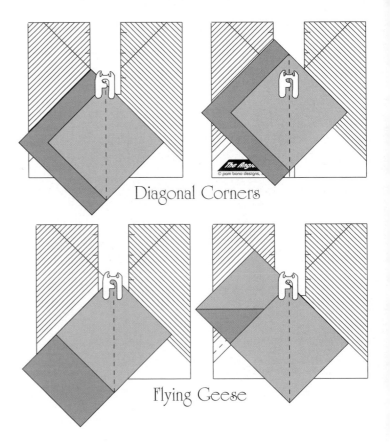

Diagonal Corners

Flying Geese

1. Align diagonal corners with raw edges matching. Line fabric up so that right side of square is aligned with first 45° line on right as shown above, with the tip of the fabric under the needle. No seam guide lines will need to be drawn unless the square is larger than 7 3/4". As feed dogs pull the fabric through the machine, keep fabric aligned with the diagonal lines on the right until center line of The Angler 2 bottom is visible.

2. Keep the tip of the square on this line as the diagonal corner is fed through the machine. Trim seam as shown in our "quick piecing" technique section and press.

3. For Flying Geese, sew first diagonal corner. Trim seam and press; then join second diagonal corner. Trim seam and press. Overlap will give you an accurate 1/4" seam allowance.

DIAGONAL ENDS

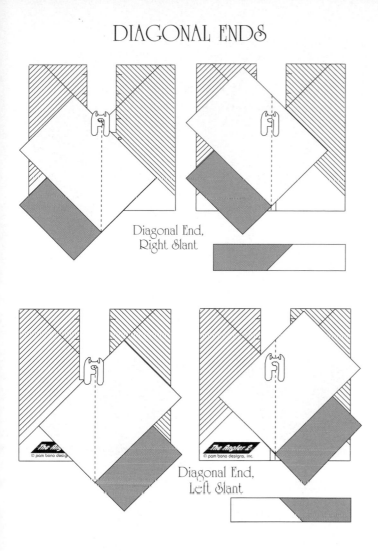

Diagonal End,
Right Slant

Diagonal End,
Left Slant

1. For both slants, prepare rectangles with raw edges matching. For right slant, align top rectangle with the first 45° line on right side of The Angler 2.

2. Bottom rectangle should align on first 45° left line as shown. As feed dogs pull fabric through machine, keep fabric aligned with the diagonal lines on the right until center line on The Angler 2 bottom is visible. Keep the top of the rectangle on this line as it is fed through the machine. Trim seam and press.

3. For left slant, line top rectangle up with the first 45° line on left side of The Angler 2 as shown. As rectangles are fed through the machine, keep top rectangle aligned with left diagonal lines on The Angler 2. This technique is great for joining binding strips.

ACCURATE 1/4" SEAMS

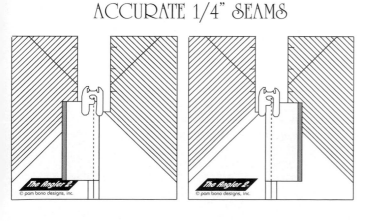

Fabric is lined up on the computer generated 1/4" seam line on The Angler 2, and stitching is along center guide line. To take a full 1/4" seam, line fabric up on 1/4" seam line. If you want a "scant" 1/4" seam, line fabric up so that the seam guide line shows. We recommend a "scant" 1/4" seam as your seams end up being more accurate after they are pressed.

When using the Angler 2, watch the point of your fabric on the center line - NOT the needle!

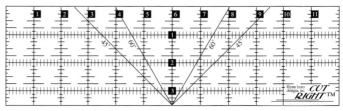

Your cutting time is cut in half with our practical rulers that minimize cutting errors.

Dear Quilting Friends,

Out of all of the different shapes and sizes of rulers that I have, I still make mistakes in my cutting, especially the 1/8" measurements; 1/8", 3/8", 5/8" and 7/8".

In talking to other quilters, it seems to be a common problem. Our new line of Pam Bono Designs rulers has helped me, and our quilting friends, especially with our changing eyesight.

Sizes:
3 1/2" x 12"
6 1/2" x 18"
8" x 24"

EMBROIDERY CHAIN STITCH

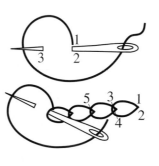

We have used this stitch throughout many of the blocks in this book. Follow the diagrams at left. This is a looped stitch with each loop or link being secured to the fabric by the next link. It can be worked along a straight line or in a circle. Come up at 1 and swing thread in a counterclockwise direction under the needle tip. Insert the needle at 2, one or two threads away from 1. Come up at 3 and pull thread through, keeping loop beneath point of needle. Pull until loop is desired fullness. Continue down at r and up at 5 until desired number of loops is completed. Anchor end of chain by inserting needle over top of loop, close to previous exit point.

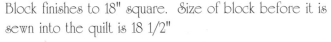

The Album Block

Block finishes to 18" square. Size of block before it is sewn into the quilt is 18 1/2"

MATERIALS

 Fabric I (background)
Need 8 5/8"   3/8 yard

 Fabric II (light peach print)
Need 3 1/2"   1/4 yard

 Fabric III (medium peach print)
Need 3 3/4"   1/4 yard

 Fabric IV (light green print)
Need 2 1/8"   1/8 yard

 Fabric V (medium green print)
Need 3 3/8"   1/4 yard

 Fabric VI (rust print)
Need 3 1/4"   1/4 yard

 Fabric VII (gold print)
Need 1 3/4"   1/8 yard

□ Fabric VIII (white on ivory print)
Need large scrap

CUTTING

□   **From Fabric I, cut: (background)**
- One 3 3/4" wide strip. From this, cut:
  * Two - 1" x 3 3/4" (D108, E108)
  * One - 3 5/8" square (D113)
  * Two - 3 1/8" x 3 5/8" (D92, E92)
  * One - 3" x 3 5/8" (E119)
  * Two - 2 1/2" x 3 5/8" (D109, E109)
  * One - 2 1/8" x 2 7/8" (A21)
  * One - 1 5/8" x 2 7/8" (A11)
  * One - 1 3/8" x 2 7/8" (A10)
  * One - 1 1/4" x 2 3/8" (A35)
  * One - 2 1/8" x 2 3/4" (C75)
  * Two - 2 1/2" squares (D107, E107)
  * One - 2 1/4" x 8" (C83)
- One 2 3/8" wide strip. From this, cut:
  * Two - 1 1/8" x 2 3/8" (D93, E93)
  * One - 2 1/8" square (A38)
  * One - 1 5/8" x 2 1/8" (C80)
  * One - 1 3/8" x 2 1/8" (E116)
  * Four - 1 7/8" squares (A33, A37, D91, E91)
  * Two - 1 5/8" x 1 7/8" (D96, E96)
  * Two - 1 1/8" x 1 7/8" (D104, E104)
  * One - 1 3/4" square (A27)
  * One - 1 1/2" x 1 3/4" (A29)
  * Five - 1 5/8" squares (C74, C81, D98a, E98a, E114c)
  * Two - 1 1/2" squares (C71c, D110a)
  * One - 1 1/2" x 4" (A22)

* One - 1 1/4" x 3" (A41)
- One 1 3/8" wide strip. From this, cut:
  * Six - 1 3/8" squares (A3b, C89, D90a, E90a, D112a)
  * Three - 1 3/8" x 1 3/4" (A9, C88)
  * Sixteen- 1 1/4" squares (A7, A18a, A20a,A39a, C77, C78a, C86b, D95b, E95b, D98b, E98b, D102a, E102a)
  * One - 1 1/8" x 1 1/4" (D111a)
  * One - 1" x 1 1/4" (A40)
  * One - 1 1/8" x 1 1/2" (E118)
  * One - 1" x 2 3/4" (E115)
- One 1 1/8" wide strip. From this, cut:
  * Eight - 1 1/8" squares (A2a, A8a, C72a, D95a, E95a, D103a, E103a, E117a)
  * Eight - 1" squares (A15a, A17, A28a, C79a, C82a, D90b, E90b)

From Fabric II, cut: (light peach print)
- One 2 1/4" wide strip. From this, cut:
  * One - 2 1/4" x 3 3/8" (A1)
  * Two - 2 1/4" x 2 3/8" (D98, E98)
  * One - 1 1/2" x 2 1/4" (A3)
  * Two - 2 1/8" x 2 5/8" (C84)
  * One - 1 3/4" x 2 3/4" (A23)
  * One - 1 3/4" square (A15)
  * One - 1 1/2" x 1 3/4" (A12)
  * One - 1 5/8" x 2 3/4" (E114)
  * Two - 1 1/2" x 2 5/8" (B67)
  * Two - 1 1/2" x 2 1/2" (C71, D110)
  * One - 1 1/4" x 1 1/2" (A26)
  * Two - 1 3/8" x 3 1/8" (C78)
- One 1 1/4" wide strip. From this, cut:
  * Two - 1 1/4" x 2 1/2" (D97, E97)
  * Four - 1 1/4" squares (C76a, C77)
  * One - 1" x 1 1/4" (B52)
  * Two - 1 1/8" x 1 3/8" (D99, E99)
  * One - 1" x 1 3/4" (B56)
  * One - 1" x 1 1/8" (A14)
  * One - 1" square (A24b)

From Fabric III, cut: (medium peach print)
- One 2 3/8" wide strip. From this, cut:
  * One - 1 1/8" x 2 3/8" (D111)
  * Two - 1 7/8" x 2 1/8" (C79)
  * One - 1 5/8" x 2 1/8" (D112)
  * One - 1 1/2" x 2 1/8" (A3a)
  * Two - 1 3/4" x 1 7/8" (D95, E95)
  * Two - 1 1/2" x 1 7/8" (D101, E101)
  * Two - 1 3/4" squares (D90c, E90c)
  * One - 1" x 1 3/4" (B59)
  * One - 1 1/2" x 1 5/8" (B49)
  * Five - 1 1/2" squares (A1a, B47a, B54, D98c, E98c)
  * Two - 1 1/4" x 2 1/4" (A25, A39)
  * Two - 1 1/4" x 2 3/8" (C76)
  * Two - 1" x 1 1/2" (A24, C73)
- One 1 3/8" wide strip. From this and scrap, cut:
  * One - 1 3/8" square (E114a)
  * Two - 1 1/4" x 1 3/8" (D100, E100)
  * Eight - 1 1/4" squares (A1b, A3c, A12a, A26a, C71b, D97a, E97a, E114b)
  * One - 1 1/8" x 3 3/8" (A2)
  * One - 1 1/8" x 3" (C72)
  * Three - 1 1/8" x 2 5/8" (C85, E117)
  * One - 1 1/8" x 1 1/4" (A13)
  * Two - 1" x 1 7/8" (B67a)
  * Two - 1" x 1 1/8" (D94, E94)
  * Four - 1 1/8" squares (C84a, D110b)
  * Seven - 1" squares (B47b, B60a, B66a, C71a, C80a, C81b)

From Fabric IV, cut: (light green print)
- One 2 1/8" wide strip. From this, cut:
  * One - 2 1/8" square (A18b)
  * One - 1 7/8" x 2" (A30)
  * One - 1 3/4" square (A15)
  * Two - 1 5/8" x 3 7/8" (D106, E106)
  * Two - 1 3/8" squares (C86a)
  * One - 1 1/8" x 1 3/8" (A8)
  * Seven - 1 1/4" squares (A20a, A23a, D102b, E102b, D103b, E103b, D112b)
  * Two - 1 1/8" x 2 3/8" (C87)
  * One - 1 1/8" x 2 1/4" (A31)
  * Two - 1 1/8" squares (C85a)
  * One - 1" x 2 3/8" (A6)
  * One - 1" x 1 1/2" (A5)
  * One - 1" x 1 1/4" (A16)
  * Three - 1" squares (A4a, A14a)

From Fabric V, cut: (medium green print)
- One 2 3/8" wide strip. From this, cut:
  * One - 2 1/8" x 2 3/8" (A18)
  * Two - 2" x 2 3/8" (C86)
  * One - 1 1/4" x 2 3/8" (A20)
  * One - 1 1/8" x 2 3/8" (A34)
  * Two - 1 7/8" x 2 1/4" (D90, E90)
  * One - 1 1/4" x 2 1/4" (A32)
  * Two - 1 3/4" x 2" (D103, E103)
  * One - 1 1/2" x 1 7/8" (A4)
  * Two - 1 3/8" squares (C89)
  * Two - 1 3/8" x 1 7/8" (D105, E105)
  * Two - 1 1/4" x 2" (D102, E102)
  * Six - 1 1/4" squares (A23b, A29a, A30a, A37a, A39b)
  * One - 1 1/4" x 1 1/2" (A28)
  * Six - 1 1/8" squares (A21a, A37b, C87a, D104a, E104a)
- One 1" wide strip. From this, cut:
  * One - 1" x 3 1/4" (A36)
  * One - 1" x 1 5/8" (C82)
  * One - 1" x 1 1/4" (A24a)
  * Two - 1" x 1 1/8" (D108a, E108a)
  * Four - 1" squares (C73a, C81a, D101a, E101a)

From Fabric VI, cut: (rust print)
- One 2 1/4" wide strip. From this, cut:
  * Two - 2 1/4" x 4" (B43)
  * One - 2 1/4" x 3 3/8" (B47)
  * One - 1 1/2" x 2 1/4" (B60)
  * Three - 1" x 2 1/4" (B53, B57, B65)
  * Four - 2" squares (B42a)
  * One - 2" x 7 1/4" (B66)
  * One - 1 3/4" square (B58)
  * One - 1" x 1 3/4" (B64)
  * One - 1 1/4" x 1 5/8" (B48)
- One 1" wide strip. From this, cut:
  * Thirteen - 1" x 1 1/4" (B44, B46, B51, B62, B70)
  * Three - 1" squares (B56a, B68)

From Fabric VII, cut: (gold print)
- One 1 3/4" wide strip. From this, cut:
  * Two - 1 3/4" squares (B55, B63)
  * Two - 1" x 1 3/4" (B69)
  * Six - 1 1/4" squares (B45, B50, B61)
  * Two - 1" x 1 7/8" (B67a)

From Fabric VIII, cut: (white on ivory print)
- One 5 1/2" x 8 3/4" (B42)

11

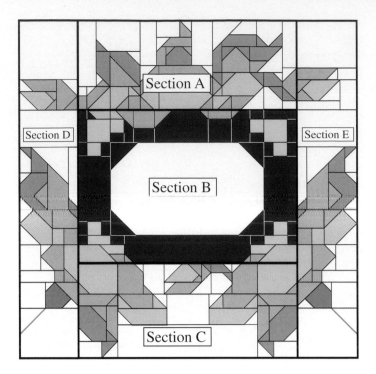

Section A
Section D
Section E
Section B
Section C

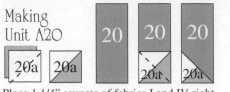

Making Unit A20

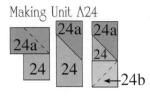

20a 20a 20 20 20
20a 20a

Place 1 1/4" squares of fabrics I and IV sides facing and raw edges matching. Stitch diagonal down the center as shown. Trim seam, open, and press. Use this triangle-square for diagonal corner A20a.

units. Join units 4 and 5; then add Unit 6 to top of these combined units. Add diagonal corner Unit 7 as shown.

6. Join units 8 and 9; then add combined units 4-7 to bottom of the 8/9 combined units. Join Unit 10 to left side; then add Unit 11 to right side. Join these combined units to the top of 1-3 combined units.

7. Join units 13 and 14; then add Unit 12 to left side matching diagonal seam. Join units 16 and 17; then add Unit 15 to right side of these combined units, matching diagonal seam. Add these combined units to the 12-14 combined units as shown.

Making Unit A24

24a 24a 24a
24   24   24 24
24b

8. Join units 18 and 20; then add Unit 21 to top of the 18/20 combined units and Unit 22 to left side. Join the 12-17 combined units to the bottom of 18-22 combined units, matching diagonal seam. These combined units may now be joined to the center combined units.

9. Join units 23 and 24. Join units 25 and 26. Add the 25/26 units to bottom of combined 23/24 units. Join diagonal corner Unit 27 to the 23-26 combined units as shown on Section A diagram. Join units 28 and 29; then add them to right side of 23-27 combined units.

10. Join units 31 and 32; then add diagonal corner Unit 33 as shown at left. Join Unit 30 to left side of these combined units. Join units 34 and 35; then add Unit 37 to left side. Join the 34-37 combined units to the 30-33 combined units; then add Unit 36 to left side. Join diagonal corner Unit 38 to top right of the combined units as shown at left. Join the 23-29 units to the bottom of 30-38 combined units.

11. Join units 39, 40, and 41 in a vertical row as shown; then add them to right side of other combined units. Join this final combined unit section to 1-22 combined units to complete the section.

SECTION A ASSEMBLY

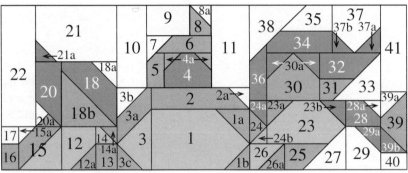

Section A. Make 1. When complete, this section should measure 5 1/4" x 12 1/4".

1. Use diagonal corner technique to make one of units 1, 2, 3, 4, 8, 12, 14, 18, 20, 21, 23, 24, 26, 28, 29, 30, 37, and 39.

2. Use diagonal end technique to make one of Unit 3 and Unit 24. Make diagonal end first; then add diagonal corners as shown.

3. Refer to diagram at bottom right for making triangle-square, Unit 15. Make the triangle-square first; then add Unit 15a diagonal corner.

Making Unit A3

3a 3a 3b
3   3a
3a
3   3
3c

4. Refer to diagram at top right for making Unit 20. Here we have used a triangle-square as a diagonal corner. Follow the instructions below the drawing.

5. To assemble "A" section, begin by joining units 1 and 2; then add Unit 3 to left side of the 1/2 combined

Making Unit A15

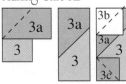

15   15   15a 15

Place 1 3/4" squares of Fabrics II and IV right sides facing and raw edges matching. Stitch diagonal down the center. Trim seam, open, and press; then add diagonal corner A15a.

SECTION B ASSEMBLY

1. Use diagonal corner technique to make one of units 42, 47, 56, 60, and 66.

2. Use diagonal end technique to make two mirror image Unit 67.

3. To assemble Section B, begin by joining units 44, 45, and 46. Make 4. Add these combined units to top and bottom of the two Unit 43's. Join these combined units to

Making Unit B67

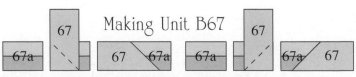

67   67
67a   67   67a   67a   67a   67

Join 1" x 1 7/8" strips of fabrics II and VII. This small strip set will now be part of diagonal end. Join Unit B67 as shown.

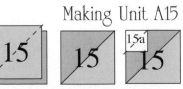

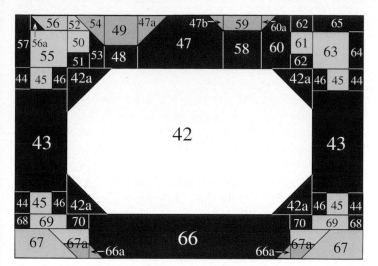

Section B. Make 1. When complete, this section should measure 8 3/4" x 12 1/4".

opposite sides of Unit 42 as shown in Section diagram. This completes the center of Section B.

4. Join units 48 and 49. Join units 58 and 59. Join the 48/49 combined units to left side of Unit 47, and combined units 58/59 to right side of Unit 47, matching diagonal seams. Join units 50, 51 and 52 in a vertical row as shown; then add diagonal corner Unit 54. Join these combined units to left side of the center combined units. Join units 55 and 56; then add Unit 57 to left side of the 55/56 combined units. Join these to left side of other combined units.

5. Join units 62, 61, and 62 in a vertical row; then add Unit 60 to left side of the row. Join to right side of other combined units. Join units 63 and 64; then add Unit 65 to top. Add these combined units to right side of other combined units, matching seams. This completes the top of Section B. Join this top section to the center section.

6. For the bottom section, refer to the diagram and note that the units are the same numbers on opposite sides of Unit 66. They are mirror images. The following instructions are for one side, so check Section diagram frequently for correct positioning of units. To begin, join units 68, 69 and 70 in a horizontal row. Join Unit 67 to bottom of the row as shown. Join the two combined unit sections to opposite sides of Unit 66 to complete the bottom section. Join the bottom section to the other combined units to complete Section B.

SECTION C ASSEMBLY

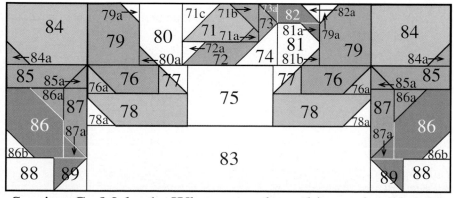

Section C. Make 1. When complete, this section should measure 5 1/2" x 12 1/4".

1. Use diagonal corner technique to make two each of mirror image units 76, 78, 79, 84, 85, 86, and 87. Make one of units 71, 72, 73, 80, 81, and 82.

2. Refer to the diagrams at right for making units 77 and 89. Follow the instructions below the drawings. Make two of each.

3. To assemble the block, begin by joining units 71 and 72; then add Unit 73 to right side of these combined units. Join diagonal corner Unit 74 to bottom as shown. Join units 81 and 82; then add them to right side of combined units 71-74, matching seams. Join units 84, 79, and 80 in a row as shown in Section C diagram. Add these combined units to left side of other combined units. Join units 79 and 84; then add them to the right side of combined units.

4. Refer to Section diagram for correct placement of mirror image units. Join units 76 and 77 as shown; then add mirror image Unit 78 to bottom of these combined units. Join the mirror image units to opposite sides of Unit 75. Join Unit 83 to bottom as shown. For side mirror image units, refer to diagram and join units 86 and 87. Join units 88 and 89. Join the 88/89 units to bottom of combined 86/87 units. Join these combined units to opposite sides of center combined units as shown. Join the two combined unit sections together, matching seams to complete Section C.

SECTIONS D and E ASSEMBLY

The bottom part of Sections D and E are the same, except that they are mirror images. Refer to the Section diagrams frequently at the top of page 16.

1. For Section D, use diagonal corner technique to make one of units 110 and 112. Use diagonal end technique to make one of Unit 111.

2. From Section E, use diagonal corner technique to make one of units 114 and 117. Use diagonal end technique to make one of Unit 111.

3. For both sections, use diagonal corner technique to make

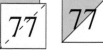

Making Unit C77

Place 1 1/4" squares of fabrics I and II right sides facing and raw edges matching. Stitch diagonal down the center as shown. Trim seam, open, and press.

Making Unit C89

Place 1 3/8" squares of fabrics I and II right sides facing and raw edges matching. Stitch diagonal down the center as shown. Trim seam, and press.

Making Mirror Image Unit D90 and E90.

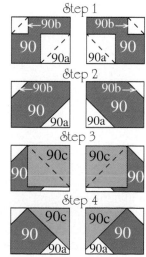

13

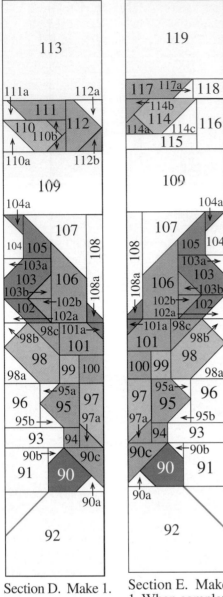

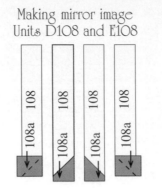

Making mirror image
Units D108 and E108

Making Unit E111

to the top of combined units 90-92.

7. Join units 99 and 100; then add Unit 101 to the top of these combined units. Join Unit 98 to the side of the combined units, matching seams. Add these units to bottom combined units.

8. Join units 102 and 103. Join units 104 and 105. Add the 104/105 combined units to the top of 102/103 combined units; then join Unit 106 to side as shown in the diagrams. Join diagonal corner Unit 107 to top corner of combined units; then join Unit 108 to side as shown.

9. Join the previously made top "D" units to the bottom "D" units to complete Section D. Join the previously made top "E" units to the bottom "E" units to complete Section E.

COMPLETING THE BLOCK

1. To complete the Album Block, join Section A to top of Section B, matching seams where necessary. Join Section C to bottom of Section B, again matching seams. Join Section D to right side; then add Section E to left side to complete the block. Block should measure 18 1/2" square.

2. We used a monogram stitch on our embroidery machine to stitch the word "Album" centered in Unit 42, Section B.

Section D. Make 1. When complete, this section should measure 3 5/8" x 18 1/2"

Section E. Make 1. When complete, this section should measure 3 5/8" x 18 1/2"

two each of mirror image units 90, 95, 97, 98, 101, 102, 103, and 104. Use diagonal end technique to make two of mirror image unit 108.

4. To assemble the top of Section D, begin by joining units 110 and 111; then add Unit 112 to right side of these combined units. Join Unit 113 to top, and 109 to bottom as shown on left.

5. To assemble the top of Section E, join units 114 and 115; then add Unit 116 to right side. Join units 117 and 118. Join these combined units to the top of the 114-116 units. Add Unit 119 to the top and Unit 109 to the bottom.

6. To assemble the bottom part of both D and E sections, remember that they are mirror images, so check the diagrams above frequently for correct placement of the units. Begin by joining units 90 and 91; then add Unit 92 to bottom of these combined units. Join units 93 and 94. Join units 95 and 96. Join the 95/96 combined units to the top of the 93/94 units; then add Unit 97 to side as shown. Join these combined units

Block finishes to 18" square. Size of block before
it is sewn into the quilt is 18 1/2"

MATERIALS

- Fabric I (background)
  Need 9 1/2"   3/8 yard

- Fabric II (navy print)
  Need 2 1/2"   1/8 yard

- Fabric III (dk. blue print)
  Need 1 1/4"   1/8 yard

- Fabric IV (med. blue print)
  Need 1 3/4"   1/8 yard

- Fabric V (light blue marble print)
  Need 1 5/8"   1/8 yard

- Fabric VI (medium brown print)
  Need 1 3/4"   1/8 yard

- Fabric VII (honey tan textured print)
  Need 3 1/2"   1/4 yard

- Fabric VIII (spotted beige print)
  Need 2 1/2"   1/8 yard

- Fabric IX (solid beige)
  Need 4 1/4"   1/4 yard

- Fabric X (solid ivory)
  Need 4 1/2"   1/4 yard

- Fabric XI (bright red print
  Need 2" x 6"   Scrap

CUTTING

From Fabric I, cut: (background)
- One 5 1/2" wide strip. From this, cut:
  * One - 5 1/2" x 6 3/4" (1)
  * One - 1 1/2" x 5 1/2" (15)
  * Two - 1 1/2" x 4 3/4" (4, 10)
  * One - 2 1/2" x 4 1/2" (2)
  * One - 1 1/2" x 4 1/2" (33)
  * One - 1 1/2" x 4 1/4" (6)
  * One - 1 3/4" x 4" (17)
  * One - 2 3/4" x 5 3/4" (5)
  * One - 2 3/4" x 3 1/2" (40)
  * One - 2" x 2 3/4" (8)
  * Two - 1 3/4" x 2 3/4" (38, 39a)
  * One - 2 1/2" x 3 1/2" (27a)
  * One - 1 1/2" x 3 1/2" (32a)
  * Two - 2 1/2" squares (3a, 25a) Stack this cut.
  - From scrap, cut:
  * Four - 1 1/2" squares (12a, 29a, 31, 37a)
- One 2 1/2" wide strip. From this, cut:
  * One - 2 1/2" x 12 1/2" (34)
  * One - 2 1/4" square (7a)
  * One - 1 3/4" x 6 1/2" (21)
  * One - 1 3/4" square (3b)
  * Two - 1 5/8" squares (A5, C5, D5) Cut in
    half diagonally.
  * One - 1 1/2" x 11 1/2" (36)
  * One - 1 1/2" x 2 1/2" (35)
- One 1 1/2" wide strip. From this, cut:
  * One - 1 1/2" x 7 1/4" (14)
  * One - 1 1/4" x 6 1/2" (16)
  * Five - 1 1/4" squares (A8, C8, C10a, D8, D10a)
  * One - 1 1/8" square (18a)

Sailing Ship

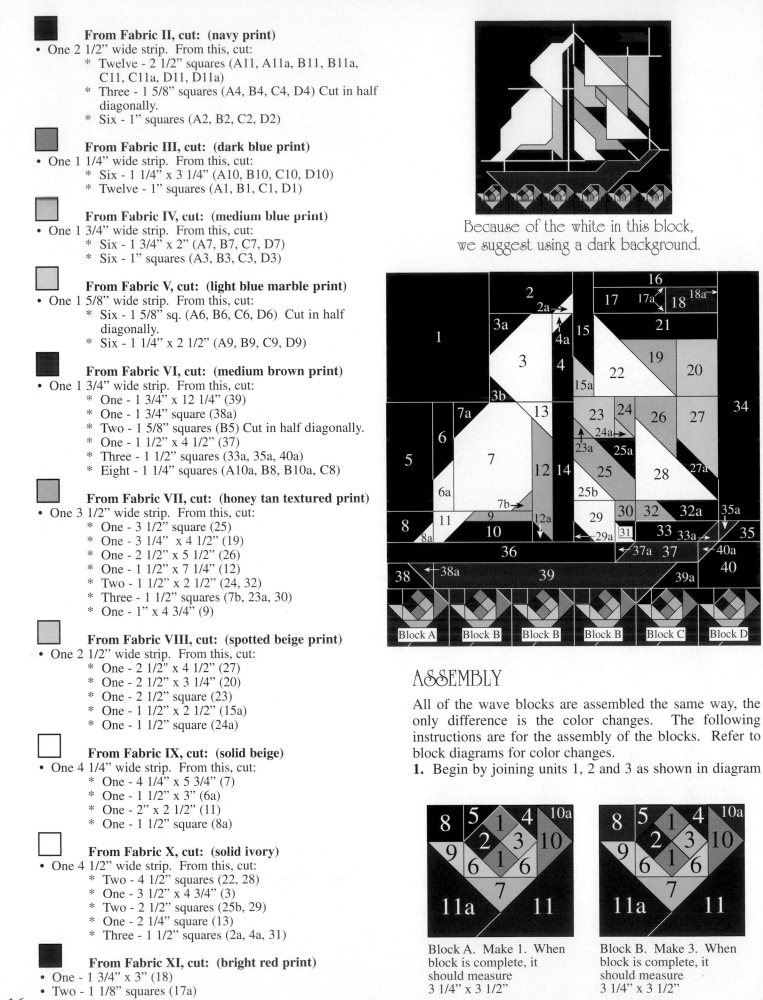

From Fabric II, cut: (navy print)
- One 2 1/2" wide strip. From this, cut:
  * Twelve - 2 1/2" squares (A11, A11a, B11, B11a, C11, C11a, D11, D11a)
  * Three - 1 5/8" squares (A4, B4, C4, D4) Cut in half diagonally.
  * Six - 1" squares (A2, B2, C2, D2)

From Fabric III, cut: (dark blue print)
- One 1 1/4" wide strip. From this, cut:
  * Six - 1 1/4" x 3 1/4" (A10, B10, C10, D10)
  * Twelve - 1" squares (A1, B1, C1, D1)

From Fabric IV, cut: (medium blue print)
- One 1 3/4" wide strip. From this, cut:
  * Six - 1 3/4" x 2" (A7, B7, C7, D7)
  * Six - 1" squares (A3, B3, C3, D3)

From Fabric V, cut: (light blue marble print)
- One 1 5/8" wide strip. From this, cut:
  * Six - 1 5/8" sq. (A6, B6, C6, D6) Cut in half diagonally.
  * Six - 1 1/4" x 2 1/2" (A9, B9, C9, D9)

From Fabric VI, cut: (medium brown print)
- One 1 3/4" wide strip. From this, cut:
  * One - 1 3/4" x 12 1/4" (39)
  * One - 1 3/4" square (38a)
  * Two - 1 5/8" squares (B5) Cut in half diagonally.
  * One - 1 1/2" x 4 1/2" (37)
  * Three - 1 1/2" squares (33a, 35a, 40a)
  * Eight - 1 1/4" squares (A10a, B8, B10a, C8)

From Fabric VII, cut: (honey tan textured print)
- One 3 1/2" wide strip. From this, cut:
  * One - 3 1/2" square (25)
  * One - 3 1/4" x 4 1/2" (19)
  * One - 2 1/2" x 5 1/2" (26)
  * One - 1 1/2" x 7 1/4" (12)
  * Two - 1 1/2" x 2 1/2" (24, 32)
  * Three - 1 1/2" squares (7b, 23a, 30)
  * One - 1" x 4 3/4" (9)

From Fabric VIII, cut: (spotted beige print)
- One 2 1/2" wide strip. From this, cut:
  * One - 2 1/2" x 4 1/2" (27)
  * One - 2 1/2" x 3 1/4" (20)
  * One - 2 1/2" square (23)
  * One - 1 1/2" x 2 1/2" (15a)
  * One - 1 1/2" square (24a)

From Fabric IX, cut: (solid beige)
- One 4 1/4" wide strip. From this, cut:
  * One - 4 1/4" x 5 3/4" (7)
  * One - 1 1/2" x 3" (6a)
  * One - 2" x 2 1/2" (11)
  * One - 1 1/2" square (8a)

From Fabric X, cut: (solid ivory)
- One 4 1/2" wide strip. From this, cut:
  * Two - 4 1/2" squares (22, 28)
  * One - 3 1/2" x 4 3/4" (3)
  * Two - 2 1/2" squares (25b, 29)
  * One - 2 1/4" square (13)
  * Three - 1 1/2" squares (2a, 4a, 31)

From Fabric XI, cut: (bright red print)
- One - 1 3/4" x 3" (18)
- Two - 1 1/8" squares (17a)

16

Because of the white in this block, we suggest using a dark background.

ASSEMBLY

All of the wave blocks are assembled the same way, the only difference is the color changes. The following instructions are for the assembly of the blocks. Refer to block diagrams for color changes.

1. Begin by joining units 1, 2 and 3 as shown in diagram

Block A. Make 1. When block is complete, it should measure 3 1/4" x 3 1/2"

Block B. Make 3. When block is complete, it should measure 3 1/4" x 3 1/2"

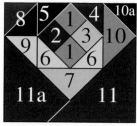

Block C. Make 1.
When block is complete, it
should measure
3 1/4" x 3 1/2"

Block D. Make 1. When
block is complete, it should
measure
3 1/4" x 3 1/2"

Making Unit 39

Making Unit 8 for Block C

Place 1 1/4" squares
of fabrics I and VI
right sides facing.
Stitch diagonal. Trim
seam and press.

Making Unit 27

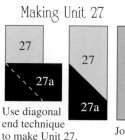

Use diagonal
end technique
to make Unit 27.

Join Unit 26 to
Unit 27 as shown.

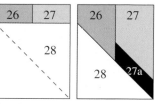

Use diagonal corner technique and
join Unit 28 to combined units 26/27.

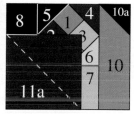

Join triangles 4, 5,
and 6 as shown.

Turn on the straight
so that center
squares are "on
point".

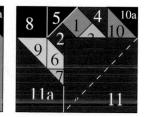

Join Unit 7 to bottom of combined
units 1-6. Join units 8 and 9. Add
them to left side of wave block.
Join unit 10 to right side.

Making the wave blocks

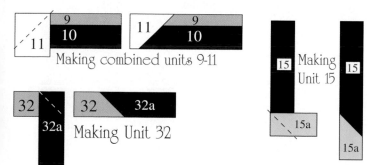

Join Unit 11a diagonal corner. Stitch diagonal seam.
Trim & press.

Join Unit 11 as shown. It
will overlap 11a. Trim seam
and press.

above. Follow the step by step instructions below each
drawing. Use diagonal corner technique to make Unit 10.
Refer to diagram at left to make Unit C8 for the "C" wave
block.

2. For the remainder of the ship block,
use diagonal corner technique to make
one of units 2, 3, 4, 7, 8, 12, 17, 18, 23,
24, 25, 29, 33, 35, 37, 38, and 40. Use
diagonal end technique to make one of
units 6, 15, 27, 32, and 39.

3. To make combined diagonal end unit
9/10/11, join units 9 and 10; then join
diagonal end as shown below left.

4. To assemble the block, join the wave
blocks as shown in block illustration. Set aside. Join units
3 and 4; then add Unit 2 to top of the combined units. Join
Unit 1 to left side of 2-4 units. Join units 5, 6, and 7 in a

row. Join Unit 8 to left side of combined 9-11 unit.
Add these to 5-7 combined units; then join Unit 12
to right side. Join diagonal corner Unit 13 to top
right of the combined units; then add Unit 14 to
right side. Join the 1-4 combined units to top of
the 5-14 combined units, carefully matching diagonal seams.

5. Join units 17 and 18; then add Unit 16 to top of
these combined units. Join units 19 and 20; then
add Unit 21 to top of 19/20 combined units. Join
diagonal corner Unit 22 to left side of the combined units; then add Unit 15 to left side as shown.

6. Join units 23 and 24; then add Unit 25 to bottom of 23/24 combined units matching seams.
Refer to diagram above to make combined 26-28 units;
then add them to right side of combined 23-25 units.
Join these combined units to
bottom of 15-22 combined
units.

7. Join units 30 and 31. Join
units 32 and 33. Join these
two combined units together
as shown; then join Unit 29
to left side. Add these combined units to bottom of
other sail units as shown in
block diagram. Join units 34
and 35; then add them to

Making Unit 31

Place 1 1/2" squares
of fabrics I and X
right sides facing.
Stitch diagonal. Trim
seam and press.

right side of sail units. Join the two sail combined
units together as shown.

8. For ship bottom, join units 36 and 37. Join units 38
and 39. Join the 36/37 units to the top of combined
units 38/39; then add Unit 40 to right side. Add the
ship to bottom of sail units. Join the combined wave
blocks to bottom of ship to complete the block.

9. The rigging was chain stitched with 6 strands of
embroidery floss. Refer to small picture at the top of
Page 16 for rigging placement.

Making combined units 9-11

Making Unit 6

Making Unit 15

Making Unit 32

MATERIALS

Fabric I (background)
Need 7 1/8"   3/8 yard

Fabric II (medium tan print)
Need 5 1/4"   1/4 yard

Fabric III (rust print)
Need 4 1/4"   1/4 yard

Fabric IV (dark brown print)
Need 1"   1/8 yard

Fabric V (light gold print)
Need 2 1/2"   1/8 yard

Fabric VI (dark red print)
Need 3 1/2"   1/4 yard

Fabric VII (green print)
Need 2"   1/8 yard

Fabric VIII (gray print)
Need 3" x 6 1/2"   Scrap

A Great Beginner Project!

CUTTING

From Fabric I, cut: (background)
• One 4 3/8" wide strip. From this, cut:
    * Two - 4 3/8" x 4 1/2" (30)
    * Two - 1 3/4" x 4 1/8" (34)
    * Two - 2 1/2" x 12" (22)
• One 1 3/4" wide strip. From this, cut:
    * One - 1 3/4" x 18 1/2" (35)
    * One - 1 1/2" x 8 1/4" (28)
    * One - 1 1/4" x 11 1/4" (33)
• One 1" wide strip. From this, cut:
    * One - 1" x 7 3/4" (31)

From Fabric II, cut: (medium tan print)
• One 5 1/4" wide strip. From this, cut:
    * Two - 1 7/8" x 5 1/4" (19)
    * Four - 1 5/8" x 5 1/4" (12, 20)
    * Two - 1 3/4" x 4 1/4" (5)
    * Two - 1 1/4" x 3 1/2" (11)
    * Six - 1 1/8" x 3 1/2" (18)
    * Two - 1" x 3 1/2" (10)
    * One - 1 1/2" x 1 3/4" (3)
    * Two - 1 1/4" x 1 1/2" (4)
    * Four - 1" squares (2a)

From Fabric III, cut: (rust print)
• One 4 1/4" wide strip. From this, cut:
    * Two - 1" x 4 1/4" (6)
    * Ten - 1" x 3 1/2" (9, 17)
    * Ten - 1" x 3" (8, 16)
    * Three - 1 1/2" x 2 1/2" (24)
    * Two - 1 1/2" x 2" (2)
    * Two - 1 1/2" x 1 3/4" (29)

Manor House

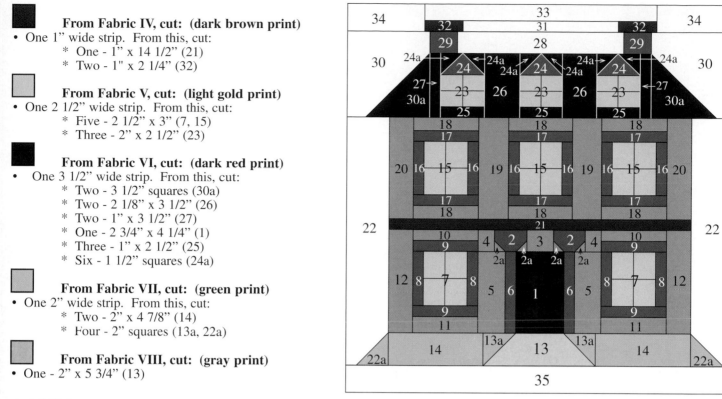

From Fabric IV, cut: (dark brown print)
• One 1" wide strip. From this, cut:
  * One - 1" x 14 1/2" (21)
  * Two - 1" x 2 1/4" (32)

From Fabric V, cut: (light gold print)
• One 2 1/2" wide strip. From this, cut:
  * Five - 2 1/2" x 3" (7, 15)
  * Three - 2" x 2 1/2" (23)

From Fabric VI, cut: (dark red print)
• One 3 1/2" wide strip. From this, cut:
  * Two - 3 1/2" squares (30a)
  * Two - 2 1/8" x 3 1/2" (26)
  * Two - 1" x 3 1/2" (27)
  * One - 2 3/4" x 4 1/4" (1)
  * Three - 1" x 2 1/2" (25)
  * Six - 1 1/2" squares (24a)

From Fabric VII, cut: (green print)
• One 2" wide strip. From this, cut:
  * Two - 2" x 4 7/8" (14)
  * Four - 2" squares (13a, 22a)

From Fabric VIII, cut: (gray print)
• One - 2" x 5 3/4" (13)

ASSEMBLY

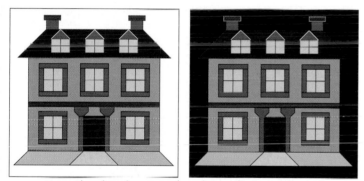

Use the background color of your choice.

1. Use diagonal corner technique to make three of Unit 24. Use this technique to make two each of units 2, mirror image units, 22, and 30. Make one of Unit 13.

2. To assemble the house, begin by joining units 24, 23, and 25 in a row. Make three. Join units 29, 28, and 29 in a long horizontal row. Refer to house block diagram, and beginning from left to right, join units 27, combined units 23-25, Unit 26, combined units 23-25, Unit 26, combined units 23-25, and Unit 27. Join the combined 28/29 units to the top of the roof; then add Unit 30 to opposite sides of roof, referring to diagram for correct placement of mirror image units.

3. Join units 32, 31, and 32 in a horizontal row; then add Unit 33 to top of this row. Join Unit 34 to opposite sides. Add these combined units to roof top.

4. For the second story of the house, join Unit 16 to opposite sides of window Unit 15. Join units 17 and 18 as shown. Join the 17/18 combined units to top and bottom of windows. Make 3. To complete the second story, working from left to right, join Unit 20, a window, Unit 19, a win-

dow, Unit 19, a window, and Unit 20. Join Unit 21 to bottom as shown.

5. To make the first story, begin by joining Unit 8 to opposite sides of window Unit 7. Join units 9 and 10; then join them to the top of each window. Join units 9 and 11; then add them to the bottom of each window. Join units 4, 2, 3, 2, and 4 in a horizontal row. Join units 5, 6, 1, 6, and 5 in a row. Referring to block diagram, join the two rows together. To complete the first story, working from left to right, join Unit 12, a window, combined units 1-6, Unit 5, a window, and Unit 12. Add the first story to the house top.

6. Join units 14, 13, and 14; then add these combined units to the bottom of the house. Join mirror image Unit 22 to opposite sides of the house as shown; then add Unit 35 to the bottom. Join the roof section to the top of the house to complete the block.

MATERIALS

Fabric I (background)
Need 9"   3/8 yard

Fabric II (light gold print)
Need 2 1/8"   1/8 yard

Fabric III (medium gold print)
Need 2 1/8"   1/8 yard

Fabric IV (dark red print)
Need 3 3/8"   1/4 yard

Fabric V (bright red print)
Need 3 3/8"   1/4 yard

Fabric VI (medium brown print)
Need 7 1/2"   3/8 yard

Fabric VII (dark brown print)
Need 2 1/8"   1/8 yard

Fabric VIII (light green print)
Need 2 5/8"   1/8 yard

Fabric IX (medium green print)
Need 2 7/8"   1/8 yard

Fabric X (yellow print)
Need 2 1/2" x 4" scrap

Steam-A-Seam 2
Need 2 1/2" x 4" scrap

CUTTING

From Fabric I, cut: (background)
• One 4 3/4" wide strip. From this, cut:
* One - 4 5/8" x 4 3/4" (47)
* One - 2 1/8" x 4 3/4" (46)
* Two - 2 1/8" squares (22, 42a) Stack this cut.
* One - 1 7/8" x 9" (51)
* One - 1 1/2" square (30a)
* One - 1 3/8" x 1 1/2" (16)
* One - 1 3/8" square (28a)
• Stack these cuts:
* Twenty-seven - 1 1/4" squares (2a, 4a, 7a, 12a, 18a, 25a, 26a, 32a, 37a, 38c, 43a)
* Twenty-seven - 1 1/8" squares (3a, 4b, 7b 13b, 14a, 19b, 20a, 26b, 32b, 38b, 39a, 43b)
• One 4 1/4" wide strip. From this, cut:
* One - 4 1/4" square (50a)
* One - 1 1/8" x 3 7/8" (40)
* One - 3 3/8" x 3 5/8" (35)
* One - 1 3/8" x 3 5/8" (34)
* One - 2 1/4" x 3 1/4" (45)
* Two - 2 1/8" x 3" (6, 9)
* Two - 1 1/2" x 3" (5, 8)
* One - 1 1/8" x 3" (44)
* One - 1 3/4" x 2 7/8" (29)
* One - 2 3/4" x 5 1/4" (10)
* One - 1 1/2" x 2 3/4" (33)
* One - 2 1/4" x 5 7/8" (41)
* One - 1 7/8" x 2 1/8" (31)
* One - 1 3/8" x 2 1/8" (15)
* One - 1 1/8" x 2 1/8" (21)

From Fabric II, cut: (light gold print)
• One 2 1/8" wide strip. From this, cut:
* Four - 2 1/8" squares (11)
* Eight - 1 3/8" squares (1a)
* Four - 1 1/4" x 2 7/8" (3)
* Four - 1 1/4" x 2 1/8" (2)

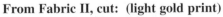

Cornucopia

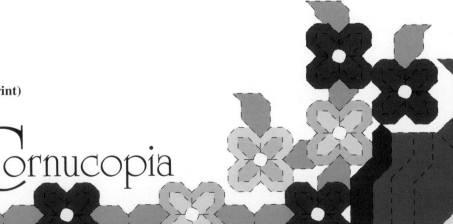

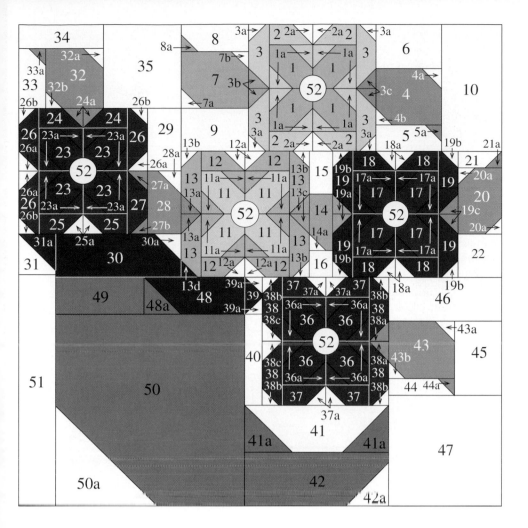

Use the background color of your choice.

52

Cut 5 from Fabric X

From Fabric III, cut: (medium gold print)
- One 2 1/8" wide strip. From this, cut:
  * Four - 2 1/8" squares (1)
  * Eight - 1 3/8" squares (11a)
  * Four - 1 1/4" x 2 7/8" (13)
  * Four - 1 1/4" x 2 1/8" (12)

From Fabric IV, cut: (dark red print)
- One 2 1/8" wide strip. From this, cut:
  * Four - 2 1/8" squares (17)
  * Sixteen - 1 3/8" squares (23a, 36a)
- One 1 1/4" wide strip. From this, cut:
  * Eight - 1 1/4" x 2 7/8" (26, 27, 38)
  * Eight - 1 1/4" x 2 1/8" (24, 25, 37)

From Fabric V, cut: (bright red print)
- One 2 1/8" wide strip. From this, cut:
  * Eight - 2 1/8" squares (23, 36)
  * Four - 1 1/4" x 2 1/8" (18)
  * Eight - 1 3/8" squares (17a)
- One 1 1/4" wide strip. From this, cut:
  * Four - 1 1/4" x 2 7/8" (19)

From Fabric VI, cut: (medium brown print)
- One 7 1/2" wide strip. From this, cut:
  * One - 7 1/2" x 7 5/8" (50)
  * One - 2 1/2" x 5 7/8" (42)
  * One - 1 7/8" x 3 3/4" (49)
  * Two - 2 1/4" squares (41a)
  * One - 1 7/8" square (48a)

From Fabric VII, cut: (dark brown print)
- One 2 1/8" wide strip. From this, cut:
  * One - 2 1/8" x 5 1/8" (30)
  * One - 1 7/8" x 4 1/4" (48)
  * One - 1 7/8" square (31a)
  * One - 1 1/8" x 1 7/8" (39)
  * One - 1 1/8" square (13d)

From Fabric VIII, cut: (light green print)
- One 2 5/8" wide strip. From this, cut:
  * One - 2 5/8" x 3" (7)
  * One - 1 3/8" x 2 5/8" (14)
  * Six - 1 1/4" squares (3b, 13c, 19a)
  * One - 1 1/8" square (8a)

From Fabric IX, cut: (medium green print)
- One 2 7/8" wide strip. From this, cut:
  * One - 1 3/4" x 2 7/8" (28)
  * Two - 2 5/8" x 3" (4, 43)
  * One - 2 5/8" x 2 3/4" (32)
  * One - 2 1/8" x 3" (20)
  * Eleven - 1 1/4" squares (3c, 13b, 19c, 24a, 27a, 38a)
  * Five - 1 1/8" squares (5a, 21a, 27b, 33a, 44a)

From Fabric X, cut: (yellow print)
- One 2 1/2" x 4" (for 1" circle flower centers)

21

ASSEMBLY

1. Use diagonal corner technique to make four each of units 1, mirror image units 2, and 3, Unit 11, mirror image units 12, and 13, Unit 17, mirror image units 18, 19, units 23, and 36, and mirror image units 37, and 38, referring to block diagram for color change in Unit 38. Use this technique to make three of Unit 26, and two each of mirror image units 24 and 25. Make one each of units 4, 5, 7, 8, 14, 20, 21, 27, 28, 30, 31, 32, 33, 39, 41, 42, 43, 44, 48, and 50.

2. All of the flowers are made the same way, therefore the following instructions are for flower #1. Make the other four flowers the same, except for color changes. Refer to the block diagram and begin to assemble the flower by joining two pairs of Unit 1 as shown. Join two pairs of mirror image Unit 2 and add them to the top and bottom of the four joined Unit 1. Refer to the diagram for correct color placement, and join two pairs of mirror image Unit 3. Add these pairs to opposite sides of the flower. Make the other four flowers as shown in block illustration.

3. Join units 8, 7, and 9 as shown in a vertical row. Join these combined units to left side of Flower #1, matching leaf seam. Join units 6, 4, and 5 in a vertical row; then add Unit 10 to right side of row. Join these combined units to right side of Flower #1, again matching leaf seam. Join units 15, 14, and 16 in a vertical row. Join this row between Flower #11, and Flower #17 as shown, matching leaf seams. Join units 21, 20, and 22 in a vertical row; then add this row to right side of Flower #17, matching seams. Join the two flower sections together, referring to block diagram for correct placement.

4. To complete the top flower section of the cornucopia, begin by joining units 32 and 33; then add Unit 34 to the top of the combined units. Join Unit 35 to right side. Join units 28 and 29; then add them to the right side of Flower #23, matching seams. Join the top combined units 32-35 to the top of the flower, matching leaf seams. Join units 30 and 31; then add these combined units to bottom of Flower #23. Join this flower section to left side of other flowers to complete the top section.

5. For the cornucopia bottom section, join units 48 and 49; then add Unit 50 to bottom of these combined units. Join Unit 51 to left side. Join units 39 and 40; then add them to left side of Flower #36. Join units 41 and 42. Join these combined units to bottom of Flower #36. Join this flower section to right side of cornucopia combined units. Join units 43 and 44; then add Unit 45 to right side of combined 43/44 units. Join Unit 46 to the top; then add Unit 47 to the bottom. Join this section to right side of Flower #36 section, matching leaf seams.

6. Join the top flower section to the bottom cornucopia section, matching seams to complete the block.

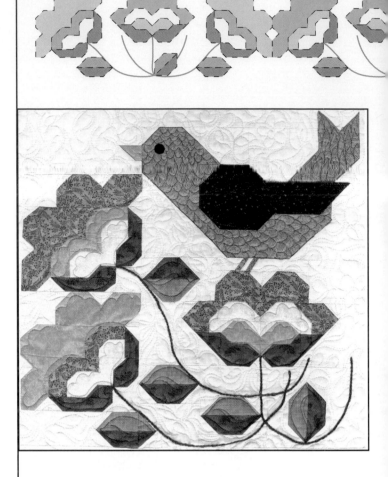

Block finishes to 18" square. Size of block before it is sewn into the quilt is 18 1/2"

MATERIALS

- Fabric I (background)
  Need 11"   1/2 yard

- Fabric II (light blue print)
  Need 3 5/8"   1/4 yard

- Fabric III (medium blue print)
  Need 3 1/8"   1/4 yard

- Fabric IV (dark gold print)
  Need 2 1/4"   1/8 yard

- Fabric V (medium gold print)
  Need 2 1/4"   1/8 yard

- Fabric VI (light yellow print)
  Need 1 7/8"   1/8 yard

- Fabric VII (light green print)
  Need 1 5/8"   1/8 yard

- Fabric VIII (medium green print)
  Need 3 1/2"   1/4 yard

CUTTING

☐ **From Fabric I, cut: (background)**
- One 5 1/2" wide strip. From this, cut:
    * One - 4 1/8" x 5 1/2" (72)
    * One - 1 1/8" x 5 1/2" (21)
    * One - 5 1/8" square (10)
    * One - 2 1/8" x 4 7/8" (45)
    * One - 1 7/8" x 4 7/8" (46)
    * One - 2 3/8" x 4 3/8" (68)
    * One - 3 3/8" x 4 1/4" (6)
    * One - 2 3/4" x 3 7/8" (31)
    * One - 2 1/8" x 3 7/8" (40)
    * One - 1 1/2" x 3 7/8" (32)
    * One - 1 1/4" x 3 7/8" (41)
    * One - 2 3/4" x 3 1/4" (22)
    * One - 2 1/2" x 3 1/8" (2)
    * Two - 3" squares (30)
    * One - 2 7/8" square (37)
- One 2 3/4" wide strip. From this, cut:
    * One - 2 5/8" x 2 3/4" (16)
    * One - 1 5/8" x 2 3/4" (11)
    * One - 1 1/4" x 2 3/4" (19)
    * One - 1 3/4" x 2 5/8" (70)
    * One - 2 1/8" x 2 1/2" (13)
    * Four - 2 1/4" squares (44a, A49, B49)
    * One - 2" square (7a)
    * One - 1 1/2" x 2" (35)
    * Three - 1 7/8" squares (12a, A62, B62)
    * Two - 1 3/4" squares (44b)
    * One - 1 1/4" x 1 3/4" (71)
    * Five - 1 5/8" squares (8a, 17a, 18a)
- One 1 1/2" wide strip. From this, cut:
    * One - 1 1/2" x 10" (9)
    * Nine - 1 1/2" squares (33a, 34a, 38a, 39a, 66a)
    * Five - 1 3/8" squares (8b, 28a, 36a, 67a)
- One 1 1/4" wide strip. From this, cut:
    * Seventeen - 1 1/4" squares (20a, 69a, A47a, B47a A48a, B48a, A50a, B50a, A54a, B54a, A60a, B60a A63b, B63b)
    * Ten - 1 1/8" squares (24b, A47b, B47b, A48b, B48b, A63a, B63a, A65, B65)
    * Four - 1" squares (A60b, B60b, A61b, B61b)

☐ **From Fabric II, cut: (light blue print)**
- One 3 5/8" wide strip. From this, cut:
    * One - 3 5/8" x 7 1/2" (8)
    * One - 2 3/4" x 3 1/4" (12)
    * One - 1 3/8" x 2 7/8" (5)
    * One - 1 1/8" x 2 1/2" (14)
    * One - 2 1/8" square (6b)
    * One - 2" x 6 7/8" (7)
    * One - 1 3/4" square (1b)
    * Four - 1 5/8" squares (1a, 2a, 11a)
    * One - 1 3/8" square (3a)

    * One - 1 1/8" square (16a)

☐ **From Fabric III, cut: (medium blue print)**
- One 3 1/8" wide strip. From this, cut:
    * One - 3 1/8" x 4" (1)
    * One - 1 7/8" x 3 1/8" (3)
    * One - 2 1/4" x 2 7/8" (4)
    * One - 2 1/4" square (15)
    * One - 1 3/8" square (6a)

☐ **From Fabric IV, cut: (dark gold print)**
- One 2 1/4" wide strip. From this, cut:
    * One - 2 1/4" x 2 7/8" (A47)
    * One - 2 1/4" x 2 5/8" (A48)
    * One - 2 1/8" x 3 7/8" (A50)
    * Two - 2 1/8" x 3" (20)
    * Two - 2" x 2 1/8" (28)
    * Two - 1 1/4" x 2 1/8" (B51, B56)
    * One - 2" x 2 3/4" (A63)
    * One - 1 1/4" x 1 7/8" (B53)
    * One - 1 1/2" x 2 5/8" (B59)
    * Three - 1 1/2" squares (27b, A59a)
    * One - 1 1/8" x 1 3/8" (A64)
    * Three - 1 1/4" squares (27a, A51a)
    * One - 1 1/8" square (A65)
    * Two - 1" squares (B52a, B55a)

☐ **From Fabric V, cut: (medium gold print)**
- One 2 1/4" wide strip. From this, cut:
    * One - 2 1/4" x 2 7/8" (B47)
    * One - 2 1/4" x 2 5/8" (B48)
    * One - 2 1/8" x 3 7/8" (B50)
    * Two - 1 1/4" x 2 1/8" (A51, A56)
    * One - 2" x 2 3/4" (B63)
    * One - 1 1/4" x 1 7/8" (A53)
    * One - 1 1/4" x 1 3/4" (69)
    * Two - 1 5/8" x 2 5/8" (23)
    * One - 1 1/2" x 2 5/8" (A59)
    * One - 1 1/2" square (B59a)
    * One - 1 1/8" x 1 3/8" (B64)
    * One - 1 1/4" square (B51a)
    * Three - 1 1/8" squares (24a, B65)
    * Two - 1" squares (A52a, A55a)

Bluebird of Happiness

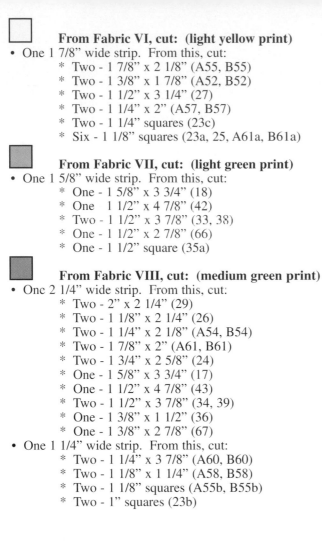

From Fabric VI, cut: (light yellow print)
• One 1 7/8" wide strip. From this, cut:
  * Two - 1 7/8" x 2 1/8" (A55, B55)
  * Two - 1 3/8" x 1 7/8" (A52, B52)
  * Two - 1 1/2" x 3 1/4" (27)
  * Two - 1 1/4" x 2" (A57, B57)
  * Two - 1 1/4" squares (23c)
  * Six - 1 1/8" squares (23a, 25, A61a, B61a)

From Fabric VII, cut: (light green print)
• One 1 5/8" wide strip. From this, cut:
  * One - 1 5/8" x 3 3/4" (18)
  * One   1 1/2" x 4 7/8" (42)
  * Two - 1 1/2" x 3 7/8" (33, 38)
  * One - 1 1/2" x 2 7/8" (66)
  * One - 1 1/2" square (35a)

From Fabric VIII, cut: (medium green print)
• Onc 2 1/4" wide strip. From this, cut:
  * Two - 2" x 2 1/4" (29)
  * Two - 1 1/8" x 2 1/4" (26)
  * Two - 1 1/4" x 2 1/8" (A54, B54)
  * Two - 1 7/8" x 2" (A61, B61)
  * Two - 1 3/4" x 2 5/8" (24)
  * One - 1 5/8" x 3 3/4" (17)
  * One - 1 1/2" x 4 7/8" (43)
  * Two - 1 1/2" x 3 7/8" (34, 39)
  * One - 1 3/8" x 1 1/2" (36)
  * One - 1 3/8" x 2 7/8" (67)
• One 1 1/4" wide strip. From this, cut:
  * Two - 1 1/4" x 3 7/8" (A60, B60)
  * Two - 1 1/8" x 1 1/4" (A58, B58)
  * Two - 1 1/8" squares (A55b, B55b)
  * Two - 1" squares (23b)

ASSEMBLY

Blocks A and B are identical except for two color changes. Refer to diagrams below for correct placement of colors. These instructions are for both blocks.

1. Use diagonal corner technique to make two each of units 47, 48, 50, 51, 52, 54, 55, 59, 60, 61, and 63. Refer to diagrams of Unit 65 to make the triangle-squares.

2. To assemble the blocks, join units 49, 47 and 48 in a row. Join units 50 and 51. Join units 52 and 53; then join Unit 54 to right side of these combined units. Join the 50/51 units to left side of the combined 52-54 units; then add this row to top row as shown. Join units 64 and 65; then join Unit 63 to bottom of these combined units. Join units 55 and 56; then join Unit 59 to left side of 55/56 units. Join units 57 and 58. Join them to right side of combined 55-

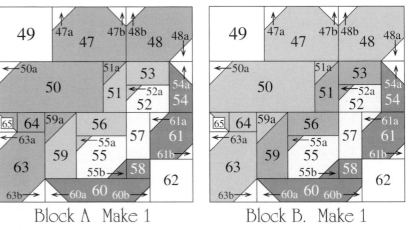

Block A Make 1   Block B. Make 1

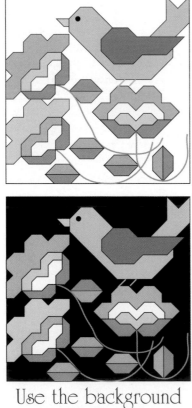

Use the background color of your choice.

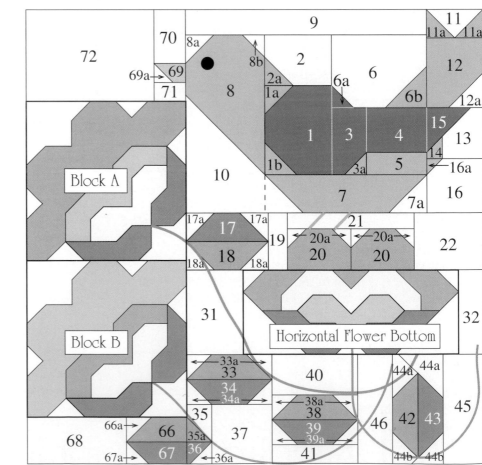

Making Unit A65

Place 1 1/8" squares of fabrics I and IV right sides together with raw edges matching. Stitch a diagonal down the center as shown. Trim seam and press.

59 units; then join Unit 60 to bottom. Join units 61 and 62. Join them to right side of 55-59 units; then join combined units 63-65 to right side. Add this completed row to block bottoms to complete A and B blocks.

Making Unit B65

Place 1 1/8" squares of fabrics I and V right sides together with raw edges matching. Stitch a diagonal down the center as shown. Trim seam and press.

3. To make the horizontal flower bottom, use diagonal corner technique and make two each of mirror image units 23, 24, 27, and 28.

Making the horizontal flower bottom.

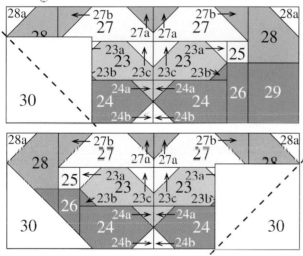

4. To assemble this section, begin by joining mirror image units 23. Join mirror image units 24. Join mirror image units 27. Join combined units 23 and 24 as shown. Join units 25 and 26; then add them to opposite sides of combined units 23/24. Join combined units 27 to top of other combined units. Join units 28 and 29; then add them to opposite sides of other combined units, matching seams. Join diagonal corner Unit 30 as shown to both sides to complete the flower bottom.

5. To make units for the remainder of the block, use diagonal corner technique to make two of Unit 20 and one of units 1, 2, 3, 6, 7, 8, 11, 12, 16, 17, 18, 33, 34, 35, 36, 38, 39, 42, 43, 44, 66, 67, and 69. When joining diagonal corners (Unit 44a and 44b), units 42 and 43 must be joined first. Refer to block diagram. Diagonal corners 44a and 44b will overlap to form the leaf.

6. To make combined units 13-15, refer to diagram at right, and join units 13 and 14; then add diagonal corner 15 as shown.

Making combined units 13-15

7. To assemble the block, begin by joining units 1 and 2. Join units 4 and 5; then add Unit 3 to left side of these combined units. Join Unit 6 to the top. Add combined units 1/2 to left side of 3-6 combined units; then add Unit 7 to bottom as shown. Join Unit 8 to left side of combined units; then add Unit 9 to the top. Join diagonal corner Unit 10 to left bottom as shown in block diagram.

8. Join units 11, 12, combined units 13-15, and Unit 16 in a vertical row. Join these units to right side of bird matching seams where necessary.

9. Join units 17 and 18; then add Unit 19 to right side of these combined units. Join two Unit 20's together as shown; then add Unit 21 to top. Join Unit 22 to right side of combined units 20/21; then add these combined units to right side of 17-19 combined units to complete the row. Join Unit 31 to left side of Horizontal Flower Bottom, and Unit 32 to right side. Join this row to the 17-22 combined unit row.

10. Join units 33 and 34. Join units 35 and 36; then add Unit 37 to right side of these combined units. Join the 33/34 leaf to top of the 35-37 combined units. Join units 40, 38, 39, and 41 in a vertical row; then add Unit 46 to right side of these combined units. Join these units to the 33-37 combined units as shown. Join units 42 and 43; then add diagonal corners 44a and 44b. Join Unit 45 to right side of these combined units; then add them to right side of the leaf row. Join this row to bottom of Horizontal Flower Bottom row. Join the leaf/horizontal flower section to the bird section.

11. To complete the flower section, begin by joining units 70, 69, and 71 in a vertical row; then add Unit 72 to left side. Join blocks A and B; then add 69-72 combined units to top of Block A as shown. Join units 66 and 67; then add Unit 68 to right side. Join these combined units to Block B bottom to complete the flower section. Join this section to left side of bird section to complete the block.

12. Chain stitch the birds feet with 6 strands of coordinating gold embroidery floss, and chain stitch the flower stems with a coordinating green floss. We cut a small black fabric circle with Steam-A-Seam 2 fused on the back and pressed it on the birds head for an eye. We suggest running a small blanket stitch around the eye.

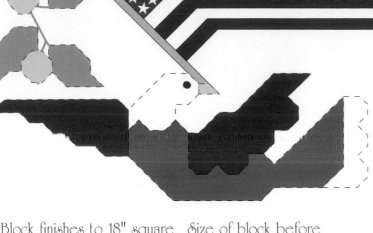

Block finishes to 18" square. Size of block before it is sewn into the quilt is 18 1/2"

MATERIALS

 Fabric I (background)
Need 12 3/8"   1/2 yard

Fabric II (medium brown print)
Need 2 3/4"   1/8 yard

Fabric III (dark brown print)
Need 2 5/8"   1/8 yard

 Fabric IV (white on white print)
Need 2 3/4"   1/8 yard

Fabric V (red print)
Need 2"   1/8 yard

 Fabric VI (dark blue print)
Need 2 1/2"   1/8 yard

 Fabric VII (medium green print)
Need 2 1/2"   1/8 yard

 Fabric VIII (light gold print)
Need 3" x 12" scrap

Fabric IX (dark gold print)
Need 4" x 10" scrap

CUTTING

From Fabric I, cut: (background)
- One 5 1/8" wide strip. From this, cut:
  * One - 5 1/8" x 6 3/4" (81)
  * One - 2" x 5 1/8" (28)
  * One - 1 1/8" x 4 7/8" (68)
  * One - 4 5/8" square (11)
  * One - 3 1/2" square (16)
  * One - 1 3/4" x 3 1/2" (13)
  * One - 2 1/2" x 3 3/8" (73)
  * One - 1" x 3 3/8" (26)

  * One - 2 3/8" x 3 1/8" (51)
  * One - 1 5/8" x 3 1/8" (67)
  * One - 1" x 3 1/8" (79)
  * One - 2 1/2" x 3" (80)
  * One - 2" x 3" (74)
  * One - 1" x 3" (23)
  * One - 2 5/8" x 7 1/8" (39)
- One 3" wide strip. From this, cut:
  * One - 3" x 8 1/2" (10)
  * One - 1 3/8" x 3" (22)
  * Two - 2 5/8" squares (47a, 63a)
  * One - 2 3/8" x 2 5/8" (29)
  * One - 2 1/4" x 2 1/2" (18)
  * One - 2" x 2 1/2" (7)
  * One - 1 1/2" x 2 1/2" (72)
  * Two - 1 1/4" x 2 1/2" (25, 75)
  * Two - 1" x 2 1/2" (71, 78)
  * One - 2 1/4" square (40a)
  * Two - 1 5/8" x 2 1/8" (30, 62a)
  * One - 2" square (7b)
  * One - 1 7/8" x 2" (27)
  * Four - 1" x 2" (21, 70)
- One 1 3/4" wide strip. From this, cut:
  * One - 1 3/4" x 11" (12)
  * One - 1 3/4" x 7 1/8" (38)
  * Two - 1 5/8" squares (33, 66a)
  * One - 1 1/4" x 1 5/8" (42)
  * One - 1 1/8" x 9 1/4" (76)
  * Three - 1 1/8" squares (32a, 46b, 60a)
  * One - 1" x 1 1/8" (48)
- One 1 1/2" wide strip. From this, cut:
  * Three - 1 1/2" squares (15a, 53, 55a)

Freedom

* One - 1 3/8" x 1 1/2" (54)
* Twelve - 1 3/8" squares (17a, 19a, 24a, 68a, 69a)
* Two - 1 1/4" squares (17b, 19b)
* One - 1" x 5 1/8" (77)
* One - 1" x 1 3/8" (35)
• One 1" wide strip. From this, cut:
  * Thirty-eight - 1" squares 5c, 6c, 14a, 20a, 36a, 37a, 41a, 58a, 59a, 61a, 64a, 65a)

From Fabric II, cut: (medium brown print)
• One 2 3/4" wide strip. From this, cut:
  * One - 1 5/8" x 2 3/4" (62)
  * One - 2 5/8" x 4 7/8" (63)
  * One - 2 5/8" x 3 3/8" (47)
  * One - 1 5/8" x 2 1/4" (46)
  * One - 1 1/2" x 2 1/4" (43)
  * One - 1 3/4" x 4 1/8" (60)
  * One - 1 1/2" x 1 3/4" (59)
  * One - 1 1/4" x 1 3/4" (44)
  * One - 1" x 1 3/4" (50)
  * Three - 1" squares (56a, 57a)
  * One - 7/8" square (49a)

From Fabric III, cut: (dark brown print)
• One 2 5/8" wide strip. From this, cut:
  * One - 2 5/8" x 2 7/8" (55)
  * One - 1 3/4" x 2 1/2" (58)
  * One - 2 3/8" square (51a)
  * One - 1 5/8" x 2 1/4" (66)
  * One - 2 1/8" x 4 1/8" (37)
  * Two - 1 5/8" x 2 1/8" (36, 61)
  * One - 1" x 2 1/2" (49)
  * One - 1 3/8" x 2" (57)
  * One - 1" x 1 5/8" (31)
  * One - 1 3/8" square (56)
  * One - 1 1/8" x 1 3/8" (34)
  * One - 1 1/8" x 3 1/2" (32)
  * One - 1 1/8" square (33a)
  * Two - 1" squares (29a, 30a)

From Fabric IV, cut: (white on white)
• One 2 3/4" wide strip. From this, cut:
  * One - 2 3/4" square (40)
  * One - 2" x 2 1/2" (6)
  * Three - 1 5/8" x 2" (41, 65)
  * One - 1 5/8" x 1 7/8" (64)
  * Five - 1 1/2" squares (3a, 5a, 16b, 63b)
  * One - 1" x 1 1/2" (3b)
  * One - 1" x 1 1/4" (45)
  • Stack these cuts:
  * Two - 1" x 10" (1)
  * One - 1" x 8 1/2" (8)
  * Four - 1" squares (2a, 43a, 46a)

From Fabric V, cut: (red print)
• One 2" wide strip. From this, cut:
  * One - 2" square (6b)
  * One - 1 1/2" x 2 1/2" (5)
  * Two - 1 1/2" squares (6a, 7b)
  • Stack these cuts:
  * One - 1" x 11" (4)
  * Two - 1" x 10" (2)
  * One - 1" x 8 1/2" (9)
  * One - 1" x 1 1/2" (3b)
  * Two - 1" squares (10a, 15b)

From Fabric VI, cut: (dark blue print)
• One 2 1/2" wide strip. From this, cut:
  * One - 2 1/2" square (16b)

* One - 1 1/2" x 2 1/2" (3)
* One - 2" square (15)
* One - 1" square (14b)

From Fabric VII, cut: (medium green print)
• One 2 1/2" wide strip. From this, cut:
  * Five - 2 1/2" x 2 5/8" (24, 68, 69)
  * Two - 2 1/2" squares (17, 19)
  * Six - 1 1/8" squares (13a, 16c, 25a, 72a, 73a, 74a)
  * One - 1" square (78a)

From Fabric VIII, cut: (light gold print)
• Five - 2" squares (20)
• One - 1" x 1 1/2" (52)

From Fabric IX, cut: (dark gold print)
• One - 3" square (16a)
• One - 2" x 2 1/2" (7a)
• One - 2" square (14)
• One - 1 1/2" square (5b)
• One - 1" x 1 1/2" (52)
• One - 1" square (41b)

ASSEMBLY

Because of the white in this block, we suggest using a dark background.

1. Use diagonal corner technique to make five of Unit 20, three of Unit 69, two of Unit 65, and one each of units 2, 3, 5, 6, 10, 13, 14, 15, 16, 17, 19, 24, 25, 29, 30, 32, 33, 36, 37, 40, 41, 43, 46, 47, 49, 51, 55, 56, 57, 58, 59, 60, 61, 63, 64, 66, 72, 73, 74, and 78. Use diagonal end technique to make one each of units 7 and 62.

Making Unit 3

Join 1" x 1 1/2" strips of fabrics IV and V. This will be used as diagonal corner 3b.

Place diagonal corner 3b, right sides facing as shown. Stitch diagonal. Trim seam and press.

2. Refer to diagram above and follow instructions to make Unit 3 using a strip set diagonal corner.

3. To make Unit 5 on left, join diagonal corners 5a. Do not trim seam as 5a is white on a darker background. Press seams. Join diagonal corner 5b, trim seam and press. Join diagonal corner 5c. Trim seam and press. For

Making Unit 5

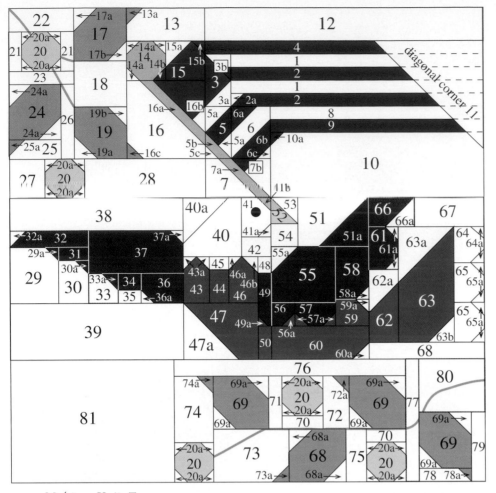

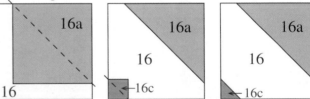
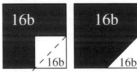
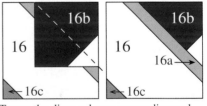

Unit 16 to the bottom, carefully matching seams. Join units 17, 18 and 19 in a row. Join Unit 21 to opposite sides of one Unit 20; then add Unit 22 to the top and Unit 23 to the bottom. Join Units 24 and 25; then add Unit 26 to right side of these combined units. Join these units to bottom of combined 20-23 units. Join combined units 17-19 to right side of combined leaf units; then add combined units 13-16 to right side as shown. Join units 27, 20 and 28 in a row. Add them to the bottom of the leaf units. Join the leaf units to the left side of the flag combined units, matching seams.

6. To make the eagle, beginning with his left wing, join units 30 and 31; then add Unit 29 to left side of these combined units. Join Unit 32 to the top. Join units 34 and 35; then add Unit 33 to left side of these combined units, and Unit 36 to right side, matching seams. Join Unit 37 to top of the combined units. Join the combined 29-32 units to the 33-37 combined units. Add Unit 38 to the top and 39 to the bottom to complete the left wing section.

7. For the eagle head and body,

Making Unit 7

Join diagonal end, Unit 7a as shown.

Join 1 1/2" square diagonal corner 7b to 2" square of Fabric I. Trim and press.

Place 7b diagonal corner right sides facing on Unit 7 as shown. Stitch diagonal and press.

Making Unit 16

Join diagonal corner 16a. Trim seam & press.

Join diagonal corner 16c. Trim seam & press.

Place 1 1/2" diagonal corner 16c from Fabric IV on 2 1/2" square of Fabric VI. Stitch diagonal. DO NOT trim seam and press.

To use the diagonal corner as a diagonal corner, place Unit 16b right sides facing as shown. Stitch diagonal, trim seam & press.

Unit 6, join diagonal corners in alphabetical order to avoid confusion. Refer to diagram of Unit 7 above and follow drawings and instructions. Refer to diagrams on right to make units 16, and combined units 52/53.

4. To assemble the block, begin by joining units 1, 2, 1, and 2 in a row. Notice that second Unit 2 has a diagonal corner. Add Unit 3 to left side of the combined stripe units. These stripe units will go all the way to the end of the block (shown by dashed lines). Add Unit 4 to top of stripe combined units. Join units 5 and 6, matching seams; then add Unit 7 to bottom of combined 5/6 units, again matching seams. Join units 8, 9 and 10. Join these combined units to right side of 5-7 combined units; then add to bottom of other combined stripe units. Join diagonal corner, Unit 11 to right side of stripes as shown. Join Unit 12 to top of the combined units.

5. Join units 14 and 15; then add Unit 13 to the top, and

Making combined units 52 and 53

Join 1" x 1 1/2" strips of fabrics VIII and IX. Place Fabric I, Unit 53 right sides facing on 52 as shown. Stitch diagonal and press.

begin by joining units 41 and 42; then add Unit 40 to left side. Join units 44 and 45; then join Unit 43 to left side and Unit 46 to right side. Join Unit 47 to bottom of these combined units. Join units 48, 49 and 50; then join them to right side of combined units 43-47 as shown. Join eagle head to eagle body, matching seams. Join these combined units to left wing units.

8. For the right wing and body, begin by joining combined units 52/53 with Unit 54; then add Unit 51 to right side. Join units 56 and 57; then add Unit 55 to top of these combined units. Join units 58 and 59; then add them to right side of combined units 55-57. Join Unit 60 to bottom as shown; then add combined units 51-54 to the top. Join this wing section to eagle head and body section, matching seams.

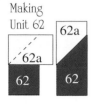

Making Unit 62
62a
62a
62
62

9. For the tail and wing tip section, join units 61 and 62; then add Unit 63 to right side of these combined units. Join units 64, and two of Units 65 together in a vertical row as shown. Add them to right side of Unit 63. Join units 66 and 67; then add the to top of tail section. Join Unit 68 to bottom of combined units. Join the tail section to the right wing section to complete the eagle. Join the eagle section to the bottom of the flag section, matching the flag pole seam.

10. To assemble the leaf/berry bottom section, begin by joining units 74 and 20 as shown. Join units 69 and 71. Join units 20 and 70. Join units 72 and 69. Referring to block diagram, join these combined units together to form a horizontal row. Join units 73, 68, and 75 together. Join Unit 70 and 20; then add them to right side of Unit 75. Join this row to top leaf row; then join combined units 74/20 to left side of row. Add Unit 76 to the top; then join Unit 81 to the left side, and Unit 77 to the right side. Join units 69 and 78; then add Unit 79 to right side. Join Unit 80 to the top. Add these combined units to right side of other combined units to complete the leaf/berry section. Join this section to bottom of eagle section to complete the blocks.

11. Using six strands of embroidery floss, chain stitch the green stems as shown. Use white french knots in the blue section of the flag if desired.

Peacock

Block finishes to 18" square. Size of block before it is sewn into the quilt is 18 1/2"

MATERIALS

☐ Fabric I (background)
Need 9 1/8"   3/8 yard

■ Fabric II (dark cobalt blue print)
Need 4 5/8"   1/4 yard

■ Fabric III (medium turquoise print)
Need 2 5/8"   1/8 yard

■ Fabric IV (dark green marble print)
Need 3 7/8"   1/4 yard

■ Fabric V (medium green marble print)
Need 4"   1/4 yard

■ Fabric VI (medium gold print)
Need 3"   1/8 yard

☐ Fabric VII (light gold print)
Need 2 7/8"   1/8 yard

■ Fabric VIII (medium brown print)
Need 1 1/8"   1/8 yard

CUTTING

From Fabric I, cut: (background)
- One 3 7/8" wide strip. From this, cut:
  * One - 2 1/8" x 3 7/8" (77a)
  * One - 3 3/4" x 5" (11)
  * One - 2 1/8" x 3 3/4" (63)
  * One - 2 1/4" x 3 1/2" (64)
  * One - 3" x 7 5/8" (78)
  * One - 2 1/2" x 3" (18)
  * Two - 1 1/2" x 3" (23, 27)
  * One - 1 3/8" x 3" (55)
  * One - 1 1/2" x 2 5/8" (26a)
  * One - 2 1/2" x 7 3/4" (13)
  * One - 2 1/2" square (90)
  * One - 1 1/2" x 2 1/2" (31a)
  * One - 2 3/8" square (17a)
- One 2 3/8" wide strip. From this, cut:
  * One - 2 3/8" x 4 3/4" (76)
  * One - 1 5/8" x 2 3/8" (71)
  * One - 2 1/4" x 5" (92)
  * One - 1 3/8" x 2 1/4" (73)
  * Four - 2" squares (8a, 9a, 67b, 91b)
  * One - 1 1/2" x 2" (79a)
  * One - 1" x 2" (10)
  * One - 1 7/8" x 12" (56)
  * One - 1 7/8" square (12a)
  * One - 1 1/8" x 1 7/8" (60)
- One 1 3/4" wide strip. From this, cut:
  * Eight - 1 3/4" squares (5, 7, 68a, 85, 86)
  * One - 1 3/8" x 1 3/4" (61)
  * One - 1 5/8" square (12b)
  * One - 1 3/8" x 1 5/8" (65)
  * Three - 1 1/8" x 1 5/8" (69, 75b)
  * One - 1" x 1 5/8" (75a)
  * Four - 1 1/2" squares (8b, 45a, 79b, 91a)
  * One - 1 1/8" x 1 1/2" (82)
  * Three - 1 3/8" squares (22a, 44a, 59b)
  * One - 1" x 1 3/8" (74)
  * Two - 1 1/4" squares (16a, 21a)
- One 1 1/8" wide strip. From this, cut:
  * Seven - 1 1/8" squares (22b, 54a, 59a, 66a, 83a)
  * One - 1" x 1 1/8" (58)
  * Thirteen - 1" squares (2a, 4b, 6a, 57a, 84a, 87a, 89a)

From Fabric II, cut: (dark cobalt blue print)
- One 4 5/8" wide strip. From this, cut:
  * One - 4 5/8" x 5 3/8" (67)
  * One - 1 3/8" x 3 7/8" (32)
  * Four - 1 3/4" x 2 1/2" (84, 87, 89)
  * Eight - 2" squares (14, 19, 24, 28, 35, 41, 46, 51)
  * One - 1 3/8" x 1 7/8" (59)
  * One - 1" x 1 1/4" (57)
  * Four - 1 1/8" squares (88a)

From Fabric III, cut: (medium turquoise print)
- One 2 5/8" wide strip. From this, cut:
  * One - 2 5/8" square (67c)
  * One - 2 1/2" x 4 5/8" (68)
  * Four - 1 3/4" x 2 1/2" (2, 3, 4)
  * One - 1 3/8" x 2 1/2" (33)
  * One - 2 1/8" x 6 7/8" (77)
  * Four - 1 1/8" squares (1a)
  * One - 1" x 1 5/8" (75b)

From Fabric IV, cut: (dark green marble print)
- One 2 3/4" wide strip. From this, cut:
  * One - 2 3/4" x 3 7/8" (75)
  * Two - 2 1/2" x 3" (8, 12)
  * One - 1 1/4" x 2 1/8" (34a)
  * One - 1 1/8" x 2" (37)
  * Three - 1" x 2" (20, 36)
  * Two - 1 3/4" squares (5)
  * One - 1" x 1 3/4" (62)
  * One - 1 5/8" x 4 5/8" (66)
  * One - 1 5/8" x 3" (21)
  * One - 1 5/8" square (67a)
  * One - 1 3/8" x 3" (22)
  * Two - 1 3/8" squares (16b, 30a)
  * One - 1 1/8" x 1 3/8" (40a)
- One 1 1/8" wide strip. From this, cut:
  * Two - 1 1/8" x 3 1/8" (38)
  * One - 1 1/8" square (34b)
  * Twelve - 1" sq. (3a, 4a, 19a, 35a, 59c, 64a)

From Fabric V, cut: (medium green marble print)
- One 3" wide strip. From this, cut:
  * One - 3" x 3 1/2" (31)
  * One - 3" x 3 1/8" (17)
  * One - 2 1/2" x 3" (91)
  * One - 1 5/8" x 3" (80)
  * Two - 1 3/8" x 3" (16, 30)
  * One - 1 1/8" x 3" (54)
  * One - 1 5/8" x 2 5/8" (26a)
  * One - 2" x 2 1/2" (9)
  * One - 1 1/2" x 2 1/2" (79)
  * Two - 1" x 2 1/2" (53)
  * Five - 1" x 2" (15, 29, 52)
  * Three - 1 3/4" squares (6, 85)
  * One - 1" x 1 1/2" (10a)
  * One - 1 3/8" square (32a)
  * Two - 1 1/4" squares (50)
- One 1" wide strip. From this, cut:
  * Fifteen - 1" squares (3b, 14a, 28a, 51a, 84b, 87b)

From Fabric VI, cut: (medium gold print)
- One 3" wide strip. From this, cut:
  * One - 3" x 3 3/8" (26)
  * One - 1 1/4" x 3" (34)
  * One - 1 1/2" x 2 1/2" (31a)
  * Two - 1" x 2" (25)
  * Two - 1" x 1 5/8" (70)
  * Four - 1" squares (24a)

From Fabric VII, cut: (light gold print)
- One 2 7/8" wide strip. From this, cut:
  * One - 1 1/8" x 2 7/8" (40)
  * Two - 2 1/2" squares (1, 88)
  * One - 1 1/4" x 2" (43)
  * One - 1 1/8" x 2" (48)
  * One - 1 1/2" x 3 1/4" (45)
  * One - 1 3/8" x 3 1/4" (44)
  * Four - 1 3/8" squares (30b, 33a, 39)
  * One - 1 1/8" squares (73a)
  * One - 1 1/8" x 1 5/8" (75a)
  * Two - 1" x 3 1/8" (49)
  * Two - 1" x 2" (42, 47)
  * Eight - 1" squares (41a, 46a)

From Fabric VIII, cut: (medium brown print)
- One 1 1/8" wide strip. From this, cut:
  * One - 1 1/8" x 1 5/8" (83)
  * One - 1" x 4 5/8" (72)
  * One - 1" x 1 1/2" (81)
  * One - 1" square (80a)

ASSEMBLY

Use the background color of your choice.

Making Unit 5

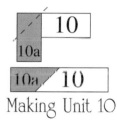

Place 1 3/4" squares of fabrics I and IV right sides together with raw edges matching. Stitch a diagonal down the center as shown. Trim seam and press.

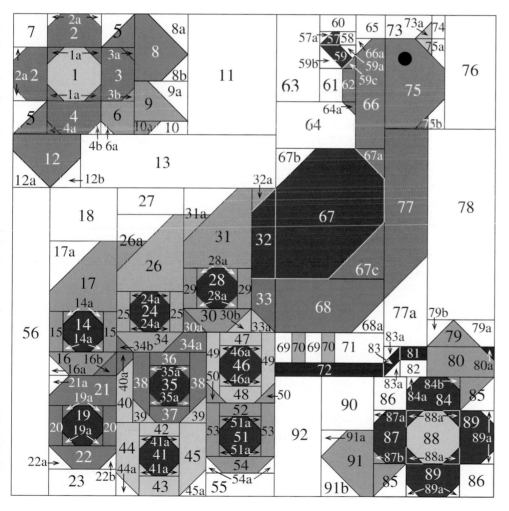

40, 77, and 79. Make triangle-squares for units 5 and 85 as shown in diagrams.

2. To assemble the block, begin in the top left corner and join units 2, 1 and 3 in a horizontal row. Join units 7, 2, and 5; then add this row to top of 2/1/3 row as shown. Join units 5, 4, and 6; then add this row to bottom of flower. Join units 8, 9, and 10 in a vertical row. Join to right side of flower; then add Unit 11 to right side as shown. Join units 12 and 13. Join these combined units to bottom of flower.

Making Unit 10

3. For peacock tail, begin by joining Unit 15 to opposite sides of Unit 14; then add Unit 16 to bottom of combined units and Unit 17 to the top. Join Unit 18 to top of Unit 17. Join Unit 20 to opposite sides of Unit 19. Join Unit 21 to top of these combined units, and Unit 22 to the bottom. Join Unit 23 to bottom of Unit 22. Join the two tail feathers together; then add Unit 56 to left side as shown.

4. Refer to diagram on page 32 to make Unit 26. Follow instructions and drawing. Join Unit 27 to top of Unit 26. Join Unit 25 to opposite sides of Unit 24. Follow instructions on page 32 for making Unit 31. Join Unit 29 to opposite sides of Unit 28; then join Unit 30 to bottom. Join combined units 24-27 and combined units 28-31 as shown. Join units 32 and 33; then add them to right side of these combined feather units. Join Unit 36 to top of Unit 35; then add Unit 37 to bottom. Join Unit 38 to opposite sides of these combined units; then join diagonal corner Unit 39 to bottom of these combined units. Join Unit 40 to left side. Join Unit 34 across the top of the combined units, matching

1. To make the units for the peacock block, use diagonal corner technique to make two of units 2 and 89. Make one each of units 1, 3, 4, 6, 8, 9, 12, 14, 16, 17, 19, 21, 22, 24, 26, (see illustration) 28, 30, 31, (see illustration), 32, 33, 35, 41, 44, 45, 46, 51, 54, 57, 59, 64, 66, 67, 68, 73, 75, (see illustration) 79, 80, 83, 84, 87, 88, 89, and 91. Use diagonal end technique to make one each of units 10, 34,

Making Unit 26

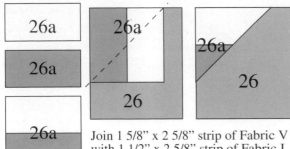

Join 1 5/8" x 2 5/8" strip of Fabric V with 1 1/2" x 2 5/8" strip of Fabric I. Use this combination as a small strip set. Place it right sides together, vertically, as shown on Unit 26. Stitch diagonal, trim seam and press.

Making Unit 31a

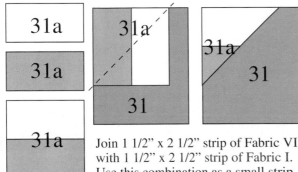

Join 1 1/2" x 2 1/2" strip of Fabric VI with 1 1/2" x 2 1/2" strip of Fabric I. Use this combination as a small strip set. Place it right sides together, vertically, as shown on Unit 31. Stitch diagonal, trim seam and press.

seams. Join Unit 42 to top of Unit 41; then add Unit 43 to bottom. Join Unit 44 to left side of these combined units; then add Unit 45 to right side. Join the green and gold feathers together in a vertical row.

5. Join Unit 47 to top of Unit 46; then add Unit 48 to bottom. Join Unit 49 to opposite sides of the combined units. Join diagonal corner, Unit 50 to opposite sides of the feather bottom as shown. Join Unit 52 to top of Unit 51. Join Unit 53 to opposite sides of combined 51/52 units; then add Unit 54 to bottom. Join Unit 55 to bottom of Unit 54. Join combined feather units 34-45 to combined feather units 46-55. Join these feathers to bottom of combined top feathers as shown; then add combined left feather units 17-23 +56 to left side to complete feather section. Join the feather section to the bottom of the flower section.

6. To assemble the peacock body, begin by joining units 57 and 58. Join Unit 59 to bottom of these combined units, and Unit 60 to the top. Join

Making Unit 34

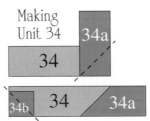

Making Unit 40

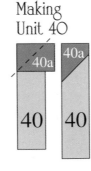

Making Unit 77

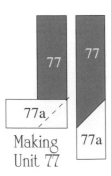

units 61 and 62; then join them to bottom of combined 57-60 units. Join Unit 63 to left side; then add Unit 64 to the bottom. Join units 65 and 66. Add these combined units to right side of other combined units. Join units 67 and 68. Add these combined units to bottom of other combined units. Join units 69, 70, 69, 70 and 71 in a horizontal row. Join this row to bottom of peacock wing section; then add Unit 72 to bottom.

Making Unit 79

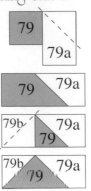

7. Refer to diagram and instructions below for making Unit 75. Join units 73 and 74. Add Unit 75 to the bottom; then join Unit 76 to right side. Join units 78, 79 and 80. Join units 81 and 82; then add Unit 83 to left side. Join Unit 77 to top of the 81-

Making Unit 75

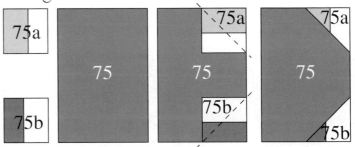

Join 1 1/8" x 1 5/8" strip of Fabric I with 1" x 1 5/8" strip of Fabric III. Use this combination as a small strip set. Place it right sides together, horizontally as shown at top right of Unit 75. Stitch diagonal, trim seam and press.
Join 1 1/8" x 1 5/8" strip of Fabric I with 1" x 1 5/8" strip of Fabric VII. Use this combination as a small strip set. Place it right sides together, horizontally as shown at bottom right of Unit 75. Stitch diagonal, trim seam and press.

83 units. Join these combined units to left side of combined units 78-80. Add the combined head units to the top.
8. For the bottom flower section, join units 86, 84 and 85 in a row. Join units 87, 88, and 89 in a row. Join units 85, 89, and 86 in a row. Join the three rows as shown. Join units 90 and 91; then add Unit 92 to left side of these combined units. Join these units to left side of flower. Join the flower section to the bottom of the peacock head/body section. Join the flower/tail section to the peacock section to complete the block.
9. Cut a small round black circle for the eye and press in place with Steam-A-Seam 2. Run a small blanket stitch around the eye with black floss.

Making Unit 85

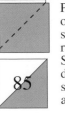

Place 1 3/4" squares of fabrics I and V right sides together with raw edges matching. Stitch a diagonal down the center as shown. Trim seam and press.

Block finishes to 18" square. Size of block
before it is sewn into the quilt is 18 1/2"

Cutting instructions shown in red indicate the quantity of
units are combined and cut in two or more different places
to conserve fabric.

CUTTING

☐ **From Fabric I, cut: (background)**
- One 4 1/8" wide strip. From this, cut:
  * Two - 4 1/8" x 5 1/4" (40)
  * Two - 2 5/8" x 4" (30)
  * Two - 2 3/4" x 3 7/8" (27)
  * Two - 1 1/2" x 3 7/8" (17)
  * Two - 1 3/4" x 3 1/2" (53)
  * Two - 1 5/8" x 3 1/2" (13)
  * Four - 1" x 3 1/2" (28, 58)
  * Two - 3" squares (38)
- One 2 5/8" wide strip. From this, cut:
  * Two - 1" x 2 5/8" (26)
  * Four - 1 3/8" x 2 1/2" (A11, B11)
  * Four - 1" x 2 1/2" (A10, B10)
  * Four - 1 1/4" x 2 3/8" (A13, B13)
  * Two - 1" x 2 3/8" (7)
  * Two - 1 1/2" x 2 1/8" (48)
  * Two - 2" squares (12)
  * Four - 1 3/4" x 2" (8, 56)
  * Three - 1 1/4" x 2" (54, 57)
  * Two - 1" x 2" (21, 55)
- One 2" wide strip. From this, cut:
  * One - 2" x 5 5/8" (39)
  * One - 1 3/4" x 5" (50)
  * Two - 1 1/4" x 1 3/4" (59)
  * Two - 1 5/8" squares (11a)
  * Two - 1 1/2" x 1 5/8" (22)
  * Four - 1 1/2" squares (4, G12, H12)
  * Two - 1 1/4" x 1 1/2" (25a)
  * Four - 7/8" x 1 1/2" (24, C11, D11) Stack this cut.
  * Three - 1" x 3" (20) Stack this cut.

MATERIALS

☐ Fabric I (background)
Need 13 3/8"   1/2 yard

■ Fabric II (navy print)
Need 5 1/8"   3/8 yard

■ Fabric III (medium blue print)
Need 2 1/2"   1/8 yard

■ Fabric IV (light blue print)
Need 2"   1/8 yard

■ Fabric V (dark gold print)
Need 3 1/4"   1/4 yard

■ Fabric VI (medium gold print)
Need 2"   1/8 yard

■ Fabric VII (light gold print)
Need 3 5/8"   1/4 yard

■ Fabric VIII (medium green print)
Need 1 5/8"   1/8 yard

■ Fabric IX (light green print)
Need 1 1/4"   1/8 yard

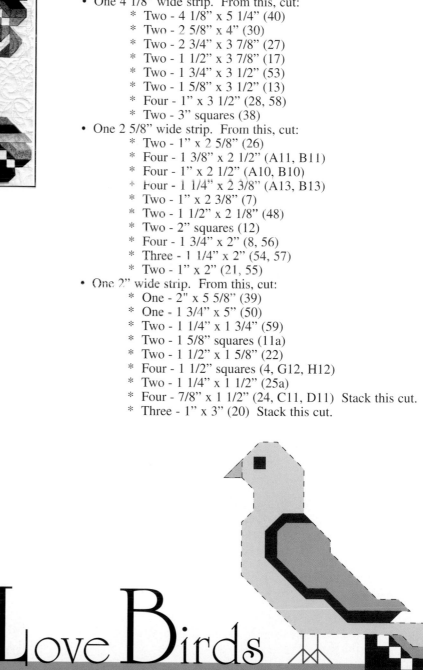

Love Birds

* One - 1" x 1 1/2" (21a)
* Two - 1 3/8" squares (44)
* Two - 1" x 1 1/4" (52)
- One 1 3/8" wide strip. From this, cut:
  * One - 1 3/8" x 7" (5)
  * Four - 1 1/8" squares (23a, C10a, D10a)
  * Thirty - 1" squares (1a, 3a, 15, 16a, 18, 36a, 49a, A1, B1, A4, B4, A6, B6, A7a, B7a, A9a, B9a, C1, D1, C4, D4, C6, D6, C7a, D7a, C9a, D9a, E1, F1, E4, F4, E6, F6, E7a, F7a, E9a, F9a, G2, H2, G4a, H4a, G5, H5, G7a, H7a, G10a, H10a, G11a, H11a)
- One 1 1/4" wide strip. From this, cut:
  * Twenty - 1 1/4" squares (6a, 25b, 51, 57b, A12a, B12a)
  * Seventeen - 1" squares (add to 1" squares above)
- Two 1" wide strips. From these, cut:
  * Sixty-one - 1" squares (add to 1" squares above)

From Fabric II, cut: (navy print)
- One 2 1/8" wide strip. From this, cut:
  * Two - 2 1/8" squares (35)
  * Two - 1" x 2 1/8" (32)
  * Two - 1 1/2" x 2" (G10, H10)
  * Eighteen - 1" x 2" (33, A5, B5, C5, D5, E5, F5)
  * Two - 1 3/4" squares (34)
  * Two - 1 1/2" x 1 3/4" (45a)
  * Two - 1" x 2 5/8" (46)
- Two 1 1/2" wide strips. From these, cut:
  * Two - 1 1/2" squares (G9, H9)
  * Thirty-eight - 1" x 1 1/2" (3, 48a, A7, B7, C7 D7, E7, F7, G7, G11, H7, H11)
  * Four - 1" x 1 3/8" (42, 43)
  * Twenty-six - 1" squares (40b, A3a, B3a, C3a, D3a, E3a, F3a, G1, G3a, G6a, G8, H1, H3a, H6a, H8)
- Cut two 1/2" squares for eyes.

From Fabric III, cut: (medium blue print)
- One 1 1/2" wide strip. From this, cut:
  * Thirty-two - 1" x 1 1/2" (2, A3, A8, B3, B8, C3, C8, D3, D8, E3, E8, F3, F8)
- One 1" wide strip. From this, cut:
  * Sixteen - 1" squares (A2, B2, C2, D2, E2, F2)

From Fabric IV, cut: (light blue print)
- Two 1" wide strips. From these, cut:
  * Sixteen - 1" x 1 1/2" (1, A9, B9, C9, D9, E9, F9)
  * Thirty-two - 1" squares (A2, A3b, B2, B3b, C2, C3b, D2, D3b, E2, E3b, F2, F3b)

From Fabric V, cut: (dark gold print)
- One 3 1/4" wide strip. From this, cut:
  * Two - 3 1/4" squares (40a)
  * Two - 1 3/8" x 3 1/8" (41)
  * Two - 1" x 2 5/8" (47)
  * Two - 1 5/8" x 2" (31)
  * Two - 1" x 2" (G6, H6)
  * Two - 1 5/8" squares (35a)
  * Two - 1" x 1 5/8" (G3, H3)
  * Two - 1" x 1 1/2" (48a)
  * Two - 1" squares (45b)

From Fabric VI, cut: (medium gold print)
- One 2" wide strip. From this, cut:
  * Two - 1 1/4" x 2" (10)
  * Two - 1" x 2" (16)
  * Eighteen - 1" squares (14, 19, 29, A6, B6, C6, D6, E6, F6)

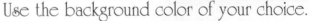
From Fabric VII, cut: (light gold print)
- One 2 5/8" wide strip. From this, cut:
  * Two - 2 5/8" x 3 1/2" (11)
  * Two - 1 1/2" x 2 1/8" (45)
  * Two - 2" x 3 1/8" (37)
  * Two - 1" x 2" (9)
  * Two - 1 7/8" squares (35b)
  * Two - 1 1/2" x 4 1/8" (36)
  * Two - 1 1/4" squares (34a)
- One 1" wide strip. From this, cut:
  * Two - 1" x 6 1/8" (49)
  * Two - 1" x 1 3/8" (G4, H4)
  * Four - 1" squares (8a, G3b, H3b)

From Fabric VIII, cut: (medium green print)
- One 1 5/8" wide strip. From this, cut:
  * Two - 1 5/8" squares (30a)
  * Four - 1 1/2" squares (4, 22a)
  * Four - 1 3/8" squares (A11a, B11a)
  * Four - 1 1/4" x 2" (57a)
  * Eight - 1 1/4" squares (50a, 51, 54a, 56a)

From Fabric IX, cut: (light green print)
- One 1 1/4" wide strip. From this, cut:
  * Eight - 1 1/4" x 2 3/8" (6, 25, A12, B12)
  * Four - 1 1/8" x 1 1/2" (23, C10, D10)

ASSEMBLY

Use the background color of your choice.

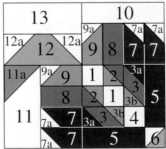
Block A Make 2

Block B Make 2

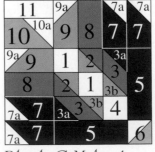
Block C Make 1

Block D Make 1

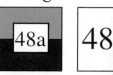

Block E Make 1   Block F Make 1

Block G Make 1   Block H Make 1

Making mirror image Unit 48

Join 1" x 1 1/2" strips of fabrics II and V.

Use joined strips as a diagonal corner. Place on Unit 48 as shown and stitch diagonal. Trim seam and press.

Make two each of mirror image units A11, and B11. Make four of Unit A12, and B12. Make two of mirror image units C10, D10, G3, H3, G4, H4, G6, H6, G11 and H11. Make one each of units G10 and H10 to complete the units for the small blocks. For the complete block, make two (mirror image) units 1, 8, 11, 22, 23, 30, 34, 35, 40, 48, 49, and 56. Make two each of Unit 6, and 16. Make one of units 50 and 54.

2. Use diagonal end technique to make two mirror image units 25 and 45. Make two of Unit 57.

3. Refer to drawings and instructions on page 36 for the triangle-

Making Unit 57

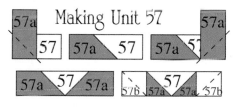

square units.

4. Blocks A and B are assembled the same, except they are mirror images. Refer to block diagrams for correct placement of mirror image units. To begin, join units 9, 8, 7 and 7 in a row. Join Unit 10 to top of row. Join units 12 and 13; then join these combined units to end of top row as shown. Join units 9, 8, 7 and 7 in a vertical row; then add Unit 11 to side of row. Join units 1 and 2, checking block diagrams for correct placement. Make two and join them together in a checkerboard. Join one of Unit 3 to bottom of the combined 1/2 units. Join units 3 and 4; then add to side of checkerboard. Join Unit 5 to bottom. Join Unit 5 and 6; then add to side of checkerboard. Add the 7-9 combined unit row to other side of center. Join the top and bottom sections to complete blocks A and B.

5. To make C and D blocks, join units 9, 8, 7 and 7 in a row. Join units 10 and 11; then join these combined units to end of top row as shown. Join units 9, 8, 7 and 7 in a ver-

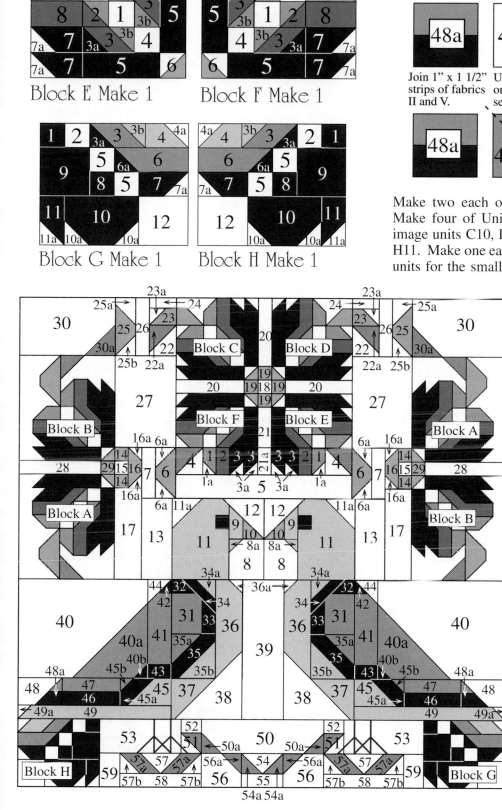

This design has many small pieces that can be chain pieced easily. The effort is very worthwhile!

1. Refer to the block diagrams for correct placement of all mirror image units. Use diagonal corner technique to make fifteen of each mirror image (thirty total) for Unit A7, B7, C7 D7, E7,F7, G7 and H7. Make a total of eighteen mirror image units A9, B9, C9, D9, E9, and F9. Make a total of sixteen mirror image units A3, B3, C3, D3, E3, and F3.

35

tical row. Join center checkerboard units the same as for blocks A and B. Add the 7-9 vertical row to end of checkerboard center as shown; then add top row.

6. To assemble blocks E and F, refer to block diagrams for correct placement of mirror image units. Make a vertical row of units 9, 8, 7, and 7. Join checkerboard center section as in Step 4. Join the vertical row to outside end of combined center units to complete the blocks.

7. For blocks G and H, make a horizontal row of units 1, 2, 3, and 4. Join units 5 and 6. Join units 8, 5, and 7; then add them to bottom of the 5/6 combined units. Join Unit 9 to outside end of these combined units. Join the top horizontal row to the 5-9 combined units, matching seams. Join units 11, 10, and 12 as shown; then add this row to bottom of other combined units to complete blocks G and H.

8. To assemble the block begin by joining units 19 and 20. Join Block C, combined units 19/20, and Block D. Join units 20, 19, 18, 19, and 20 in a long horizontal row. Add this row to the C and D block row. Join units 19 and 21. Join Block F, combined units 19/21 and Block E as shown. Add them to bottom of other combined units.

9. Refer to block diagram for correct placement of mirror image units. Join units 24, 23, and 22 in a row. Join units 25 and 26. Add these two combined units to side of combined units 22-24. Join Unit 27 to bottom of the combined units. Make two. They will be mirror images. Join these two combined unit sections to opposite sides of center flower.

10. Make a row, beginning from left to right of units 4, 1, 2, 3, 3, 21a, 3, 3, 2, 1, and 4. Join Unit 5 to bottom of this row. Join units 6 and 7; then add them to opposite sides of the combined 1-5 unit section. Join units 9 and 10; then add mirror image Unit 8 to bottom of these combined units. Join Unit 11 to outside edge of combined 8-10 units; then add diagonal corner, Unit 12 as shown. Make two that are mirror images. Join the two bird heads; then add Unit 13 to outside ends of the row. Join the bird heads and flower bottom rows together. Join units 14, 15 and 14 in a vertical row; then add Unit 16 as shown. Join Unit 17 to bottom. Make two mirror images and add them to opposite ends of bird head section. Join this section to bottom of center flower.

Making Unit 2 for blocks A, B, C, D, E, and F.

Place 1" squares of fabrics III and IV right sides facing and raw edges matching. Stitch down the center diagonally as shown. Trim seam and press. Make 16.

Making Unit 6 for blocks A, B, C, D, E, and F.

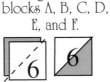

Place 1" squares of fabrics I and VI right sides facing and raw edges matching. Stitch down the center diagonally as shown. Trim seam and press. Make 8.

Making Unit 4

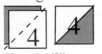

Place 1 1/2" squares of fabrics I and VIII right sides facing and raw edges matching. Stitch down the center diagonally as shown. Trim seam and press. Make 2.

Making Unit 51

Place 1" squares of fabrics I and VIII right sides facing and raw edges matching. Stitch down the center diagonally as shown. Trim seam and press. Make 2.

11. Join units 28 and 29. Make 2. Make a row of Unit 30, Block B, combined units 28/29, and Block A. Join these combined block sections to opposite sides of other combined units.

12. Refer to diagram below for combined mirror image units 31-34. Join these combined units with Unit 35; then add Unit 36 to side; then join Unit 37 to bottom. Join diagonal corner Unit 38. Join Unit 39 between the two combined unit sections. Refer to diagram below for making combined mirror image units 41-44. Join these units to Unit 40. Join units 46 and 47; then add mirror image unit 48 to outside end and Unit 45 to opposite end. Join Unit 49 to bottom of the combined units. Add these units to bottom of combined units 40-44. Join the bird breast section to the bird wing section. Join this section to bottom of flower section.

13. To make bottom leaf section, begin in the center and join units 54 and 55;

Making combined mirror image units 31-34

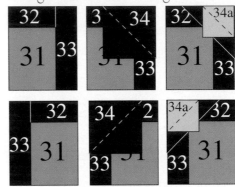

Making combined mirror image units 41-44

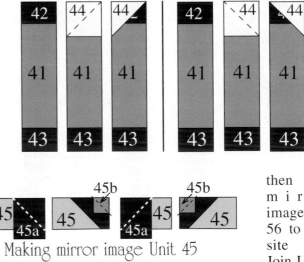

Making mirror image Unit 45

then add mirror image Unit 56 to opposite ends. Join Unit 50 to top. Join units 51 and 52; then add Unit 53 as shown. Join units 57 and 58; then join Unit 59 to outside end. Join these combined leaf sections to combined units 51-53; then add to opposite ends of combined units 50-56. Join blocks G and H to opposite ends of leaf section as shown. Join this section to bottom of birds to complete the block.

14. We cut 1/8" wide strips of Fabric VII for the birds feet, and pressed them down with Steam-A-Seam 2. Do the same for the eyes and blanket stitch around them if desired.

Block finishes to 18" square. Size of block before it is sewn into the quilt is 18 1/2"

MATERIALS

■ **Fabric I** (background)
Need 11"   1/2 yard

□ **Fabric II** (white on ivory print)
Need 3 1/8"   1/4 yard

□ **Fabric III** (white on white print)
Need 5 1/2" x 11 1/2"   large scrap

■ **Fabric IV** (dark green print)
Need 3 3/8"   1/4 yard

■ **Fabric V** (medium green print)
Need 2 3/4"   1/8 yard

■ **Fabric VI** (light green print)
Need 2 3/4"   1/8 yard

■ **Fabric VII** (burgundy print)
Need 2 1/4"   1/8 yard

■ **Fabric VIII** (dark rose print)
Need 2 1/4"   1/8 yard

■ **Fabric IX** (medium rose print)
Need 2 1/4"   1/8 yard

■ **Fabric X** (light rose solid)
Need 2 3/8"   1/8 yard

■ **Fabric XI** (pale pink print)
Need 2 1/4"   1/8 yard

■ **Fabric XII** (medium blue print)
Need 3" x 8"   scrap

□ **Fabric XIII** (light blue print)
Need 3" x 5"   scrap

■ **Fabric XIV** (dark gold print)
Need 2" square   scrap

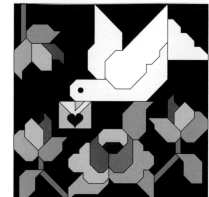

Because of the white in this block,
we suggest using a dark background.

Love Letter

CUTTING

From Fabric I, cut: (background)
- One 4 3/4" wide strip. From this, cut:
  * One - 4 3/4" square (17)
  * One - 2 1/8" x 4 3/4" (80)
  * One - 1 1/8" x 4 3/4" (15)
  * One - 1 1/2" x 4 5/8" (35)
  * One - 2 5/8" x 4 1/4" (34)
  * One - 2 1/8" x 4 1/4" (96)
  * One - 1 3/4" x 4 1/4" (82a)
  * One - 1 1/8" x 4 1/4" (66)
  * One - 1 1/8" x 4 1/8" (1)
  * One - 2 3/8" x 4" (3)
  * One - 2 1/8" x 3 1/2" (31)
  * One - 1 3/8" x 3 1/2" (11)
  * One - 3 3/8" square (50b)
  * One - 3" x 3 3/8" (53)
  * One - 1 3/4" x 3 3/8" (83)
  * One - 1" x 3 3/8" (48)
  * One - 2" x 3 1/4" (93)
  * One - 1" x 3 1/4" (95)
  * One - 3 1/8" square (16a)
- One 3" wide strip. From this, cut:
  * One - 3" x 3 1/8" (27)
  * One - 1 1/2" x 3" (92)
  * One - 2 3/4" square (50a)
  * One - 1 3/4" x 2 3/4" (62)
  * One - 1 1/2" x 2 3/4" (57)
  * Two - 1 1/4" x 2 3/4" (46)
  * One - 1 1/8" x 2 3/4" (40)
  * One - 1" x 2 3/4" (45)
  * One - 2 1/2" square (24a)
  * One - 2 3/8" x 5 5/8" (13)
  * One - 2 1/8" x 7 3/8" (14)
  * One - 1 1/2" x 2 1/8" (36)
  * One - 1 3/8" x 2 1/4" (7a)
- One 2" wide strip. From this, cut:
  * One - 1 3/4" x 2" (81)
  * One - 1 1/4" x 2" (55)
  * One - 1 1/8" x 2" (4a)
  * One - 1 7/8" square (65a)
  * One - 1 3/4" x 1 7/8" (25)
  * One - 1 5/8" x 1 7/8" (5a)
  * Two - 1 3/4" squares (29, 89b)
  * One - 1 3/8" x 1 3/4" (88)
  * Three - 1 5/8" squares (38b, 43b, 54a)
  * Four - 1 1/2" squares (44b, 49b, 64a, 76)
  * Three - 1 1/4" x 1 1/2" (56, 74, 90)
  * Four - 1 3/8" squares (8b, 9a, 18a, 85b)
  * Six - 1 1/8" squares (4b, 6a, 14b, 32a, 49a, 59a)
- One 1 1/4" wide strip. From this, cut:
  * One - 1 1/4" x 1 3/8" (42)
  * Eleven - 1 1/4" squares (6b, 26a, 28a, 30a, 33a, 39a, 73a, 89a, 93b, 94a)
  * Thirteen - 1" squares (10b, 14c, 37a, 43c, 58a, 72a, 75a, 77a, 79a, 83b, 87b)
  * One - 1" x 7 1/2" (12)

From Fabric II, cut: (white on ivory print)
- One 3 1/8" wide strip. From this, cut:
  * One - 3 1/8" x 4 3/4" (16)
  * One - 2 1/8" x 3 1/8" (18)
  * One - 3" square (28)
  * One - 2 1/2" x 3 7/8" (24)
  * Two - 2 1/8" x 2 1/2" (14a, 19)
  * One - 2" square (20b)
  * Two - 1 3/4" squares (26, 30)

  * One - 1 1/4" x 1 3/4" (23)
  * One - 1 5/8" x 4 3/8" (21)
  * Two - 1 1/2" squares (20a)
  * Two - 1 1/4" squares (17a, 22a)
  * One - 1 1/8" square (15a)

From Fabric III, cut: (white on white print)
- One - 4 3/4" square (17)
- One - 4" x 4 3/8" (20)
- One - 1 3/4" square (22)

From Fabric IV, cut: (dark green print)
- One 3 3/8" wide strip. From this, cut:
  * One - 3 3/8" x 3 1/2" (50)
  * One - 2" square (93a)
  * One - 1 3/4" square (83a)
  * One - 1 1/4" square (82b)
  * One - 1" x 4 1/8" (2)
  * One - 1" x 1 1/2" (91)
  * One - 1" x 1 1/4" (47)
  * Two - 1" squares (44c, 86b)

From Fabric V, cut: (medium green print)
- One 2 3/4" wide strip. From this, cut:
  * One - 2 3/4" x 3" (54)
  * One - 2 3/4" square (44)
  * One - 1 3/4" x 2 3/4" (87)
  * One - 2 1/4" x 3 1/4" (94)
  * One - 2 1/8" square (80a)
  * One - 2" x 3 3/8" (49)
  * One - 1 3/4" x 3 3/8" (89)
  * Two - 1 1/2" x 1 3/4" (73, 79)
  * One - 1 5/8" x 3 3/4" (5)
  * One - 1 1/2" square (70)
  * Three - 1 1/4" squares (50c, 55a, 93c)
  * One - 1 1/8" x 3 1/8" (4)
  * One - 1 1/8" square (78a)
  * One - 1" square (45a)

From Fabric VI, cut: (light green print)
- One 2 3/4" wide strip. From this, cut:
  * One - 2 3/4" square (43)
  * Two - 1 3/4" x 2 3/4" (82, 86)
  * One - 1 7/8" x 2 1/2" (65)
  * One - 1 1/2" x 2 7/8" (64)
  * One - 1 1/8" x 1 1/2" (37)
  * One - 1 3/8" x 3" (7)
  * One - 1 1/4" x 3 7/8" (6)
  * Two - 1 1/8" squares (56a, 66a)
  * Four - 1" squares (2a, 5b, 63a)

From Fabric VII, cut: (burgundy print)
- One 2 1/4" wide strip. From this, cut:
  * One - 1 1/2" x 2 1/4" (68)
  * One - 2 1/8" square (38a)
  * One - 1 1/2" x 1 5/8" (10)
  * Two - 1 1/2" squares (60a, 85a)
  * One - 1 1/4" x 1 1/2" (33)

From Fabric VIII, cut: (dark rose print)
- One 2 1/4" wide strip. From this, cut:
  * One - 2 1/4" square (61)
  * One - 1 1/2" x 2 1/4" (60)
  * One - 1 5/8" x 2" (9)
  * One - 1 1/8" x 2" (84)
  * Two - 1 1/4" x 1 3/4" (44a, 62a)
  * One - 1 1/8" x 1 3/4" (86a)
  * Three - 1 1/2" squares (8a, 38a, 85a)

* One - 1 1/4" x 2 3/4" (39)
* One - 1 1/8" x 1 1/4" (32)
* One - 1" square (10a)

From Fabric IX, cut: (med. rose print)
• One 2 1/4" wide strip. From this, cut:
    * One - 2 1/4" x 2 3/4" (71)
    * One - 1 1/2" square (68b)
    * One - 1" x 2 3/4" (69)

From Fabric X, cut: (light rose solid)
• One 2 3/8" wide strip. From this, cut:
    * One - 2 3/8" x 3" (8)
    * One - 2 1/4" x 2 1/2" (77)
    * One - 1 1/2" x 2 3/4" (72)
    * One - 1 1/2" x 1 3/4" (78)
    * One - 1 1/2" square (75)
    * One - 1 3/8" square (71b)
    * One - 1" square (71a)

From Fabric XI, cut: (pale pink print)
• One 2 1/4" wide strip. From this, cut:
    * One - 2 1/4" x 2 3/4" (38)
    * One - 1 3/4" x 2 1/4" (67)
    * One - 1 1/2" x 2 1/4" (58)
    * One - 2" x 2 3/8" (85)
    * Two - 1 3/4" squares (43a, 87a)
    * One - 1 1/8" x 1 3/4" (86a)
    * One - 1" x 1 3/4" (44a)
    * One - 1 1/2" x 3 1/4" (59)
    * One - 1 1/2" x 2 7/8" (63)
    * One - 1 1/2" x 1 3/4" (62a)
    * Three - 1 1/4" squares (60a, 61a, 68a)
    * One - 1" square (61b)

From Fabric XI, cut: (medium blue print)
• One - 2" x 3" (52)
• One - 1 3/8" x 3" (41)
• One - 1 1/8" x 2 1/8" (51a)

From Fabric XIII, cut: (light blue print)
• One - 2" square (52a)
• One - 1 1/8" x 2" (51)
• One - 1 3/8" square (41a)

From Fabric XIV, cut: (dark gold print)
• One 1 3/8" square (52b)

ASSEMBLY

1. Use diagonal corner technique to make one of units 2, 6, 8, 9, 10, 14a, 15, 16, 18, 20, 22, 24, 26, 28, 30, 32, 33, 37, 38, (see diagram) 39, 41, 43, 44, (see diagram) 45, 49, 50, 52, 54, 55, 56, 58, 59, 60, (see diagram) 61, 63, 64, 65, 66, 68, 71, 72, 73, 75, 77, 78, 79, 80, 83, 85, (see diagram) 86, (see diagram) 87, 89, 93, and 94.

2. Refer to diagrams and use diagonal end technique to make one each of units 4, 5, 7, 51, 62, and 82. Refer to diagram on left to make triangle-square, Unit 17.

3. To assemble the block, begin by

Cut one from burgundy for letter

Making Unit 4

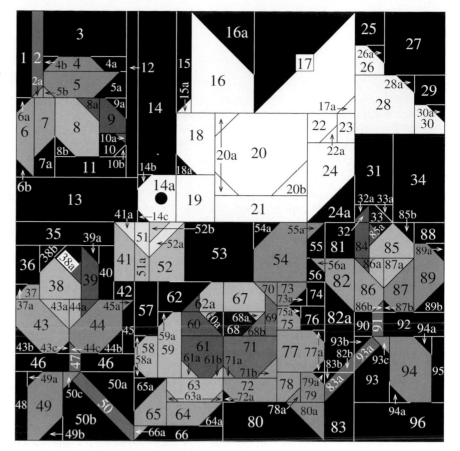

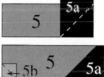

Making Unit 5

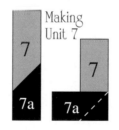

Making Unit 7

joining units 1 and 2. Join units 4 and 5; then add Unit 3 to top of 4/5 combination. Join combined units 1/2 to left side. Join units 9 and 10; then add Unit 8 to left side of the 9/10 combined units. Join Unit 11 to the bottom. Join units 6 and 7; then join them to left side of combined units 8-11. Join this rose bud section to leaf combined units; then join Unit 12 to right side. Join Unit 13 to the bottom to complete top rose bud.

4. Join units 14 and 14a. Join units 15 and 16; then add Unit 17 to right side of combined 15/16 units. Join units 18 and 19. Join units 20 and 21. Join the 18/19 combined units to left side of combined units 20/21. Join units 22 and 23; then add Unit 24 to bottom of these combine units. Join these units to right side of wing as shown. Join combined units 15-17 across the top of the

Making Unit 17

Place 4 3/4" squares of Fabrics I and III right sides facing, and raw edges matching. Stitch diagonal. DO NOT trim seam on Fabric I. Press; then join 17a.

17

17

17a →

39

combined units; then add combined units 14/14a to left side to complete the dove body and wing. Join this section to rose bud section as shown.

5. Join units 25 and 26; then add Unit 27 to right side. Join units 29 and 30; then add Unit 28 to left side of these combined units. Join the two combined tail unit sections together as shown in block diagram. Join units 32 and 33; then add Unit 31 to top. Join Unit 34 to the right side; then join these combined units to bottom of tail. Join the tail section to right side of the body section to complete the top of the block.

6. Refer to diagram and instructions below for making Unit 38. Join units 36 and 37; then add Unit 38 to right

Making Unit 38

This unit is made by using a diagonal corner unit as a diagonal corner on a larger unit. Use the 1 1/2" square of Fabric VIII as the diagonal corner on the 2 1/8" square of fabric VII. Place the completed 38a unit right sides facing and raw edges matching on Unit 38. Stitch diagonal, trim seam and press; then add diagonal corner 38b.

side of these combined units. Join units 39 and 40. Join these combined units to right side of Unit 38; then add Unit 35 across the top. Join units 41 and 42; then join them to right side of other bud units. Join units 43, 44, and 45 in a

Making Unit 44

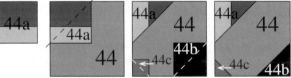

Join the 1 1/4" x 1 3/4" strip of Fabric VIII with the 1" x 1 3/4" strip of Fabric XI as shown. Use this as diagonal corner 44a and place on Unit 44, right sides facing as shown. Stitch the diagonal, trim and press. Join diagonal corners 44b and 44c.

row. Join units 46, 47, and 46 in a row. Add this row to bottom of leaf row. Join units 48 and 49; then join Unit 50 to right side of the 48/49 combined units. Join these combined units to bottom of rose bud stem as shown, matching seams. When making Unit 50, add diagonal corners in alphabetical order.

7. To piece the letter and large rose, begin by joining units 51, 52, 53, and 54 in a row. Join units 55 and 56; then add them to right side of the row. Refer to diagram at top right for making Unit 60. Join units 60 and 61; then add Unit 59 to left side. Join Unit 62 across the top, matching seams. Join units 57 and 58. Add them to left side of combined units 59-62. Join units 63 and 64; then add Unit 65 to left side. Join Unit 66 across the bottom. Add these combined units to bottom of combined units 57-62. Join units 67 and 68; then add Unit 69 to right side of these combined units. Join diagonal corner, Unit 70 as shown. Join Unit 71 to bottom of these combined units;

Making Unit 51

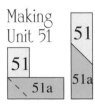

Making Unit 60

Join diagonal corner 60a first. Use the 1 1/4" square of Fabric XI as the diagonal corner on the 1 1/2" square of fabric VII. Place the completed 60a unit right sides facing and raw edges matching on Unit 60. Stitch diagonal, trim seam and press.

Making Unit 62

Unit 62 is a diagonal end which is made as you would make any diagonal end. The small joined 62a units are used as the second part of the diagonal end. Join the 1 1/4" x 1 3/4" strip of Fabric VII and the 1 1/2" x 1 3/4" strip of Fabric XI as shown. Stitch the diagonal as shown. Trim and press.

Making Unit 82

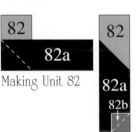

Making Unit 85

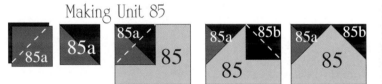

Place 1 1/2" squares of fabrics VII and VIII right sides facing and raw edges matching. Stitch the diagonal, trim seam and press. Use this triangle square and a diagonal corner as shown. Stitch the 85a unit. Trim seam and press; then add diagonal corner 85b.

Making Unit 86

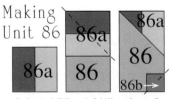

Join 1 1/8" x 1 3/4" strips of fabrics VIII and X1. Use this strip set as a diagonal corner. Stitch the diagonal as shown, trim seam and press. Add diagonal corner 86b.

then add Unit 72 to bottom. Join units 73 and 74. Join units 75 and 76. Join these two combined unit sections together; then add Unit 77 to the bottom. Join units 78 and 79. Add these units to bottom of Unit 77. Join these combined units to combined units 67-72; then add Unit 80 across the bottom. Join the two rose sections together, matching seams; then add combined units 51-56 across the top, again matching seams. Join this section to bottom left rose bud section.

8. For bottom right rose bud, begin by joining units 81, 82 and 83 in a row. Join units 84 and 85. Join units 86 and 87. Join these two combined unit sections together. Join units 88 and 89. Add to right side of combined units 84-87. Join units 90, 91, and 92 in a row. Join to bottom of rose bud. Join units 93, 94, and 95; then add Unit 96 to bottom of these combined units. Join these units to bottom of rose bud stem; then add combined units 81-83 to right side. Join this rose bud section to right side of large rose. Join this bottom section to the top section, matching seams to complete the block. Press heart on letter with Steam-A-Seam 2.

Block finishes to 18" square. Size of block before
it is sewn into the quilt is 18 1/2"

MATERIALS

☐ Fabric I (background)
Need 11 1/2"   1/2 yard

■ Fabric II (bronze brown print)
Need 3 7/8"   1/4 yard

☐ Fabric III (medium gold print)
Need 4 3/8"   1/4 yard

■ Fabric IV (orange print)
Need 2 1/2"   1/8 yard

■ Fabric V (bright red print)
Need 2 1/2"   1/8 yard

■ Fabric VI (dark green print)
Need 2 1/2"   1/8 yard

■ Fabric VII (medium green print)
Need 1 7/8"   1/8 yard

CUTTING

☐ **From Fabric I, cut: (background)**
• One 3 3/4" wide strip. From this, cut:
   * Two - 3 3/4" squares (21)
   * Two - 7/8" x 3 3/4" (45)
   * Two - 2 7/8" x 3 1/2" (37)
   * Two - 1 7/8" x 3 1/2" (49)
   * Two - 2 1/2" x 3" (10)
   * Two - 1 3/4" x 2 1/2" (9)
   * Eight - 1 1/4" x 2 1/2" (5)
   * Two - 1 1/8" x 2 3/8" (24)
• One 2 3/4" wide strip. From this, cut:
   * Two - 2 3/4" x 9 3/4" (13)
   * Two - 2 1/2" x 4 1/4" (11)
   * Eight - 1 1/8" x 2 1/2" (8)
   * Two - 1 7/8" x 2 3/8" (29)
• One 2 1/4" wide strip. From this, cut:
   * Two - 1 5/8" x 2 1/4" (33)
   * Four - 2 1/8" squares (44)
   * Two - 1" x 2 1/8" (47)
   * Two - 1 7/8" squares (48)

   * Two - 1 3/8" x 1 7/8" (31)
   * Two - 1" x 1 7/8" (32)
   * Two - 1 5/8" x 5 1/8" (38)
   * Two - 1 5/8" squares (36)
• One 1 3/4" wide strip. From this, cut:
   * One - 1 3/4" x 14" (12)
   * Twenty - 1 1/8" squares (1c, 2b, 6a, 30a, 46a)
• One 1" wide strip. From this, cut:
   * Twenty - 1" squares (34a, 38b, 41a, 42a, 43a)

■ **From Fabric II, cut: (bronze brown print)**
• One 3 7/8" wide strip. From this, cut:
   * One - 3 7/8" x 8" (18)
   * One - 2 1/8" x 3" (14)
   * Two - 2 1/8" x 2 3/8" (15)
   * One - 1 3/8" x 1 1/2" (25)
   * One - 1 1/8" x 1 1/2" (22)
   * Two - 1 3/8" squares (26)

Apples & Oranges

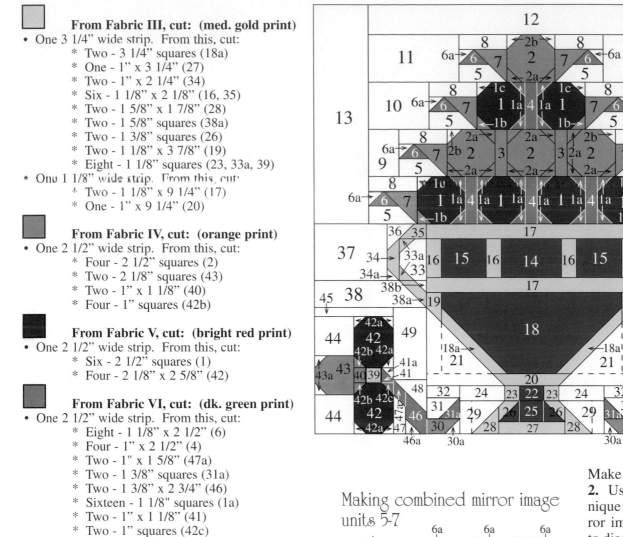

From Fabric III, cut: (med. gold print)
- One 3 1/4" wide strip. From this, cut:
  * Two - 3 1/4" squares (18a)
  * One - 1" x 3 1/4" (27)
  * Two - 1" x 2 1/4" (34)
  * Six - 1 1/8" x 2 1/8" (16, 35)
  * Two - 1 5/8" x 1 7/8" (28)
  * Two - 1 5/8" squares (38a)
  * Two - 1 3/8" squares (26)
  * Two - 1 1/8" x 3 7/8" (19)
  * Eight - 1 1/8" squares (23, 33a, 39)
- One 1 1/8" wide strip. From this, cut:
  * Two - 1 1/8" x 9 1/4" (17)
  * One - 1" x 9 1/4" (20)

From Fabric IV, cut: (orange print)
- One 2 1/2" wide strip. From this, cut:
  * Four - 2 1/2" squares (2)
  * Two - 2 1/8" squares (43)
  * Two - 1" x 1 1/8" (40)
  * Four - 1" squares (42b)

From Fabric V, cut: (bright red print)
- One 2 1/2" wide strip. From this, cut:
  * Six - 2 1/2" squares (1)
  * Four - 2 1/8" x 2 5/8" (42)

From Fabric VI, cut: (dk. green print)
- One 2 1/2" wide strip. From this, cut:
  * Eight - 1 1/8" x 2 1/2" (6)
  * Four - 1" x 2 1/2" (4)
  * Two - 1" x 1 5/8" (47a)
  * Two - 1 3/8" squares (31a)
  * Two - 1 3/8" x 2 3/4" (46)
  * Sixteen - 1 1/8" squares (1a)
  * Two - 1" x 1 1/8" (41)
  * Two - 1" squares (42c)

From Fabric VII, cut: (med. green print)
- One 1 7/8" wide strip. From this, cut:
  * Eight - 1 7/8" squares (7)
  * Two - 1 1/8" x 1 7/8" (30)
  * Sixteen - 1 1/8" squares (1b, 2a)
  * Two - 1" x 2 1/2" (3)

Use the background color of your choice.

ASSEMBLY

1. Use diagonal corner technique to make eight of mirror image Unit 6. Make six of Unit 1 and four of Unit 2. Use this technique to make four mirror image Unit 42, and two each of mirror image units 30, 31, 34, 38, 41, 43, and 46.

Making combined mirror image units 5-7

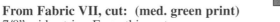

Making Unit 26

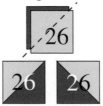

Place 1 3/8" squares of fabrics II and III right sides together with raw edges matching. Stitch diagonal. Trim seam, open, and press. Make 2.

Make two of Unit 33.

2. Use diagonal end technique to make two of mirror image Unit 47. Refer to diagram below for triangle-square Unit 26.

3. To assemble the block, refer to diagram on left and join units 5 and 6; then add diagonal corner Unit 7 as shown. Refer to block diagram above, and join Unit 8 to the top of all combined units 5-7. This will now be referred to as leaves. Join mirror image leaves to opposite sides of one Unit 2; then add Unit 11 to opposite sides of these combined units. Add Unit 12 across the top. Join Unit 10, leaves, Unit 1, Unit 4, Unit 1, leaves, and another Unit 10. Join this row to top row. For row three, join Unit 9, leaves, Unit 2, Unit 3, Unit 2, Unit 3, Unit 2, leaves, and another Unit 9. Join this row to second row. For fourth row, join leaves, Unit 1, Unit 4, Unit 1, Unit 4, Unit 1, Unit 4, Unit 1, and leaves. Join this row to third row; then join Unit 13 to opposite sides of fruit to complete the block top.

4. For bottom half of block, begin by joining units 16, 15,

Making combined units 18-21

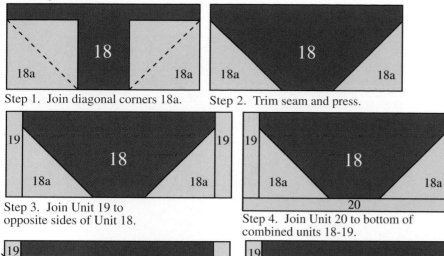

Step 1. Join diagonal corners 18a.

Step 2. Trim seam and press.

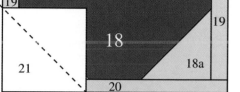

Step 3. Join Unit 19 to opposite sides of Unit 18.

Step 4. Join Unit 20 to bottom of combined units 18-19.

Step 5. Join diagonal corner 21 to combined units. DO NOT trim seam as diagonal corner 21 is a light colored fabric on top of a darker colored fabric

Step 5. Press diagonal corners 21 in place.

Making combined units 25-29

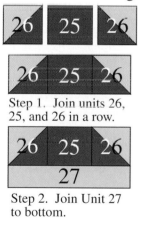

Step 1. Join units 26, 25, and 26 in a row.

Step 2. Join Unit 27 to bottom.

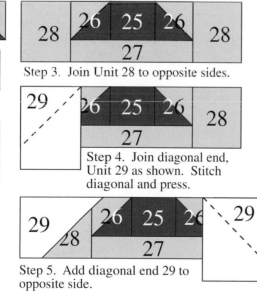

Step 3. Join Unit 28 to opposite sides.

Step 4. Join diagonal end, Unit 29 as shown. Stitch diagonal and press.

Step 5. Add diagonal end 29 to opposite side.

16, 14, 16, 15, and 16 in a vertical row as shown. Join Unit 17 to top and bottom of this row. Refer to diagram above for making combined units 18-21. Follow instructions for making this section; then add it to the bottom of the combined 14-17 row. Join units 32, 31, and 30 as shown. Join units 24, 23, 22, 23, and 24 in a vertical row. Refer to diagram directly above and follow drawings and instructions to make combine units 25-29. Join the 22-24 combined unit row to top of the 25-29 combined units. Join combined mirror image units 30-32 to opposite sides of urn to complete this section.

5. Join units 33 and 34; then add Unit 35 to top. Join diag-

onal corner 36 as shown to these combined units. Refer to block diagram for correct placement of mirror image. Join Unit 37 to outer ends of combined units 33-36. Join mirror image, Unit 38 to bottom of these combined units.

6. Join units 40, 39, and 41 in a row. Join mirror image Unit 42 to top and bottom of this row. Refer frequently to block diagram for mirror image placement. Join units 44, 43, and 44; then add them to combined units 39-42 as shown. Join Unit 45 to top of these combined units. Refer to diagrams below and make combined units 46-48. Join Unit 49 to top of these combined units; then add this row to flowers as shown. Join this flower section to bottom of combined units 33-38; then add to opposite sides of urn. Join this completed bottom section to top section to complete the block.

Making Mirror Image Unit 47

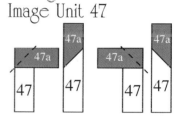

Making combined mirror image units 46-48

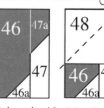

Join diagonal corner 46a. DO NOT trim seam. Press only.

Join units 46 and 47.

Join diagonal corner Unit 48. DO NOT trim seam.

Press Unit 48.

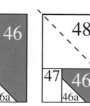

Block finishes to 18" square. Size of block before
it is sewn into the quilt is 18 1/2"

MATERIALS

 Fabric I (background)
Need 9 1/2"   3/8 yard

 Fabric II (bright red print)
Need 4"   1/4 yard

 Fabric III (dark green print)
Need 2 1/8"   1/8 yard

 Fabric IV (medium green print)
Need 2" x 6"   scrap

 Fabric V (dark gold print)
Need 4 1/8"   1/4 yard

 Fabric VI (medium gold print)
Need 2 1/4"   1/8 yard

Fabric VII (pale gold print)
Need 2 5/8"   1/8 yard

Fabric VIII (tan print)
Need 1 5/8"   1/8 yard

Fabric IX (orange print)
Need 2" x 9"   scrap

Fabric X (light peach print)
Need 4" square   scrap

Fabric XI (dark salmon print)
Need 2"   1/8 yard

CUTTING

From Fabric I, cut: (background)
• One 5 7/8" wide strip. From this, cut:
  * One - 2 7/8" x 5 3/4" (28)
  * One - 1 7/8" x 5 1/2" (56)
  * Two - 3 1/4" x 5 3/8" (67)
  * One - 1 1/8" x 5 1/4" (69)
  * One - 2 5/8" x 4 1/2" (55)
  * Two - 1 5/8" x 4 1/4" (70)
  * Two - 1" x 4" (63a)
  * One - 3 1/4" square (34)
  * One - 2" x 3 1/4" (7)
  * One - 1 5/8" x 3 1/4" (1)
  • Stack these cuts:
  * Two - 2 7/8" squares (61a)
  * Two - 1" x 2 7/8" (77)
  * Eight - 1 1/2" squares (5b, 25a, 38b, 42a,
    47a, 75)
  * Seven - 1" squares (2b, 26b, 35a, 47b, 49a, 50b)
  • From scrap, cut:
  * Four - 1 1/4" squares (23a, 51a, 76)
  * Four - 1 1/8" squares (39a, 42b, 74a)
• One 3 5/8" wide strip. From this, cut:
  * One - 3 5/8" x 9 7/8" (57)
  * Two - 3 3/8" x 6 1/2" (78)
  * One - 1 1/8" x 2 1/4" (33)
  * One - 2 1/8 square (31b)
  * One - 1 7/8" x 2 1/8" (3)
  * Two - 1 5/8" x 2 1/8" (48, 53)
  * One - 1 1/2" x 2 1/8" (52)
  * One - 1 1/2" x 2" (27)
  * One - 1" x 1 7/8" (6)
  * One - 1 3/4" square (12a)
  * Two - 1 5/8" x 1 3/4" (71) Stack this cut.
  * One - 1" x 1 3/4" (44)

Bowl of Fruit

* One - 1 1/8" x 1 5/8" (45)
* Two - 1 3/8" square (50a, 50c)

From Fabric II, cut: (bright red print)
• One 4" wide strip. From this, cut:
* One - 2 3/8" x 4" (50)
* One - 1 1/2" x 4" (49)
* One - 1 5/8" x 3 3/4" (2)
* One - 2 1/8" x 2 5/8" (47)
* One - 1 5/8" x 2 5/8" (35)
* One - 1 1/8" x 1 5/8" (37)
* One - 1 1/2" square (42a)
* Three - 1 1/8" squares (38a, 40a, 46a)
* Two - 1" squares (42c, 44a)

From Fabric III, cut: (dark green print)
• One 2 1/8" wide strip. From this, cut:
* One - 2 1/8" x 2 3/8" (51)
* One - 2 1/8" x 2 1/4" (31)
* One - 1" x 2 1/8" (30)
* One - 1 5/8" x 2" (1a)
* One - 1 5/8" x 1 7/8" (4)
* One - 1 3/4" x 2 3/8" (12)
* Two - 1 5/8" squares (5a, 18a)
* One - 1" x 1 5/8" (54)
* One - 1 1/2" x 3 3/8" (25)
* Two - 1 1/2" squares (2a, 34a)
* One - 1 1/8" x 1 1/2" (32)
* One - 1 3/8" square (50c)
* One - 1 1/8" square (23b)
* One - 1" x 1 1/8" (11)
* Five - 1" squares (9a, 13a, 21a, 50d, 55a)

From Fabric IV, cut: (medium green print)
• One 1 5/8" wide strip. From this, cut:
* One - 1 5/8" x 2 1/8" (29)
* One - 1 5/8" x 1 3/4" (18)
* One - 1 5/8" square (31a)

From Fabric V, cut: (dark gold print)
• One 3 1/8" wide strip. From this, cut:
* Two - 3 1/8" x 4" (61)
* One - 1 5/8" x 3" (66)
* One - 1 3/8" x 3" (64)
* Four - 1 5/8" x 2 1/2" (59)
* Two - 1 5/8" squares (67b)
* Two - 1 3/8" squares (67a)
* Two - 1 1/4" x 7 1/2" (60)
• One 1" wide strip. From this, cut:
* One - 1" x 5 1/4" (68)

From Fabric VI, cut: (medium gold print)
• One 1 1/4" wide strip. From this, cut:
* One - 1 1/4" x 3" (65)
* Four - 1 1/8" x 2 7/8" (74)
* Two - 1 1/8" x 1 5/8" (73)
* Two - 1 1/8" squares (71a)
* One - 1" x 12 3/4" (62)
* One - 1" x 6 3/4" (63)
• One 1" wide strip. From this, cut:
* Five - 1" x 2 1/2" (58)
* Two - 1" x 1 5/8" (72)
* Two - 1" squares (71b)

From Fabric VII, cut: (pale gold print)
• One 2 5/8" wide strip. From this, cut:
* One - 2 5/8" x 3 1/2" (42)
* One - 2" x 2 1/2" (8)
* One - 1 3/4" x 2 1/2" (13)

* One - 1 1/8" x 2 3/8" (40)
* One - 1 3/4" x 2 1/8" (43)
* One - 1 1/2" x 2" (9)
* One - 1 7/8" x 3 5/8" (5)
* One - 1 5/8" x 3 1/2" (39)
* Two - 1 1/8" x 1 1/2" (10, 46)
* One - 1" x 1 1/2" (21a)
* One - 1 3/8" square (7a)
* One - 1 1/4" x 1 3/8" (14)
* One - 1" x 1 1/4" (16)
* One - 1 1/8" square (45a)
* One - 1" square (26a)

From Fabric VIII, cut: (tan print)
• One 1 5/8" wide strip. From this, cut:
* One - 1 5/8" x 3 3/4" (38)
* One - 1" x 1 5/8" (36)
* One - 1 1/2" x 1 7/8" (27a)
* One - 1" x 1 1/2" (26)
* One - 1" x 2 3/8" (41)
* One - 1" x 1 3/8" (15)
* Five - 1" squares (13b, 17, 35b, 39b)

From Fabric IX, cut: (orange print)
• One 1 5/8" wide strip. From this, cut:
* One - 1 5/8" x 3 3/4" (24)
* One - 1 1/2" square (38b)
* One - 1 3/8" square (19a)
* Two - 1 1/8" squares (19b, 38a)

From Fabric X, cut: (light peach print)
• One - 2 7/8" x 3 3/4" (19)

From Fabric XI, cut: (dark salmon print)
• One 2" wide strip. From this, cut:
* One - 2" square (21)
* One - 1 3/4" x 3 3/4" (23)
* One - 1 3/4" square (22)
* One - 1" x 1 1/2" (21a)
* One - 1" x 3 3/4" (20)

ASSEMBLY

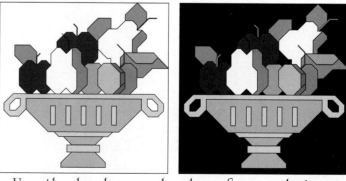

Use the background color of your choice.

1. Refer to block diagram on page 46, and use diagonal corner technique to make two each of mirror image units 61, 67, 71, and 74. Refer to diagram at bottom of page 47. There are two of Unit 74; one with a diagonal corner and one without. Use diagonal corner technique to make one of units 2, 5, 7, 9, 12, 13, 18, 19, (see diagram) 23, 25, 26, 31, (see diagram) 34,

Making Unit 1

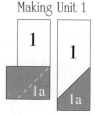

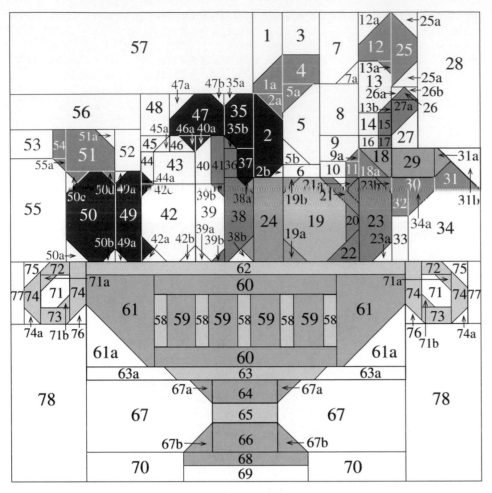

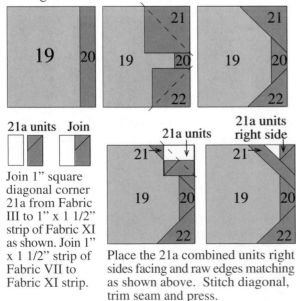

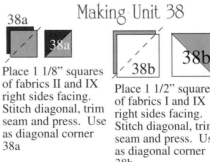

tical row. Join these combined units to combined 1/2 units. Join units 10 and 11. Join units 7, 8, 9, and 10/11 combination in another vertical row. Join to right side of other combined units. Join units 14 and 15. Join units 16 and 17. Join these two combined units together as shown in block diagram at left. Join units 12, 13, and combine 14-17 units, and Unit 18 in a row. Add to right side of other combined units. Join units 24, combined units 19-22, and Unit 23 in a row. Add to bottom of other combined units.

4. Join units 25, 26, and 27; then add Unit 28 to right side of these combined units. Join unit 29 and 30; then add Unit 31 to right side of combined 29/30 units. Join units 32 and 33; then add Unit 34 to right side of these units. Join combined units 25-28 to top of combined units 29-34. Join this combined unit section to right side of other combined units.

5. Join units 36 and 37; then add Unit

Making Unit 18

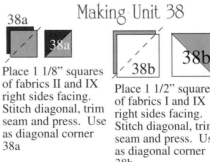

Join diagonal corner 18a from Fabric III to 1 5/8" x 2 3/4" piece of Unit 18.

35, 38, (see diagram) 39, 40, 42, 44, 45, 46, 47, 49, 50, and 51.

2. Use diagonal end technique to make one of units 1, 27, and 63. Refer to diagram for making triangle-square Unit 18.

3. To assemble the fruit top of the bowl, begin by joining units 1 and 2. Join units 3, 4, 5 and 6 in a ver-

Making Unit 31

Join diagonal corner 31a. Trim seam and press. Join diagonal corner 31b. If this background is a light color on dark, do not trim seam. Press.

Making Unit 38

Place 1 1/8" squares of fabrics II and IX right sides facing. Stitch diagonal, trim seam and press. Use as diagonal corner 38a

Place 1 1/2" squares of fabrics I and IX right sides facing. Stitch diagonal, trim seam and press. Use as diagonal corner 38b

Making combined units 19-21a

Join 1" square diagonal corner 21a from Fabric III to 1" x 1 1/2" strip of Fabric XI as shown. Join 1" x 1 1/2" strip of Fabric VII to Fabric XI strip.

Place the 21a combined units right sides facing and raw edges matching as shown above. Stitch diagonal, trim seam and press.

Making Unit 42

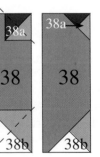

Place 1 1/2" squares of fabrics I and IX right sides facing. Stitch diagonal, trim seam and press. Use as diagonal corner 42a.

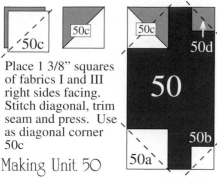

50c

50c

50c
50d

50

50b

50a

Making Unit 50

Place 1 3/8" squares of fabrics I and III right sides facing. Stitch diagonal, trim seam and press. Use as diagonal corner 50c

35 to top and Unit 38 to bottom. Join units 40 and 41; then add Unit 39 to bottom of these combined units. Join units 45 and 46. Join units 43 and 44. Join these two combined unit sections together; then add Unit 42 to bottom. Join these combined units to combined units 39-41. Join units 47 and 48. Add them to top of other combined pear units. Join combined units 35-38 to right side of pear units. Join units 51 and 52. Join units 49 and 50. Join these two unit sections together as shown. Join units 53 and 54; then add Unit 55 to bottom of these combined units. Join these units to combined units 49-51; then add Unit 56 to top. Join this apple section to left side of pear/apple section; then join Unit 57 across top. Join the two fruit sections together to complete the top of the block.

6. For the bowl, refer to block diagram and join five of Unit 58 with four of Unit 59 as shown; then add Unit 60 to top and bottom of the 58/59 combined units. Join mirror image Unit 61 to opposite sides of bowl center; then add Unit 62 to the top and Unit 63 to the bottom. Join units 64, 65, and 66 in a vertical row. Join mirror image Unit 67 to opposite sides of the 64-66 units. Join units 68 and 69; then add Unit 70 to opposite sides of the 68/69 combined units. Join this section to combined units 64-67; then add these combined units to bowl bottom.

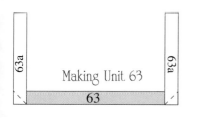

63a

Making Unit 63

63a

63

7. For the bowl handles, refer to diagram below, and make mirror image units 71-76. Join Unit 77 to these combined units as shown; then add Unit 78 to bottom of the handle combined units. Join these combined units to opposite sides of bowl. Join the fruit top of the block to the bowl bottom to complete th block.

8. Using 6 strands of dark brown embroidery floss, chain stitch the fruit stems.

Making mirror image combined units 71-76

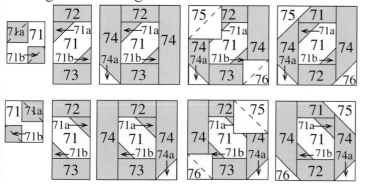

Floral Fantasy

Block finishes to 18" square. Size of block before it is sewn into the quilt is 18 1/2"

MATERIALS

- [ ] Fabric I (background)
  Need 12 3/4"   1/2 yard

- [ ] Fabric II (pale yellow print)
  Need 2"   1/8 yard

- [ ] Fabric III (light pink print)
  Need 2 5/8"   1/8 yard

- [ ] Fabric IV (medium rose print)
  Need 2 5/8"   1/8 yard

- [ ] Fabric V (light lavender print)
  Need 2 5/8"   1/8 yard

- [ ] Fabric VI (dark lavender print)
  Need 2 5/8"   1/8 yard

- [ ] Fabric VII (light green print)
  Need 4 1/2" square   scrap

- [ ] Fabric VIII (medium green print)
  Need 2 1/4"   1/8 yard

- [ ] Fabric IX (dark green print)
  Need 2 1/4"   1/8 yard

Cutting instructions shown in red indicate the quantity of units are combined and cut in two or more different places to conserve fabric.

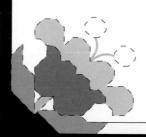

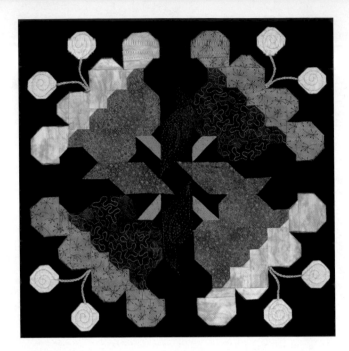

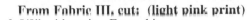

CUTTING

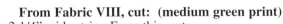

From Fabric I, cut: (background)
- One 2 7/8" wide strip. From this, cut:
  * Four - 2 7/8" x 3 1/2" (A28, B28)
  * Eight - 2" x 2 7/8" (A19, A25, B19, B25)
  * Four - 1 1/8" x 2 7/8" (A24, B24)
  * One - 2 1/4" square (Q9)
- One 2 1/4" wide strip. From this, cut:
  * Four - 2 1/4" x 4 1/4" (Q4, Q8)
  * Four - 1 1/8" x 2 1/4" (A27, B27)
  * Four - 1 3/8" x 2 1/8" (A13a, B13a)
  * Four - 1 7/8" squares (A1, B1)
  * Four - 1 5/8" squares (A12, B12)
- Two 2" wide strip. From these, cut:
  * Twelve - 1 3/8" x 2" (A18, A23, B18, B23, Q3, Q7)
  * Four - 1 1/8" x 1 5/8" (A21, B21)
  * Sixteen - 1 3/8" squares (A3a, B3a, Q1a, Q2a, Q5a, Q6a)
- One 1 1/2" wide strip. From this, cut:
  * Eight - 1 1/2" x 2 5/8" (A16, A31, B16, B31)
  * Four - 1 1/4" x 1 3/8" (A4, B4)
  * Eight - 1" x 1 3/8" (A15a, A30a, B15a, B30a)
  * Eight - 1" squares (A1a, A2a, A3b, A17a, A22a, B1a, B2a, B3b, B17a, B22a)
- One 1 1/8" wide strip. From this, cut:
  * Thirty-two - 1 1/8" squares (A14a, A20a, A26a, A29a, B14a, B20a, B26a, B29a)
- One 1" strip. From this, cut:
  * Thirty-six - 1" squares (add to 1" squares above)

From Fabric II, cut: (pale yellow print)
- One 2" wide strip. From this, cut:
  * Eight - 2" squares (A17, A22, B17, B22)

From Fabric III, cut: (light pink print)
- One 2 5/8" wide strip. From this, cut:
  * Four - 2" x 2 5/8" (A14, A29)
  * Two - 1 5/8" x 2 5/8" (A11)
  * Two - 1 1/2" x 2 5/8" (A10)
  * Four - 1 1/8" x 2 3/8" (A20, A26)
  * Four - 1" x 2 1/4" (A15, A30)
  * Two - 1 5/8" squares (A8)
  * Eight - 1" squares (A5a, A6a, A7a, A9a)

From Fabric IV, cut: (medium rose print)
- One 2 5/8" strip. From this, cut:
  * Two - 2 5/8" squares (A6)
  * Two - 2 3/8" x 3 1/2" (A3)
  * Two - 1" x 1 7/8" (A2)
  * Four - 1 1/2" x 1 5/8" (A7, A9)
  * Two - 1 1/4" x 1 1/2" (A5)
  * Two - 1 3/8" x 3" (A13)

From Fabric V, cut: (light lavender print)
- One 2 5/8" wide strip. From this, cut:
  * Four - 2" x 2 5/8" (B14, B29)
  * Two - 1 5/8" x 2 5/8" (B11)
  * Two - 1 1/2" x 2 5/8" (B10)
  * Four - 1 1/8" x 2 3/8" (B20, B26)
  * Four - 1" x 2 1/4" (B15, B30)
  * Two - 1 5/8" squares (B8)
  * Eight - 1" squares (B5a, B6a, B7a, B9a)

From Fabric VI, cut: (dark lavender print)
- One 2 5/8" strip. From this, cut:
  * Two - 2 5/8" squares (B6)
  * Two - 2 3/8" x 3 1/2" (B3)
  * Two - 1" x 1 7/8" (B2)
  * Four - 1 1/2" x 1 5/8" (B7, B9)
  * Two - 1 1/4" x 1 1/2" (B5)
  * Two - 1 3/8" x 3" (B13)

From Fabric VII, cut: (light green print)
- Four 1 7/8" squares (A1, B1)

From Fabric VIII, cut: (medium green print)
- One 2 1/4" wide strip. From this, cut:
  * Two - 2 1/4" x 3 3/8" (5)
  * Two - 1 3/8" x 2" (6)
  * Two - 1 3/8" squares (9b)

From Fabric IX, cut: (dark green print)
- One 2 1/4" wide strip. From this, cut:
  * Two - 2 1/4" x 3 3/8" (1)
  * Two - 1 3/8" x 2" (2)
  * Two - 1 3/8" squares (9a)

ASSEMBLY

This block is divided into two blocks with leaves as the sashing between the smaller blocks. Blocks A and B are the same. They have the same unit numbers, however their colors are different and they are mirror images. Refer to these block diagrams frequently for correct placement of mirror image units. Assembly and unit construction instructions below are for *one* block.

1. Use diagonal corner technique to make one each of the following *A & B block* units: 2, 3, 5, 6, 7, 9, 14, 17, 20, 22, and 26.

2. Use diagonal end technique to make one each of unit 13, 15, and 30.

3. For center leaf sashing, use diagonal corner technique to make two each of units 1, 2, 5, and 6. Make one of Unit 9.

4. Refer to diagram above and make one of Unit 1 for both A and B blocks.

5. To assemble both A and B blocks, begin by joining units 1 and 2; then add Unit 3 to side as shown. Join units 4 and 5. Join to side of Unit 3, matching seams. Join units 11 and 12. Join units 9 and 10; then join these two combined unit sections together as shown. Join units 7 and 8; then add Unit 6 to bottom of these combined units. Add these units to side of combined units 9/10; then add Unit 13 to side of the 6-12 combined units. Join combined units 1-5 to bottom as illustrated.

6. Join units 20 and 21. Join units 17 and 18; then add Unit 19 to bottom of combined units 17/18. Join combined units 20/21 to side of 17-19 combined units as shown. Join units 16, 14, and 15; then add them to bottom of other combined units. Join this section to side of flower, referring to block diagrams for correct placement.

7. Join units 22 and 23; then join Unit 24 to one side of combine units, and Unit 25 to other side as shown. Join units 26 and 27. Add them to the bottom of combined units 22-25. Join Unit 28 to side as illustrated. Join units 31, 29, and 30 in a row; then add this row to other combined units. Join this section to top of flower to complete A and B blocks.

8. Referring to completed block diagram below, for leaf sashing, join units 2 and 3; then add Unit 4 to one end and Unit 1 to the other end. Refer to block diagram and join one A and one B block to opposite sides of the leaf combined units, forming two rows as shown. For center leaf sashing, join units 6 and 7; then add Unit 8 to one end and Unit 5 to the other as shown. Join the two leaf sashing sections to opposite sides of center Unit 9. Join the block rows to opposite sides of the center sashing to complete the block.

9. Use 6 strands of medium green embroidery floss and chain stitch the stamens.

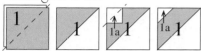

Making A1 & B1

Place 1 7/8" squares of fabrics I and VII sides facing and raw edges matching. Stitch diagonal as shown. Trim seam and press. Add diagonal corner 1a.

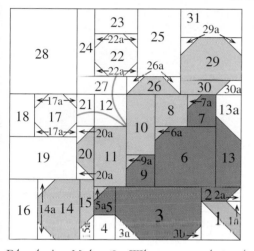

Block A. Make 2 When completed should measure 8 5/8" square

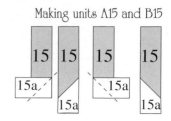

Making units A15 and B15

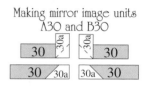

Making mirror image units A30 and B30

gram above and make one of Unit 1 for both A and B blocks.

Block B. Make 2 When completed should measure 8 5/8" square

Making mirror image units A13 & B13.

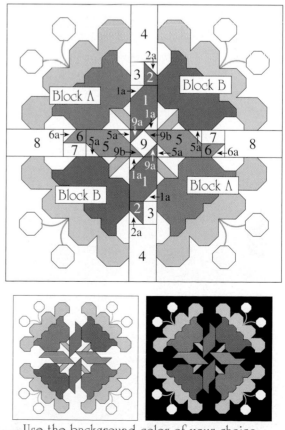

Use the background color of your choice.

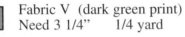

Fresh from the Vine

MATERIALS

Fabric I (background)
Need 9"   3/8 yard

Fabric II (light gold print)
Need 5 1/4"   1/4 yard

Fabric III (dark gold print)
Need 3 7/8"   1/4 yard

Fabric IV (light green print)
Need 3 5/8"   1/4 yard

Fabric V (dark green print)
Need 3 1/4"   1/4 yard

Fabric VI (dark grape print)
Need 2 1/2"   1/8 yard

Fabric VII (light grape print)
Need 2 1/2"   1/8 yard

CUTTING

From Fabric I, cut: (muslin)
- One 3 3/4" wide strip. From this, cut:
  * One - 2" x 3 3/4" (46)
  * Two - 3 1/8" squares (39a)
  * Two - 2 3/8" x 3 1/8" (6)
  * Two - 2 7/8" x 4 5/8" (40)
  * One - 1 5/8" x 2 3/4" (14)
  * Two - 2 1/8" x 2 1/2" (30)
  * Two - 1 3/8" x 2 1/2" (44)
  * Two - 1 1/4" x 1 3/4" (4)
- One 2 1/2" wide strip. From this, cut:
  * Two - 2 1/2" x 8" (41)

  * Two - 2 1/4" squares (11)
  * One - 2" x 2 1/4" (47)
  * Two - 2 1/8" squares (23a)
  * Two - 2" squares (22a)
  * Three - 3/4" x 2" (10)
  * Four - 1 1/2" squares (1b, 7a)
- One 1 3/4" wide strip. From this, cut:
  * Two - 1 3/4" squares (22b)
  * Two - 1 1/4" x 7 1/4" (31)
  * Eight - 1 1/4" squares (1a, 2b, 3b, 16a)
  * Two - 1 1/8" x 5 1/8" (5)
  * Two - 1 1/8" squares (45a)
- One 1" wide strip. From this, cut:
  * Twenty-six - 1" squares (2a, 3a, 8a, 9a)
  * One - 7/8" x 5 1/2" (12)

From Fabric II, cut: (light gold print)
- One 3 5/8" wide strip. From this, cut:
  * Two - 3 5/8" x 4 5/8" (39)
  * One - 2 1/2" x 3 1/2" (42)
  * One - 1" x 3 1/4" (35)
  * Two - 2" x 2 5/8" (38)
  * Two - 1 3/8" x 2 5/8" (37)
  * Two - 2 3/8" x 2 1/2" (26)
  * Two - 1 1/8" x 2 1/2" (29)
  * Two - 1 7/8" x 2 1/8" (24)
  * Two - 1 7/8" squares (13a)
  * Two - 1 5/8" x 1 7/8" (27)
  * Two - 1 3/8" x 1 7/8" (34)
  * Two - 1" squares (33a)
- One 1 5/8" wide strip. From this, cut:
  * Two - 1 5/8" squares (36a)
  * One - 1 3/8" x 8" (43)
  * Six - 1 3/8" squares (32b, 41a, 44a)

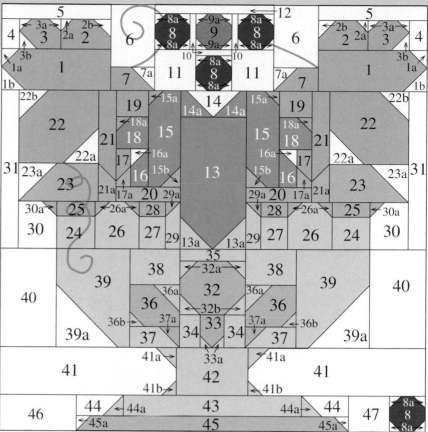

* Two - 1 1/4" squares (32a)
* Four - 1 1/8" squares (36b, 41b)

From Fabric III, cut: (dark gold print)
* One 2 3/4" wide strip. From this, cut:
    * One - 2 3/4" x 3 1/4" (32)
    * Two - 2 1/4" x 2 5/8" (36)
    * Two - 2 1/8" x 3 7/8" (23)
    * Two - 1 1/4" x 2 1/8" (21a)
    * Two - 1 1/8" x 2 1/8" (25)
    * One - 1 1/2" x 1 7/8" (33)
    * Two - 1 1/8" x 1 5/8" (28)
    * Four - 1 3/8" squares (15b, 37a)
    * One - 1 1/8" x 12" (45)
* One 1 1/8" wide strip. From this, cut:
    * Two - 1 1/8" x 3 1/4" (20)
    * Two - 1 1/8" x 1 3/8" (17a)
    * Eight - 1 1/8" squares (26a, 29a, 30a)

From Fabric IV, cut: (light green print)
* One 3 5/8" wide strip. From this, cut:
    * Two - 3 5/8" x 3 7/8" (22)
    * Two - 1 3/4" x 2 5/8" (2)
    * Two - 1 1/2" x 2 3/8" (7)
    * Two - 2 1/4" x 5 1/8" (1)
    * Two - 1 3/4" x 2 1/4" (3)
    * Two - 1 5/8" x 1 7/8" (19)
    * Two - 1 1/4" x 4 3/8" (21)
    * Two - 1 1/8" x 1 7/8" (17)
    * Four - 1 1/8" squares (15a, 18a)

From Fabric V, cut: (dark green print)
* One 3 1/4" wide strip. From this, cut:
    * One - 3 1/4" x 6 1/8" (13)
    * Two - 1 1/4" x 2 1/8" (16)
    * Two - 1 7/8" x 4 5/8" (15)
    * Two - 1 7/8" squares (18)
    * Two - 1 5/8" x 1 7/8" (14a)

From Fabric VI, cut: (dark grape print)
* One 2 1/2" wide strip. From this, cut:
    * One - 2 1/2" x 11 1/2" (appliqued grapes)
    * Four - 2" squares (8)

From Fabric VII, cut: (light grape print)
* One 2 1/2" wide strip. From this, cut:
    * Four - 2 1/2" squares (appliqued grapes)
    * One - 2" square (9)

ASSEMBLY

1. Use diagonal corner technique to make four of Unit 8. Use this technique to make two of mirror image units 1, 2, 3, 7, 15, 16, 18, 22, 23, 30, 36, 37, 39, 41, and 44. Make two of Unit 26. Make one of units 9, 13, 32, 33, and 45.

2. Use diagonal end technique to make two of mirror image 17 and 21. Use this technique to make one of Unit 14.

3. Refer frequently to block diagram for correct placement of mirror image units. To assemble the top grapes and leaf tops, begin by joining units 4, 3, and 2 in a row; then join Unit 5 across the top of these combined units. Join Unit 1 to the bottom. Join units 6 and 7; then add them to other combined units. Join units 8, 10, 9, 10, and 8 in a horizontal row. Join Unit 12 across the top of the combined units. Join units 8 and 10. Join Unit 11 to opposite sides of combined 8/10 units. Add these units to bottom of combined 8-10 units. Join the combined 1-7 mirror image units to opposite sides of grape units to complete the grape top.

Making Unit 14

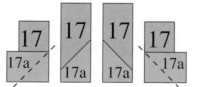

1/4" seam overlap

Making mirror image Unit 17

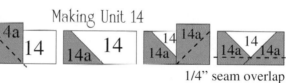

Making mirror image Unit 21

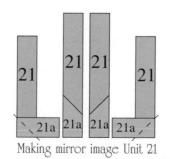

4. For bottom of leaves, begin by joining units 13 and 14. Join units 16 and 17. Join units 18 and 19. Join combined 18/19 to top of combined 16/17 units. Join Unit 15 to side of these combined units, checking block diagram for correct placement of mirror image units. Join Unit 20 to bottom of combined units; then add Unit 21 to sides as shown. Join units 22 and 23; then add them to outside end of other combined units. Join units 24 and 25. Join units 27 and 28. Join Unit 30, combined units 24/25, Unit 26, combined units 27/28 and Unit 29. Make two mirror image rows, and add them to other combined leaf units; then add Unit 31 to outside end. Join these combined units to opposite sides of combined units 13 and 14 to complete the leaf section.

Join this section to the bottom of grape/leaf section.

5. For vase section, join Unit 34 to opposite sides of Unit 33; then add Unit 32 to top of 33/34 combined units. Add Unit 35 to top of Unit 32. Join units 37, 36, and 38, referring to block diagram for placement of mirror image units. Make two of this mirror image row. Join the row to opposite sides of combined units 33-38; then add Unit 40 to outside edges. Join mirror image Unit 41 to opposite sides of Unit 42 as shown. Join mirror image Unit 44 to opposite sides of Unit 43; then add Unit 45 to the bottom of these combined units. Join Unit 46 to left side and Unit 47 to right side. Join Unit 8 to right side of Unit 47. Join this section to bottom of vase to complete the pieced block.

Placement of appliqué grapes

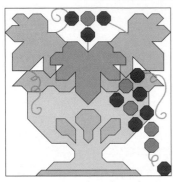 

Use the background of your choice.

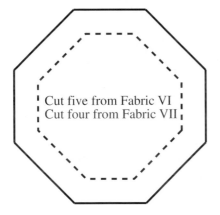

Cut five from Fabric VI
Cut four from Fabric VII

6. The pattern above is for the appliqued grapes. You may appliqued the grapes by hand or by machine. To appliqued by hand, turn under the 1/4" seam, clip corners and hand whip stitch the grapes in place. You may use a scrap of Steam-A-Seam 2, and follow manufacturer's instructions. You will cut the grapes on the dashed line. Press them in place. Use a machine or hand blanket stitch around the grapes.

7. Use 6 strands of medium green embroidery floss and chain stitch the vine tendrils.

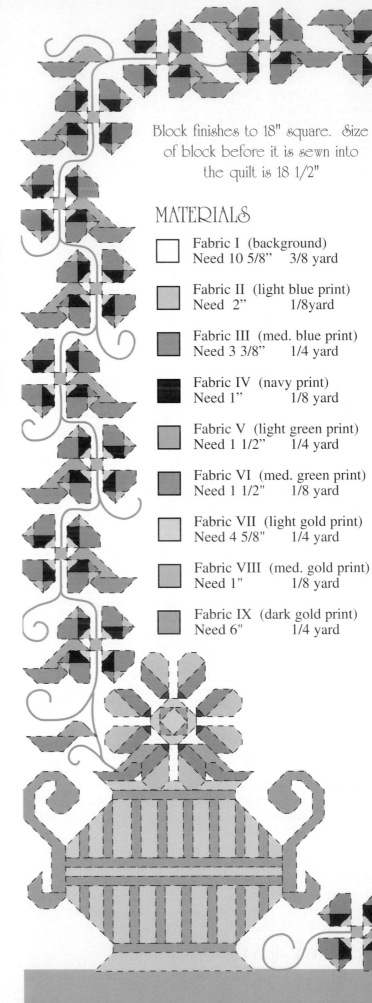

Block finishes to 18" square. Size of block before it is sewn into the quilt is 18 1/2"

MATERIALS

☐ Fabric I (background)
Need 10 5/8"   3/8 yard

☐ Fabric II (light blue print)
Need 2"   1/8yard

☐ Fabric III (med. blue print)
Need 3 3/8"   1/4 yard

☐ Fabric IV (navy print)
Need 1"   1/8 yard

☐ Fabric V (light green print)
Need 1 1/2"   1/4 yard

☐ Fabric VI (med. green print)
Need 1 1/2"   1/8 yard

☐ Fabric VII (light gold print)
Need 4 5/8"   1/4 yard

☐ Fabric VIII (med. gold print)
Need 1"   1/8 yard

☐ Fabric IX (dark gold print)
Need 6"   1/4 yard

CUTTING

From Fabric I, cut: (background)
- One 3 7/8" wide strip. From this, cut:
  * Two - 3 3/4" x 3 7/8" (62)
  * Two - 3 1/8" x 3 7/8" (1)
  * Two - 1 3/4" x 3 7/8" (57)
  * Two - 2" x 3 1/8" (6)
  * Four - 3" squares (46, 47)
  * Two - 2" x 3" (50)
  * Two - 1 1/2" x 3" (51)
- One 2 1/4" wide strip. From this, cut:
  * Two - 2 1/8" x 2 1/4" (52)
  * Two - 1" x 2 1/4" (23)
  * Two - 1 1/2" x 2 1/8" (18)
  * Two - 2" squares (56)
  * Two - 1 1/2" x 2" (13)
  * Two - 1" x 2 1/8" (19)
  * Three - 1" x 2" (12, 35)
  * Ten - 1" x 1 7/8" (A10, B10, C10, C12, D10, D12)
  * Two - 1 1/2" x 1 5/8" (14)
  * Four - 1 1/2" squares (17, 32b)
- One 1 3/8" wide strip. From this, cut:
  * Sixteen - 1 3/8" squares (A4, A9a, B4, B9a, C4, C9a, D4, D9a)
  * Two - 1 1/4" x 5 1/4" (5)
  * Two - 1 1/4" x 2 5/8" (58)
  * Two - 1 1/8" x 1 1/4" (53)
- One 1 1/8" wide strip. From this, cut:
  * One - 1 1/8" x 4" (38)
  * One - 1 1/8" x 2 3/4" (39)
  * Two - 1 1/8" x 2 5/8" (2)
  * Two - 1 1/8" x 2 1/2" (4a)
  * Six - 1 1/8" squares (7a, 61a)
  * Two - 1" x 4 1/2" (8)

  * Three - 1" x 3" (33, 59)
- Two 1" wide strips. From these, cut:
  * Two - 1" x 2 1/2" (10)
  * Forty-six - 1" squares (9a, 9c, 11a, 20a, 29, 30, 31b, 32d, 54a, A5, A7a, A12a, B12a B5, B7a, C5, C7a, D5, D7a)

 From Fabric II, cut: (light blue print)
- One 2" wide strip. From this, cut:
  * Six - 2" x 2 1/2" (9, 11, 32)
  * Two - 2" squares (34a)
  * Two - 1" x 2" (37)
  * Sixteen - 1" x 1 3/8" (A3, A9, B3, B9, C3, C9, D3, D9)

 From Fabric III, cut: (medium blue print)
- One 2" wide strip. From this, cut:
  * Four - 2" x 2 1/2" (32a, 34)
  * Four - 2" squares (9b, 11b)
  * Four - 1" x 1 1/2" (31)
  * Sixteen - 1" squares (A5, A8, B5, B8, C5, C8, D5, D8)
- One 1 3/8" wide strip. From this, cut:
  * Sixteen - 1 3/8" squares (A3, A9, B3, B9, C3, C9, D3, D9)

 From Fabric IV, cut: (navy print)
- One 1" wide strip. From this, cut:
  * Sixteen - 1" x 1 3/8" (A6, B6, C6, D6)
  * Eight - 1" squares (31a, 32c, 34c)

 From Fabric V, cut: (light green print)
- One 1 1/2" wide strip. From this, cut:
  * Two - 1 1/2" squares (34b)
  * Two - 1" x 1 1/2" (12a)
  * Four - 1 1/4" squares (1a, 6a)
  * Two - 1 1/8" x 1 3/4" (4)
  * Two - 1 1/8" squares (38a)
  * Six - 1" x 1 7/8" (A7, A12, B7, B12, C7, D7)
  * Twelve - 1" squares (11c, 19a, 21a, A8, B8, C8, D8)

 From Fabric VI, cut: (medium green print)
- One 1 1/2" wide strip. From this, cut:
  * Two - 1 1/2" squares (21)
  * Six - 1 3/8" squares (A9a, B9a, C9a, D9a)
  * Two - 1 1/8" x 2 3/8" (2a)
  * Two - 1 1/8" x 2" (7)
  * Two - 1 1/8" x 1 3/4" (39a)
  * Two - 1 1/8" squares (3)
  * Two - 1" x 2 1/8" (20)

 From Fabric VII, cut: (light gold print)
- One 3 5/8" wide strip. From this, cut:
  * Two - 1 1/2" x 3 5/8" (43)
  * Eight - 1 3/8" x 3 5/8" (42)
  * Eight - 1 1/4" x 3 5/8" (40)
  * One - 2" square (25)
  * One - 1 1/2" x 7" (49)
  * Six - 1 1/2" squares (28, 50a)
- One 1" wide strip. From this, cut:
  * One - 1" x 12" (45)
  * Nineteen - 1" squares (21b, 36, A6a, B6a, C6a, D6a)

Urn of Flowers

From Fabric VIII, cut: (medium gold print)
• One 1" strip. From this, cut:
  * Two - 1" x 3" (27)
  * Two - 1" x 2" (26)
  * Four - 1" squares (A11, B11, C11, D11)

From Fabric IX, cut: (dark gold print)
• One 3" wide strip. From this, cut:
  * Two - 1 1/4" x 3" (60)
  * Two - 1 1/8" x 3" (55)
  * Two - 1 3/8" x 2 1/2" (61)
  * Two - 2 1/8" squares (52a)
  * Two - 1 1/8" x 2" (16)
  * Two - 1" x 2" (24)
  * Two - 1 1/2" x 1 3/4" (18a)
  * Two - 1" x 1 3/4" (22)
  * Two - 1 1/4" x 1 5/8" (58a)
  * Two - 1" x 1 5/8" (15)
  * Two - 1 1/4" x 1 1/2" (54)
  * Six - 1 1/4" squares (25a, 46a)
  * Two - 1 1/8" squares (14a)
• Three 1" wide strips. From these, cut:
  * Two - 1" x 12" (44)
  * One - 1" x 7" (48)
  * Sixteen - 1" x 3 5/8" (41)
  * Seven - 1" squares (14b, 37a, 37b)

ASSEMBLY OF BLOCKS A, B, C, AND D.

1. For blocks A and B, use diagonal corner technique to make eight of Unit 6, and two of Unit 7. Make two of mirror image, Unit 12. For Blocks C and D, use diagonal corner technique to make eight of Unit 6 and two of Unit 7. Refer to the diagram below for making combined units 3 and 4 for all four blocks. Refer to the block diagrams for correct placement of this combined mirror image unit. A diagram at right is shown for making triangle-squares A, B, C and D5 and 8. Make 8 of Unit 5, and six of Unit 8 for all four blocks.

2. The illustration at right shows how to make Unit 9 for blocks A, B, C, and D.

3. Blocks A and B are assembled the same way, however they are mirror images. To assemble them, begin by joining units 5 and 6; then add combined units 3/4 to side. Make four. One for the top of the block and one for the bottom.. Join units 6 and 8; then add Unit 9 to top of these combined units. Make four. Join combined units 3-6 to one side of Unit 10; then add the remaining combined units to the opposite side of Unit 10 as shown. Repeat this for the bottom of the block. Join units 7, 11, and 12. Join the flower top and bottom to the center combined units to complete the blocks.

4. The assembly for blocks C and D are similar. Join units 5

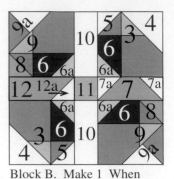
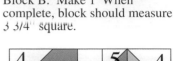

Block A. Make 1 When complete, block should measure 3 3/4" square.

Block B. Make 1 When complete, block should measure 3 3/4" square.

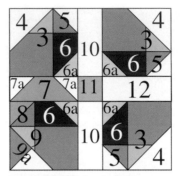
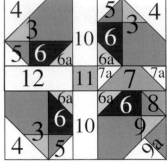

Block C. Make 1 When complete, block should measure 3 3/4" square.

Block D. Make 1 When complete, block should measure 3 3/4" square.

Making units 5 and 8 for A, B, C, and D blocks

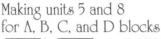

Place 1" squares of fabrics I and III right sides facing, and raw edges matching. Stitch diagonal, trim seam and press.

Place 1" squares of fabrics I and V right sides facing, and raw edges matching. Stitch diagonal, trim seam and press.

and 6; then add combined units 3/4 to the side of the combined units. Make six. Join units 6 and 8; then add Unit 9 to bottom of these combined units as shown. Join the top combined units to opposite sides of Unit 10. Repeat for the bottom. Join units 7, 11 and 12 for the center. Join the flower top and bottom to the center combined units to complete the blocks.

Making combined mirror image units A3, B3, C3, D3.

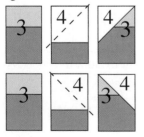

Join 1 3/8" square of Fabric III and 1" x 1 3/8" strip of fabric II. This now becomes Unit 3. Join Unit 4 diagonal corner. If you are using a muslin background, DO NOT trim seam as darker color behind will show through. Press.

Making combined mirror image units A9, B9, C9, D9

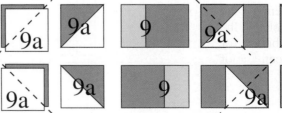

Place 1 3/8" squares of fabrics I and VI right sides facing, and raw edges matching. Stitch diagonal, trim seam and press.

Join 1 3/8" square of Fabric III and 1" x 1 3/8" strip of fabric II. This now becomes Unit 9.

Use the 9a triangle-square as a diagonal corner. Place right sides facing as shown and stitch diagonal. Trim seam and press.

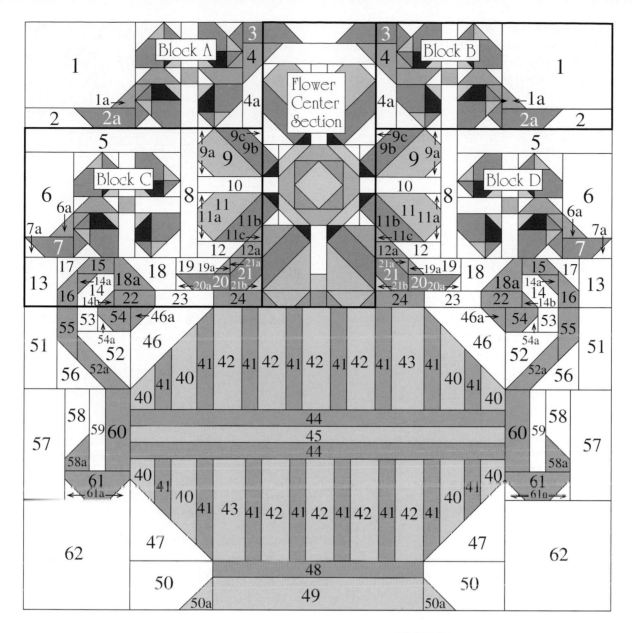

BLOCK TOP ASSEMBLY

1. Refer to the large block diagram above and use diagonal corner technique to make two of mirror image units 1, 6, 7, 9, 11, 14, 19, 20, and 21.

2. Use diagonal end technique to make two of mirror image units 2, 4, 12, and 18.

3. To assemble the block top, refer to the diagram above for correct placement of mirror image units.

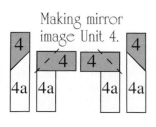

Making mirror image Unit 4.

Making mirror image Unit 2

Begin by joining units 1 and 2. Referring to block illustration, join Block A to the right side of the combined 1/2 units and Block B to the left side as shown.. Join units 3 and 4 as shown; then add them to the inside ends of the A and B

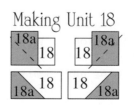

Making mirror image Unit 12

Making Unit 18

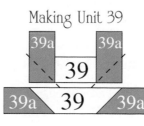

Making Unit 39

blocks. Join unit 6 and 7. Join Block C to right side of the combined 6/7 units and Block D to the left side. Join Unit 5 to top of the combined block units; then add Unit 8 as shown.

Join mirror image units 9, 10, 11, and 12 in a vertical row. Join this row to Unit 8. Join the Block A and B combined units to the top of blocks C and D combined units. Join units 14 and 15. Add Unit 16 to side of these combined units; then join diagonal corner, Unit 17 to top outside edge as shown. Refer to diagram of these units on page 56. Join Unit 13 to these combined units. Join units 19 and 20; then add Unit 18 to one end of these combined units, and Unit 21 to opposite side, referring to block

55

diagram for correct placement. Join units 22, 23 and 24; then add them to the bottom of combined units 18-21. Join combined units 13-17 to outer edge of the combined 18-24 units. Join these combined units to bottom of block combined units, and set aside.

CENTER SECTION ASSEMBLY

1. Refer to center section diagram below. To assemble this section, use diagonal corner technique to make four each of

Making mirror image Unit 32

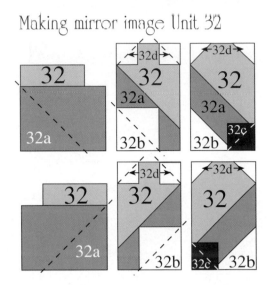

Flower Center Section

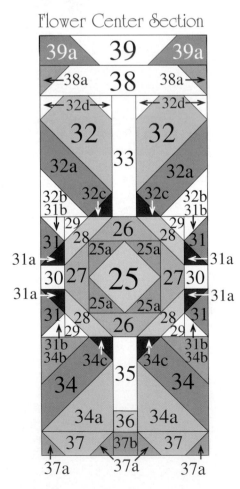

mirror image units 31, and two of mirror image Unit 34. Make two of Unit 37, and one of combined units 25-29, and one of Unit 38. Use diagonal end technique to make two of mirror image Unit 32, referring to diagram below. To assemble Unit 25, refer to diagram at right. Use diagonal corner technique to make Unit 25. Join Unit 26 to top and bottom; then add Unit 27 to opposite sides. Join diagonal corner Unit 28 as shown; then join diagonal corner, Unit 29 to all four corners.

2. To assemble the center section, beginning at the top, join units 38 and 39. Join mirror image Unit 32 to opposite sides of Unit 33; then join combined 38/39

Making combined mirror image units 14-17

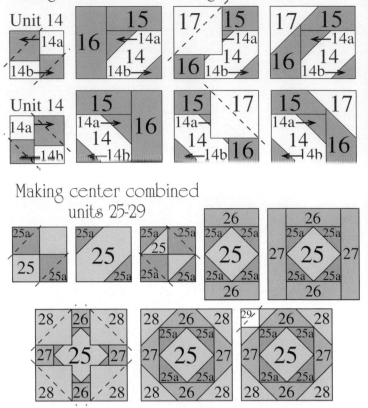

Making center combined units 25-29

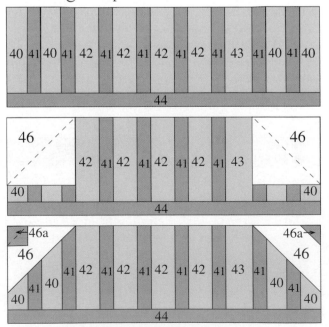

units to the top. Make two rows of mirror image units 31, 30 and 31, referring to diagram for correct placement of mirror image units. Join these rows to opposite sides of Unit 25. Add these combined units to bottom of top combined units, matching seams. Join units 35 and 36; then join Unit 34 to opposite sides of combined units 35/36. Join units 37, 37b and 37 in a horizontal row. Add these units to bottom of combined units 34-36; then join the bottom section of the flower to the bottom of Unit 25 to complete the Center Flower Section.

Making Strip Set center sections

Making combined mirror image units 52-56

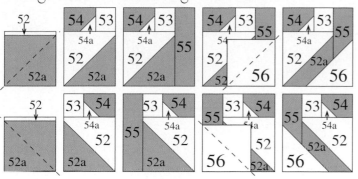

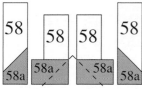

Making mirror image Unit 58

BLOCK BOTTOM ASSEMBLY

1. To complete the bottom of the block, use diagonal corner technique to make two each of mirror image units 50, 52, and 54. Use diagonal end technique to make two of mirror image unit 58.

2. Refer to the diagram on page 56 and join units 40, 41, 42 and 43 strips as shown for the top part of the Urn. Join Unit 44 to the bottom of the combined strips; then add diagonal corner 46. If you are using muslin as your background color, do not trim Unit 46 seam, as the dark colors behind it will show through. Add diagonal corner Unit 46a to top edges.

3. Refer to block diagram on page 55 and join units 40-43 as shown. Join horizontal strips 45 and 44 as shown. Join these combined units to the top of the joined strips; then add diagonal corner, Unit 47 to bottom ends as shown. Join these combined strip units to the bottom of the other joined strip units as shown. Join units 48 and 49; then add mirror image Unit 50 to opposite sides of the 48/49 combined units. Join these combined units to the bottom of the urn as shown.

4. For the urn sides, refer to block diagram, and use diagonal corner technique to make two of Unit 61. Use diagonal end technique to make one of Unit 58.

5. For side assembly, refer to the diagram above and use diagonal corner technique to make Unit 52. Join units 53 and 54; then join Unit 52 to bottom of these combined units. Join Unit 55 to side as shown; then add diagonal corner Unit 56. Add Unit 51 to outside end of the combined 52-56 units. Join units 58, 59 and 60; then join Unit 61 to the bottom of these com-

bined units. Join Unit 57 to sides as shown; then add Unit 62 to the bottom. Join these combined units to combined units 51-56 to complete the urn handles. Join these combined units to opposite sides of urn center; then add the urn bottom to the flower top to complete the block.

Use the background color of your choice.

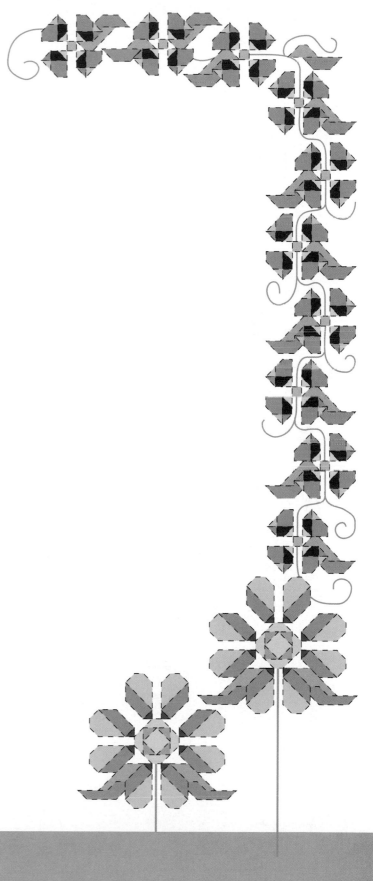

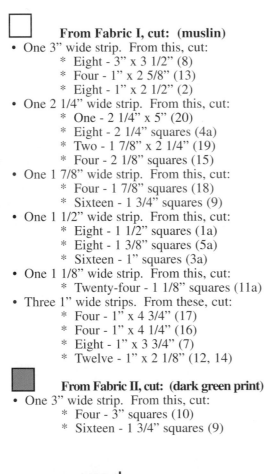

MATERIALS

☐ Fabric I (background)
Need 12 3/4"   1/2 yard

■ Fabric II (dark green print)
Need 3"   1/4yard

■ Fabric III (med. green print)
Need 3 5/8"   1/4 yard

■ Fabric IV (tan print)
Need 2 1/2"   1/8 yard

■ Fabric V (rust print)
Need 2"   1/8 yard

CUTTING

☐   **From Fabric I, cut: (muslin)**
• One 3" wide strip. From this, cut:
* Eight - 3" x 3 1/2" (8)
* Four - 1" x 2 5/8" (13)
* Eight - 1" x 2 1/2" (2)
• One 2 1/4" wide strip. From this, cut:
* One - 2 1/4" x 5" (20)
* Eight - 2 1/4" squares (4a)
* Two - 1 7/8" x 2 1/4" (19)
* Four - 2 1/8" squares (15)
• One 1 7/8" wide strip. From this, cut:
* Four - 1 7/8" squares (18)
* Sixteen - 1 3/4" squares (9)
• One 1 1/2" wide strip. From this, cut:
* Eight - 1 1/2" squares (1a)
* Eight - 1 3/8" squares (5a)
* Sixteen - 1" squares (3a)
• One 1 1/8" wide strip. From this, cut:
* Twenty-four - 1 1/8" squares (11a)
• Three 1" wide strips. From these, cut:
* Four - 1" x 4 3/4" (17)
* Four - 1" x 4 1/4" (16)
* Eight - 1" x 3 3/4" (7)
* Twelve - 1" x 2 1/8" (12, 14)

■   **From Fabric II, cut: (dark green print)**
• One 3" wide strip. From this, cut:
* Four - 3" squares (10)
* Sixteen - 1 3/4" squares (9)

Block finishes to 18" square. Size of block before it is sewn into the quilt is 18 1/2"

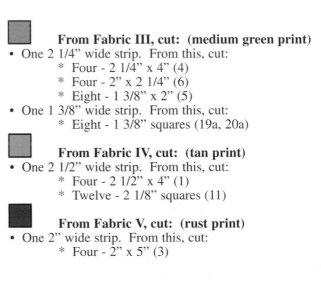

■   **From Fabric III, cut: (medium green print)**
• One 2 1/4" wide strip. From this, cut:
* Four - 2 1/4" x 4" (4)
* Four - 2" x 2 1/4" (6)
* Eight - 1 3/8" x 2" (5)
• One 1 3/8" wide strip. From this, cut:
* Eight - 1 3/8" squares (19a, 20a)

■   **From Fabric IV, cut: (tan print)**
• One 2 1/2" wide strip. From this, cut:
* Four - 2 1/2" x 4" (1)
* Twelve - 2 1/8" squares (11)

■   **From Fabric V, cut: (rust print)**
• One 2" wide strip. From this, cut:
* Four - 2" x 5" (3)

Fall

This pattern is great for a beginner.

ASSEMBLY

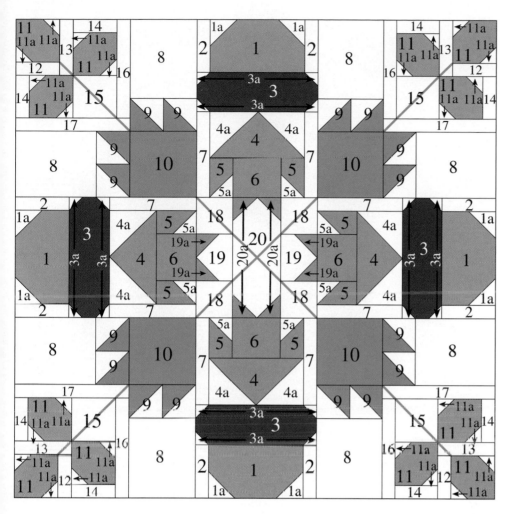

Use the background color of your choice.

joined units. Join Unit 8 the combined 9 units. Make eight. Join Unit 10 to four combined 8/9 units.

6. For one side section, beginning at top left, join one combined 8/9 unit section to right side of corner. Join combined 8-10 units to bottom of these combined units. Make two. Join these combined leaf sections to opposite sides of acorn/leaf section to complete one side. Make two side sections.

7. For the center section of the block, join units 18, 19 and 18 in a row. Make two. Join these rows to opposite sides of Unit 20. Join the combined acorn/leaf sections to top and bottom of combined 18-20 units.

8. Use six strands of green embroidery floss and make a chain stitch for the stems.

1. Use diagonal corner technique to make twelve of Unit 11. Make eight of mirror image Unit 5, and four each of units 1, 3, and 4. Make two of Unit 19, and one of Unit 20.

2. Refer to diagram below for making sixteen of Unit 9.

Making Unit 9

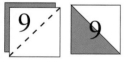

Place 1 3/4" squares of fabrics I and II, right sides facing and raw edges matching. Stitch a diagonal down the center as shown. Trim seam, open and press.

3. To assemble the block, begin by joining Unit 2 to opposite sides of Unit 1; then add Unit 3 to top of the 1/2 combined units. Make four. Referring to block diagram above, join mirror image units 5 to opposite sides of Unit 6; then add Unit 4 to top of these combined units. Join Unit 7 to opposite sides of the 4-6 combined units. Join these combined units to top of acorn as shown.

4. For the corners, join one Unit 11 and Unit 12; then add Unit 13 to top of these combined units. Join another unit 11 and Unit 14. Add these combined units to combined units 11-13. Join units 15, 11, and 14 in a vertical row; then add them to side of other leaves. Join Unit 16 to side as shown; then join Unit 17 to top to complete the corners. Make four.

5. Join two of Unit 9's together, referring to block diagram for correct positioning of the units. Make eight of these

59

MATERIALS

▢ Fabric I (background)
Need 12 1/4"   1/2 yard

◼ Fabric II (brown print)
Need 5 3/8"   1/4yard

▨ Fabric III (light.green print)
Need 2 3/8"   1/8 yard

▨ Fabric IV (medium green print)
Need 2 3/8"   1/8 yard

CUTTING

▢ **From Fabric I, cut: (background)**
• One 5" wide strip. From this, cut:
  * One - 5" x 7 1/2" (11)
  * One - 3 1/8" x 5" (24)
  * One - 1 5/8" x 3 3/4" (7)
  * Two - 2 1/8" x 3 5/8" (30)
  * Two - 1 5/8" x 3 5/8" (31)
  * Eight - 1 1/2" x 3 5/8" (32)
  * Two - 3 3/8" squares (13b)
  * Four - 1 1/8" squares (16a, 18a)
  * Four - 1" squares (8a)
• One 3 1/8" wide strip. From this, cut:
  * Two - 3 1/8" x 3 3/8" (19)
  * Two - 2" x 3 1/8" (17)
  * Two - 1 5/8" x 3 1/8" (6)
  * Two - 1 1/4" x 2 5/8" (21)
  * Two - 1 1/2" x 2 5/8" (9)
  * Twelve - 1 1/2" x 2 3/8" (25, 26, 28, 29)
  * Two - 1 1/8" x 2 3/8" (1)
  * Two - 1 5/8" x 2 1/8" (3)

• One 2 3/4" wide strip. From this, cut:
  * Two - 2 3/4" squares (5a)
  * Two - 2" x 2 1/8" (22)
  * Two - 1 1/2" x 2" (23)
  * One - 1 5/8" x 5 1/4" (15)
  * Two - 1 5/8" squares (13a)
  * One - 1 1/2" x 12 1/4" (10)
  * Fourteen - 1 1/4" squares (20b, 27b)
• One 1 3/8" wide strip. From this, cut:
  * Fourteen - 1 3/8" squares (20a, 27a)

◼ **From Fabric II, cut: (brown print)**
• One 5 3/8" wide strip. From this, cut:
  * Two - 1 1/2" x 5 3/8" (8)
  * One - 2 1/4" x 5 1/4" (14)
  * Two - 2 7/8" x 5" (12)
  * Two - 3 3/8" x 4" (13)
  * One - 1 5/8" x 3 3/4" (4)
  * One - 1 3/4" x 3 1/8" (16)
  * Two - 1 3/8" x 3 1/8" (18)
  * Two - 2 3/4" x 2 7/8" (5)
  * Two - 2 1/8" x 2 3/8" (2)
  * Two - 1 5/8" x 2 1/4" (7b)
  • From scrap, cut:
  * Ten - 1 1/8" squares (1a, 3a, 6a, 19a)
  * Six - 1" squares (3b, 17a)

▨ **From Fabric III, cut: (light green print)**
• One 2 3/8" wide strip. From this, cut:
  * Eight - 2 3/8" x 2 5/8" (20)
  * Eight - 1" squares (10a, 24a, 25a)

▨ **From Fabric IV, cut: (med. green print)**
• One 2 3/8" wide strip. From this, cut:
  * Six - 2 3/8" x 2 5/8" (27)
  * Six - 1" squares (23a, 29a)

Lyre

Block finishes to 18" square. Size of block before it is sewn into the quilt is 18 1/2"

ASSEMBLY

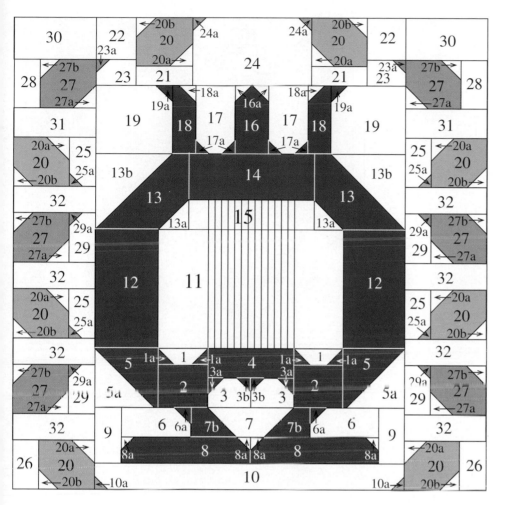

image Unit 13 to opposite ends of the combined 14/15 units. Add these combined units to the top of combined 11/12 units. Working from left to right, join units 19, 18, 17, 16, 17, 18, and 19 in a horizontal row. Add this row to top of combined units 13-15, matching seams. Join units 22 and 23. Join units 20 and 21. Join these two combined units together as shown. Join these mirror image units to opposite sides of Unit 24; then add them to the Lyre top to complete the center section of the block.

5. The sides are identical, except that they are mirror images. These instructions are for the left side. Refer to the block diagram for correct placement of mirror image units for the right side. Beginning at top left, join units 27 and 28; then add Unit 30 to the top of the combined units, and Unit 31 to the bottom. Join units 20 and 25; then add Unit 32 to the bottom of these combined units. Join these units to the bottom of Unit 31. Join units 27 and 29; then add Unit 32 to the bottom. Join these combined units to the bottom of the leaf row. Join units 20 and 25; then add another Unit 32 to the bottom. Join to bottom of leaf row. Join units 27 and 29; then add Unit 32 to bottom. Add these units to bottom of leaf row. Join units 20 and 26; then add them to leaf row bottom. Repeat for right side row checking for correct placement of mirror image units..

6. Join the sides to opposite sides of the center section to complete the block.

7. For the strings, we used gold metallic thread and a triple stitch on the sewing machine. Mary added to the look by quilting with gold metallic thread next to the strings and around the Lyre. Use six strands of medium green embroidery floss and stitch a chain stitch for the vines.

This pattern is great for a beginner.

1. Use diagonal corner technique to make eight of mirror image Unit 20, and six of Unit 27. Use this technique to make four of mirror image units 25 and 29, and two each of units 3, 5, 6, 13, 18, 19, and 23. Make two of units 1, 8, and 17. Make one of units 10, 16, and 24.

2. Use diagonal end technique to make one of Unit 7 shown below.

3. To assemble the block, begin by joining units 1 and 2. Join the two unit 3's; then add Unit 4 to the top of the combined 3 units. Join combined units 1/2 to opposite sides of combined units 3/4; then join mirror image unit 5 to opposite ends as shown. Refer to block diagram above for correct placement of mirror image units, and join units 6, 7, and 6 in a row. Join the two unit 8's; then add them to the bottom of combined units 6/7/6. Join Unit 9 to opposite ends of the combined units; then add Unit 10 to the bottom. Join these combined units to the bottom of combined units 1-5.

4. Join Unit 12 to opposite sides of Unit 11. Add these combined units to Lyre bottom combined units. Join units 14 and 15; then add mirror

Making Unit 7

Use the background color of your choice.

LaurelWreath

MATERIALS

☐ Fabric I (background)
   Need 13"   1/2 yard

▨ Fabric II (light green print)
   Need 2 1/2"   1/8 yard

▨ Fabric III (medium.green print)
   Need 2 1/2"   1/8 yard

▨ Fabric IV (dark gold print)
   Need 2"   1/8 yard

CUTTING

☐ **From Fabric I, cut: (background)**
- Two 2 1/2" wide strips. From these, cut:
  * Eight - 2 1/2" squares (B5, C7)
  * Four - 2" x 2 1/2" (B3)
  * Eight - 1 3/4" x 2 1/2" (C3)
  * Twenty - 1 1/2" x 2 1/2" (A5, A7, B7, C5)
  * Four - 1" x 2 1/2" (A3)
  * Sixteen - 1" squares (A1a, B1a, C1a) Stack this cut.
- Four 1 1/2" wide strips. From these, cut:
  * Four - 1 1/2" x 8 1/2" (C8)
  * Four - 1 1/2" x 5 1/2" (B8)
  * Sixty-four - 1 1/2" squares (A4a, A6a, B4a, B6a, C4a, C6a)
- Two 1" wide strips. From these, cut:
  * Twelve - 1" x 2" (A2, B2, C2)
  * Thirty-two - 1" squares (add to 1" squares above)

▨ **From Fabric II, cut: (light green print)**
- One 2 1/2" wide strip. From this, cut:
  * Sixteen - 2 1/2" squares (A6, B6, C6)

▨ **From Fabric III, cut: (medium green print)**
- One 2 1/2" wide strip. From this, cut:
  * Sixteen - 2 1/2" squares (A4, B4, C4)

▨ **From Fabric IV, cut: (dark gold print)**
- One 2" wide strip. From this, cut:
  * Twelve - 2" squares (A1, B1, C1)

Cutting instructions shown in red indicate the quantity of units are combined and cut in two or more different places to conserve fabric.

Block finishes to 18" square. Size of block before it is sewn into the quilt is 18 1/2"

This pattern is great for a beginner.

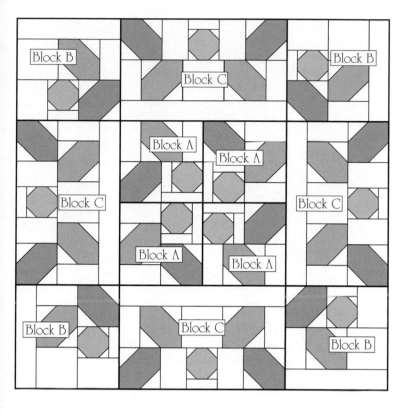

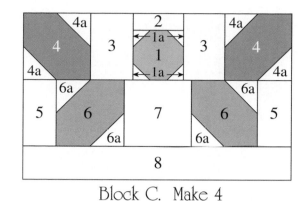

Block C. Make 4

5. Refer to the complete block diagram at left and join the four A blocks together as shown. Join Block C to top and bottom of the combined A blocks to complete the center section. For the sides, refer to block diagram for correct placement and join blocks B, C, and B in a row. Make two of these rows. Join the side rows to opposite sides of the center section to complete the block.

6. Refer to the photograph on page 62. With a blue, disappearing marker, mark a circle around the leaves. Mark the center design. Using 6 strands of medium green embroidery floss, chain stitch the circle and the center design.

1. Refer to block diagrams and use diagonal corner technique to make sixteen of units 4 and 6 and twelve of Unit 1 for blocks A, B, and C.

2. To assemble Block A, join units 1 and 2; then add Unit 3 to left side as shown. Join Unit 4 to top of combined units 1-3. Join units 5, 6, and 7 in a row; then add them to right side of other combined units to complete Block A. Make 4.

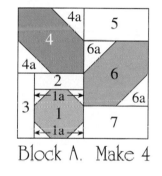

Block A. Make 4

3. To assemble Block B, join units 1 and 2; then add Unit 3 to the top of the 1/2 combined units, and Unit 4 to the bottom. Join units 5, 6, and 7 in a row as shown; then add Unit 8 to right side of the row. Join the two sections together to complete Block B. Make four.

4. To assemble Block C, begin by joining units 1 and 2; then add Unit 3 to opposite sides of combined 1/2 units. Refer to the block diagram for correct placement, and join Unit 4 to opposite sides of Unit 3 to complete the top row. Again referring to the diagram of Block C, join units 5, 6, 7, 6, and 5 in a row; then add Unit 8 to the bottom. Join the two rows together to complete the block. Make 4.

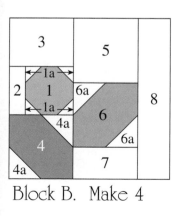

Block B. Make 4

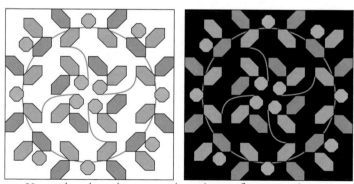

Use the background color of your choice.

Block finishes to 18" square. Size of block before it is sewn into the quilt is 18 1/2"

MATERIALS

☐ Fabric I (background)
Need 9 1/4"   3/8 yard

☐ Fabric II (light gold print)
Need 4 7/8"   1/4 yard

☐ Fabric III (medium gold print)
Need 2 3/4"   1/8 yard

☐ Fabric IV (dark gold print)
Need 1"   1/8 yard

☐ Fabric V (dark grape print)
Need 4 1/4"   1/4 yard

☐ Fabric VI (medium grape print)
Need 2 3/4"   1/8 yard

☐ Fabric VII (navy print)
Need 1 1/8"   1/8 yard

☐ Fabric VIII (light green print)
Need 3 7/8"   1/4 yard

☐ Fabric IX (medium green print)
Need 4 1/4"   1/4 yard

This block is one of my favorites. It has many pieces, but if diagrams and instructions are followed, it works like a jig saw puzzle. The end results are very rewarding. Put some coordinating borders around it and it will be a lovely wall piece for your home or office.

CUTTING

☐ **From Fabric I, cut: (background)**
• One 3 5/8" wide strip. From this, cut:
  * Three - 3 1/8" x 3 5/8" (22, 96)
  * Two - 1" x 3 5/8" (27)
  * One - 1 3/4" x 3 3/8" (19)
  * One - 1 1/2" x 3 3/8" (18)
  * One - 2" x 3 1/4" (91)
  * One - 1 1/4" x 3 1/4" (11)
  * One - 1" x 3 1/4" (10)
  * One - 1 1/4" x 3 1/8" (110)
  * One - 7/8" x 3 1/8" (67)
  * One - 2 3/8" x 2 7/8" (84)
  * One - 2" x 2 7/8" (121)
  * One - 1 7/8" x 2 7/8" (47)
  * One - 2 5/8" x 3 7/8" (74)
  * Two - 2 5/8" x 2 3/4" (31)
  * One - 1 1/4" x 2 5/8" (87)

• One 2 5/8" wide strip. From this, cut:
  * One - 1 3/8" x 2 5/8" (83)
  * One - 1 7/8" x 2 1/2" (76)
  * One - 1 1/4" x 2 3/8" (43b)
  * One - 2 1/4" square (101a)
  * One - 2" x 2 1/4" (117)
  * One - 1 1/2" x 2 1/4" (71)
  * Two - 2 1/8" squares (24b)
  * One - 1 1/4" x 2 1/8" (99)
  * One - 1 1/8" x 2 1/8" (100)
  * One - 2" x 6 5/8" (122)
  * One - 2" x 4 1/4" (113)
  * Two - 2" squares (29)
  * Two - 1 1/8" x 2" (112, 120)
  * Two - 1" x 2" (36, 85a)
  * One - 1 3/4" x 1 7/8" (79)
  * One - 1 1/8" x 1 7/8" (89a)

• One 1 3/4" wide strip. From this, cut:

Vase with Flowers

* One - 1 3/4" square (66a)
* One - 1 1/2" x 1 3/4" (119)
* One - 1 1/4" x 1 3/4" (94)
* One - 1 1/8" x 1 3/4" (77)
* Four - 1 5/8" squares (72c, 86a, 90, 97a)
* Two - 1" x 1 5/8" (8)
* Ten - 1 1/2" squares (16a, 17a, 20a, 68a, 73a)
* One - 1 1/4" x 1 1/2" (107)
* One - 1 1/8" x 1 1/2" (34)
* One - 1" x 1 3/8" (92)
* One - 1 1/8" x 1 1/4" (108a)
• One 1 1/4" wide strip. From this and scrap, cut:
* Nine - 1 1/4" squares (5a, 30a, 54a, 66b, 98a, 102a)
* Nine - 1 1/8" squares (9a, 30c, 52b, 53a, 70c, 72b, 95a)
* One - 1" x 2 1/4" (82)
* Two - 1" x 1 1/8" (64)
* Nineteen - 1" squares (9b, 25a, 32b, 38a, 43c, 49c, 65a, 70b, 80a, 114a, 118a)

From Fabric II, cut: (light gold print)
• One 4 7/8" wide strip. From this, cut:
* One - 4 7/8" x 5 5/8" (46)
* One - 3 1/8" x 3 7/8" (44)
* One - 1 1/8" x 3 1/8" (53)
* One - 1" x 2 7/8" (48)
* One - 1 5/8" square (52a)
* One - 1 1/2" square (51a)
* Two - 1" x 2 1/2" (13, 56)
* Three - 1 1/4" squares (47a, 49a)

From Fabric III, cut: (medium gold print)
• One 2 3/4" wide strip. From this, cut:
* One   2 3/4" x 5 1/8" (101)
* One - 2 1/2" square (46b)
* One - 1 3/4" x 2 1/2" (57)
* One - 1 1/4" x 2 1/2" (12)
* One - 1 1/2" x 2 1/4" (102)
* One - 1 1/2" x 2 1/8" (1)
* One - 1 1/2" x 2" (45)
* One - 1 1/2" x 1 5/8" (58)
* Two - 1 1/2" squares (46a, 103b)
* One - 1" x 3 5/8" (104)
* Two - 1" squares (2a)

From Fabric IV, cut: (dark gold print)
• One 1" wide strip. From this, cut:
* One - 1" x 6 3/8" (115)
* One - 1" x 2" (106)
* One - 1" x 1 3/4" (41)
* One - 1" x 1 1/2" (43a)

From Fabric V, cut: (dark grape print)
• One 3 1/8" wide strip. From this, cut:
* One - 1 7/8" x 3 1/8" (66)
* One - 1 3/4" x 3 1/8" (52)
* Two - 1 5/8" x 3 1/8" (17)
* One - 1" x 2 1/2" (7)
* One - 2 1/4" x 2 3/8" (49)
* One - 2 1/4" square (70)
* Two - 1 5/8" x 2 1/4" (16)
* Two - 1 5/8" x 2 1/8" (9)
* Two - 1 1/2" x 2 1/8" (5)
* One - 2" x 3 1/2" (65)
* Two - 1 3/8" x 2" (54)
* One - 1 1/2" x 1 3/4" (51)
* One - 1" x 1 3/4" (118)

* One - 1 1/2" x 1 5/8" (68)
* One - 1 3/8" x 1 5/8" (83a)
* One - 1" x 1 5/8" (82a)
* One - 1 1/2" x 3 1/2" (32)
• One 1 1/8" wide strip. From this, cut:
* Eight - 1 1/8" squares (4b, 6a, 61a, 81a, 120a)
* Twenty-eight - 1" squares (3, 4a, 8a, 14a, 15a, 50a, 55a, 60, 62a, 63a, 69a, 81b, 117b)

From Fabric VI, cut: (medium grape print)
• One 1 3/4" wide strip. From this, cut:
* Four - 1" x 1 3/4" (14, 62)
* Two - 1 5/8" x 2 1/8" (4)
* One - 1 1/2" x 1 5/8" (81)
* Two - 1" x 1 5/8" (2)
* Two - 1 1/8" x 2 1/2" (6, 61)
* Two - 1 1/8" x 1 1/2" (50, 69)
* Two - 1 1/8" squares (49b, 70a)
* Two - 1" x 2 1/8" (63)
* Two - 1" x 1 1/8" (59)
* Four - 1" x 2" (15, 55)
• One 1" wide strip. From this, cut:
* Fourteen - 1" squares (1a, 3, 13a, 56a, 57a, 58a, 60)

From Fabric VII, cut: (navy print)
• One 1 1/8" wide strip. From this, cut:
* One - 1 1/8" x 2 5/8" (108)
* Two - 1 1/8" squares (35a, 37a)
* Two - 1" x 6 3/8" (114, 116)
* One - 1" x 2" (105)
* One - 1" x 1 3/4" (42)
* One - 1" x 1 1/2" (43a)
* Two - 1" squares (117a, 122a)

From Fabric VIII, cut: (light green print)
• One 2 5/8" wide strip. From this, cut:
* One - 2 1/2" x 2 5/8" (86)
* One - 1 1/2" x 2 5/8" (45a)
* Two - 2 1/2" x 3 1/8" (24)
* One - 2 3/8" x 3 5/8" (43)
* One   1 5/8" x 2 1/8" (38)
* Two - 1 1/4" x 2" (30)
* One   1" x 1 7/8" (85)
* One - 1 5/8" x 1 3/4" (37)
* One - 1 1/2" x 1 3/4" (80)
* One - 1 1/2" x 3 7/8" (73)
* Three - 1 1/2" squares (28, 40)
* One - 1 1/4" x 1 1/2" (33)
* Two - 1 3/8" squares (47b, 98b)
* One - 1 1/4" x 1 3/8" (93)
* Three - 1" squares (32a, 83b, 88a)
• One 1 1/4" wide strip. From this, cut:
* Three - 1 1/4" x 3 1/8" (21, 109)
* Five - 1 1/4" squares (72a, 94a, 95b, 103a, 113a)

From Fabric IX, cut: (medium green print)
• One 2 5/8" wide strip. From this, cut:
* One - 2 5/8" square (44a)
* One - 2 1/4" x 2 5/8" (103)
* One - 1 1/2" x 2 5/8" (39)
* One - 1" x 2 5/8" (88)
* Two - 1" x 2 1/2" (25)
* One - 1 5/8" x 2 3/8" (43b)
* One - 2 1/8" x 3" (97)
* Three - 2 1/8" squares (23, 75)
* One - 1 7/8" x 2 1/8" (95)
* One - 1 3/8" x 2 1/8" (98)
* One - 1 1/8" x 2" (35)

* One - 2" square (111)
* One - 1 7/8" x 3 7/8" (72)
* Two - 1 7/8" x 3 1/8" (20)
* Two - 1 1/4" x 1 7/8" (30b)
* One - 1 1/2" square (102b)
• One 1 5/8" wide strip. From this, cut:
  * Three - 1 5/8" squares (24a, 86b)
  * Two - 1 1/4" squares (76a, 79a)
  * One - 1 1/4" x 1 3/4" (78)
  * One - 1 1/8" x 3" (89)
  * One - 1 1/8" square (38b)
  * Two - 1" x 3 5/8" (26)

image Unit 30 shown below. Refer to the diagram at the bottom of the page for making triangle-square, Unit 3.

3. To assemble the top flower portion of the block, begin

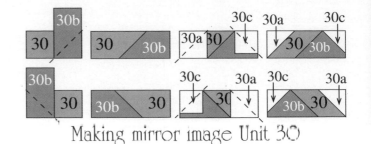

Making mirror image Unit 30

ASSEMBLY

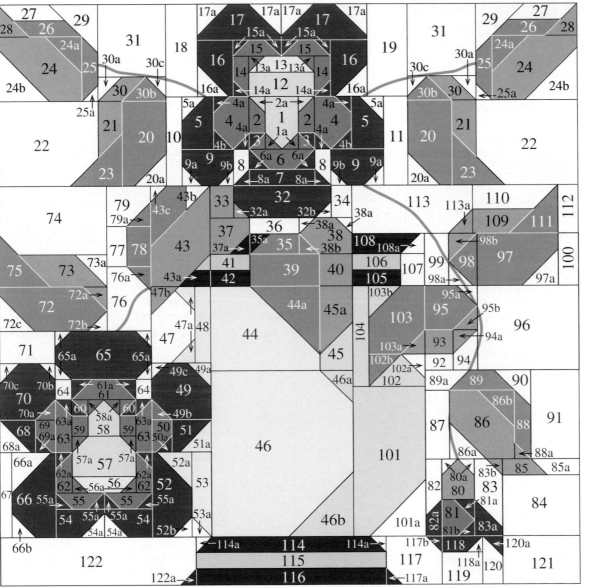

by joining mirror image units 2 and 3. Join these combined units to opposite sides of Unit 1 as shown. Join Unit 4 to opposite sides of the 1-3 combined units; then add mirror image Unit 5 to opposite sides of Unit 4. Join units 6 and 7; then add mirror image Unit 8 to opposite sides of the 6/7 combined units. Join mirror image Unit 9 to opposite sides of Unit 8. Join these combined units to bottom of combined units 1-5; then add Unit 10 to left side of the combined units, and Unit 11 to right side.

4. Join units 12 and 13; then add mirror image Unit 14 to opposite sides of these combined units. Join the two unit 15's; then add them to combined units 12-

14. Join mirror image Unit 16 to opposite sides of these combined Units. Join the two unit 17's as shown. Join these units to top of combined units 12-16; then add Unit 18 to left side of combined units, and Unit 19 to right side. Join flower top to flower bottom combined units.

5. Refer to block diagram and join mirror image Unit 30 and Unit 31. Join units 21 and 22; then add diagonal corner Unit 23 to bottom corner as shown. Join mirror image Unit 20 to side of these combined units. Refer to the dia-

1. For top flower section, use diagonal corner technique to make two of mirror image units 2, 4, 5, 8, 9, 14, 16, 20, 24, and 25. Make two of units 15 and 17, and one of units 1, 6, and 13.

2. Use diagonal end technique to make two of mirror

Making Unit 3

Place 1" squares of fabrics V and VI right sides facing and raw edges matching. Stitch diagonal, trim seam and press.

66

Making combined mirror image units 24-29.

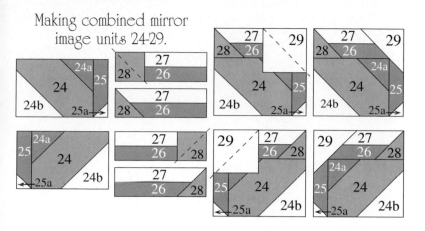

gram above, and join mirror image units 24 and 25. Join units 26 and 27; then add diagonal corner Unit 28 as shown. Join the combined 26-28 units to the top of combined units 24/25; then add diagonal corner Unit 29 as shown above. Join these combined units to combined units 30 and 31; then join combined units 20-23 to bottom of combined units 25-31 as shown. Join these leaf sections to opposite sides of flower to complete the top flower section.

6. For the block bottom, use diagonal corner technique to make two of mirror image units 54, 62, and 63. Make two of Unit 55. Make one of units 35, 37, 38, 44, 46, 47, 49, 50, 51, 52, 53, 56, 57, 58, 61, 65, 66, 68, 69, 70, 72, 73, 76, 79, 80, 81, 86, 88, 94, 95, 97, 98, 101, 102, 103, 108, 113, 114, 117, 118, 120, and 122.

Making Unit 45

7. Use diagonal end technique to make one of Unit 45, 82, 83, 85, and 89. Refer to diagram below and make triangle-square, Unit 60.

8. To assemble the bottom of the block, begin by joining units 33, 32, and 34 in a row. Join units 35 and 36. Join Unit 37 to left side of these combined units, and Unit 38 to right side. Join this row to bottom of combined units 32-34. Join units 41 and 42. Join units 39 and 40. Referring to block diagram, join these units together in a row; then add them to the bottom of combined units 32-38. Join units 44 and 45, matching seams; then add Unit 46 to bottom of these combined units, again matching seams. Join these combined units to vase top units to complete the main part of the vase.

Making Unit 60

Place 1" squares of fabrics V and VI right sides facing. Stitch a diagonal down the center. Open and press.

9. Join units 47 and 48. Refer to diagram below for making Unit 43. Add Unit 43 to the top of combined units 47/48. Join units 50 and 51; then add Unit 49 to

top of these combined units. Join these units to combined units 43/47/48. Join units 52 and 53. Join these combined units to bottom of other combined units. Set aside.

10. Join units 77 and 78; then add Unit 79 to top of these combined units, matching seams. Join Unit 76 to bottom, again matching seams. Join units 73 and 74; then add diagonal corner Unit 75 as shown. Join Unit 72 to bottom of combined units 73-75. Add these combined units to left side of combined units 76-79.

11. Join Unit 64 to opposite sides of Unit 61; then add Unit 65 to top of these combined units. Join units 59 and 60, referring to block diagram for correct positioning of Unit 60. Join the 59/60 units to opposite sides of Unit 58. Join units 56 and 57; then add these units to bottom of combined units 58-60. Join units 62 and 63. Refer to block diagram for correct placement of mirror image units. Join these combined units to opposite sides of combined units 56-60. Join units 55 as shown. Join mirror image units 54 as shown. Join the combined 54 units to bottom of combined 55 units; then add them to bottom of other flower center units. Join combined units 61/64/65 to top of flower center units.

12. Join units 70 and 71. Join units 68 and 69. Add the combined units together. Join units 66 and 67; then add them to bottom of other combined units. Join this combined unit section to left side of flower center units. Join combined units 72-79 to top of flower, then add combined units 43-53 to right side of flower. Join to left side of vase combined units, matching seams where necessary.

Making Unit 108

13. For the right side of the vase, begin by joining units 105 and 106; then join Unit 107 to right side of these combined units. Join Unit 108 to the top as shown. Join units 102 and 103; then add Unit 104 to left side of these com-

Making combined units 86-90

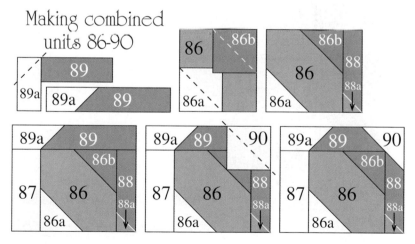

bined units. Join Unit 101 to the bottom. Join combined units 105-108 to top of other combined units. Set aside.

14. Join units 99, 98, 97, and 100 in a horizontal row. Join units 92 and 93; then add Unit 94 to right side of these combined units, matching seams. Join Unit 95 to the top; then add Unit 96 to the right side. Join these combined units to bottom

Making Unit 43

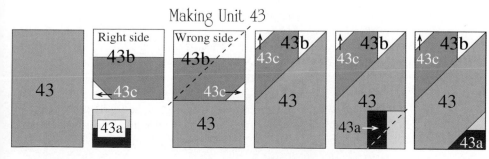

side. Join these combined units to bottom of combined units 97-100 as shown. Refer to diagram on page 67 for making combined units 86-90. Complete these combined units; then join Unit 91 to right side. Join to the bottom of combined leaf units 92-100. Join units 80 and 81; then add Unit 82 to left side of these combined units, and Unit 83 to right side. Join units 84 and 85; then add them to right side of other combined bud units. Join these units to bottom of other combined leaf units. Add these units to right side of combined units 101-108. Join units 109 and 110; then add diagonal corner 111 to right side of these combined units. Join Unit 112 to right side, and 113 to left side to complete the row. Join this row to the top of the combined bud and leaf units.

Making Unit 82.

Making Unit 83

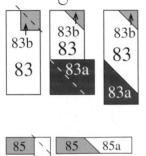

15. Join the combined flower and leaf units made in steps 9-12 to left side of vase; then add the bud and leaf units to the right side of the vase. Join units 114, 115, and 116; then add Unit 122 to left side of these combined units, and Unit 117 to the right side. Join units 118 and 119; then add Unit 120 to right side of these combine units. Join Unit 121 to right side of Unit 120. Join the bottom units together; then add them to the bottom of the vase, matching vase and bud seams. Join the bottom section to the top section, matching flower bottom seams.

Making Unit 85.

16. Use six strands of medium green embroidery floss and chain stitch the stems as shown.

Use the background color of your choice.

68

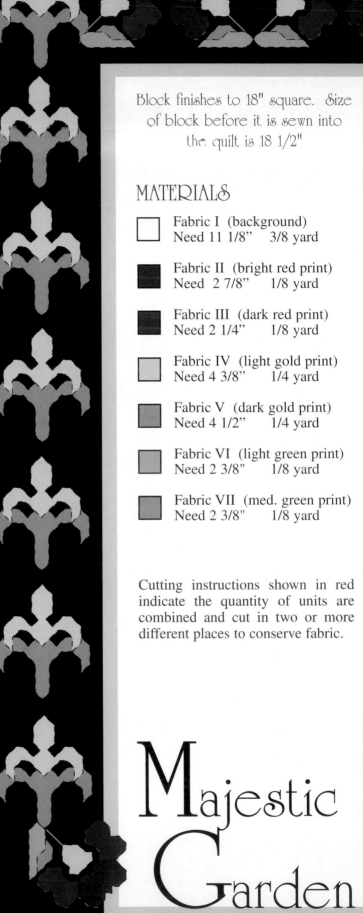

Block finishes to 18" square. Size of block before it is sewn into the quilt is 18 1/2"

MATERIALS

☐ Fabric I (background)
Need 11 1/8"   3/8 yard

■ Fabric II (bright red print)
Need 2 7/8"   1/8 yard

■ Fabric III (dark red print)
Need 2 1/4"   1/8 yard

☐ Fabric IV (light gold print)
Need 4 3/8"   1/4 yard

■ Fabric V (dark gold print)
Need 4 1/2"   1/4 yard

■ Fabric VI (light green print)
Need 2 3/8"   1/8 yard

■ Fabric VII (med. green print)
Need 2 3/8"   1/8 yard

Cutting instructions shown in red indicate the quantity of units are combined and cut in two or more different places to conserve fabric.

Majestic Garden

CUTTING

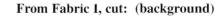
From Fabric 1, cut: (background)
- One 2 3/4" wide strip. From this, cut:
  * Eight - 2 1/2" x 2 3/4" (22, 32)
  * Eight - 2" x 2 3/4" (30, 33, B37)
  * Four - 1" x 2 3/4" (15)
- One 2" wide strip. From this, cut:
  * Four - 2" x 2 1/4" (18)
  * Eight - 2" x 2 1/8" (29)
  * Four - 1 1/2" x 2" (1)
  * Four - 1 7/8" x 2 3/8" (36a, B38a)
- One 1 5/8" wide strip. From this, cut:
  * Four - 1 5/8" x 1 3/4" (19)
  * Twelve - 1 5/8" squares (13, 17)
  * Eight - 1" x 1 5/8" (9)
  * Four - 1 1/8" x 1 1/2" (21a)
- One 1 1/2" wide strip. From this, cut:
  * Four - 1 1/2" squares (7)
  * Twenty-eight - 1 1/4" squares (2a, 6a, 8a, 14b, 23a, 24a)
- One 1 1/4" wide strip. From this, cut:
  * Twenty - 1 1/4" squares (add to 1 1/4" squares above)
  * Four - 1 1/8" squares (34b, B39b)
- Two 1" wide strips. From these, cut:
  * Sixty-eight - 1" squares (2b, 4a, 5a, 6b, 8b, 11, 14a, 16a, 24b, 25a, 27)
  * Four - 1" x 1 1/2" (3)

From Fabric II, cut: (bright red print)
- One 2 7/8" wide strip. From this, cut:
  * Four - 1 7/8" x 2 7/8" (5)
  * Four - 1 1/2" x 2 7/8" (6)
  * Four - 1 1/2" x 2 3/8" (2)
  * Four - 1 3/8" x 1 1/2" (4)

From Fabric III, cut: (dark red print)
- One 2 1/4" wide strip. From this, cut:
  * Eight - 2 1/4" x 2 3/8" (8)
  * Eight - 1 5/8" x 2 1/4" (14)
  * Eight - 1 1/8" x 1 1/2" (12)
- From scrap, cut:
  * Eight - 1" squares (9a)

From Fabric IV, cut: (light gold print)
- One 1 5/8" wide strip. From this, cut:
  * Four - 1 5/8" x 2 1/8" (16)
  * Eight - 1 5/8" squares (29c)
  * Four - 1" x 1 5/8" (15a)
  * Four - 1 1/2" squares (7)
- One 1 1/2" wide strip. From this, cut:
  * Eight - 1 1/2" x 2 1/2" (23)
  * Eight - 1 1/8" x 2" (26)
  * Eight - 1 1/4" squares (25)
- One 1 1/4" wide strip. From this, cut:
  * Eight - 1 1/4" x 3" (24)
  * Eight - 1" x 1 1/8" (10)
  * Eight - 1" squares (27)

From Fabric V, cut: (dark gold print)
- One 1 7/8" wide strip. From this, cut:
  * Eight - 1 7/8" squares (29a)
  * Four - 1 1/8" x 1 3/4" (20)
  * Eight - 1 3/8" squares (30a, 33a, B37a)
  * Four - 1" x 2 3/8" (36a, B38a)
- One 1 1/2" wide strip. From this, cut:
  * Eight - 1 1/2" squares (29b)
  * Twelve - 1" x 1 1/2" (28, 36b, B38b)
  * Four - 1 1/8" x 3" (21)
- One 1 1/8" wide strip. From this, cut:
  * Twenty - 1 1/8" squares (18a, 26a, 30c, 33b, B37c)
  * Four - 1" x 2 7/8" (35)
  * Four - 1" x 2" (31)

From Fabric VI, cut: (light green print)
- One 2 3/8" wide strip. From this, cut:
  * Two - 2 3/8" x 3 1/4" (36)
  * Two - 1 3/8" x 2 3/4" (B39)
  * Four - 1 3/8" squares (30b, 34a)
  * Two - 1" x 1 1/2" (B38b)

From Fabric VII, cut: (medium green print)
- One 2 3/8" wide strip. From this, cut:
  * Two - 2 3/8" x 3 1/4" (B38)
  * Two - 1 3/8" x 2 3/4" (34)
  * Four - 1 3/8" squares (B37b, B39a)
  * Two - 1" x 1 1/2" (36b)

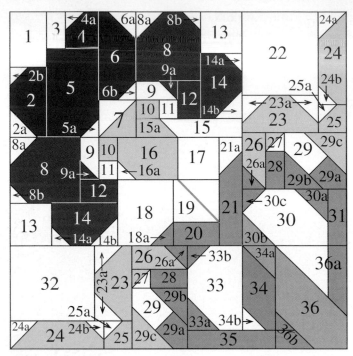

Block A. Make 2. When complete, block should measure 9 1/2" square.

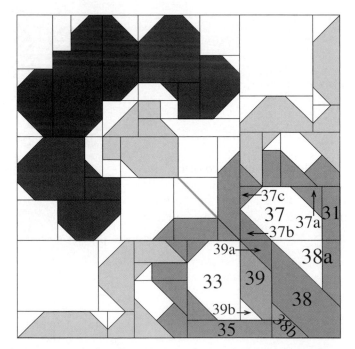

Block B. Make 2. When complete, block should measure 9 1/2" square. This block is the same as Block A, except for the unit numbers shown. These unit numbers ONLY will be shown as "B" + unit number in the cutting list.

ASSEMBLY

1. Referring to both block diagrams at left, for all four blocks, use diagonal corner technique to make eight of mirror image units 8, 9, 14, 24, 26, and 29. Make eight of Unit 23. Use this technique to make four of units 2, 4, 5, 6, 16, and 18. Make two of units 30, 33, 34, 36, 37, 38, and 39. Use diagonal end technique to make four of units 15, and 21. Refer to the diagrams for triangle-square units 7 and 27.

2. The two blocks are basically the same, except for the units that are shown with numbers in Block B. These units have different colors for the leaves. The following assembly instructions are for both blocks: Begin by joining units 1 and 2. Join units 3 and 4; then add Unit 5 to the bottom of these combined units. Join the combined 1/2 units to left side of combined units 3-5. Join units 6 and 7; then add them to right side of other combined units.

Making Unit 7

Place 1 1/2" squares of fabrics I and IV right sides facing, and raw edges matching. Stitch a diagonal seam down the center. Open and press.

3. Join units 10 and 11; then add mirror image Unit 9 to the top of these combined units as shown. Join Unit 12 to right side; then add mirror image Unit 8 to the top. Join units 13 and 14. Join these combined units to combined units 8-12. Join Unit 15 across the bottom, matching seams.   Add these combined units to right side of combined units 1-7 to complete the top part of the flower..

Making Unit 15

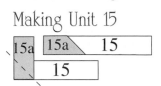

4. For the bottom part of the flower, referring to block diagrams, once again join units 10 and 11; then add Unit 9 to left side of combined units 10/11. Join Unit 12 to the bottom of these combined units; then add Unit 8 to the left side. Join units 13 and 14. Join these units to the bottom of other combined units. Join units 16 and 17. Join units 19 and 20; then add Unit 18 to left side of combined units 19/20. Join combined units 16/17 to top of combined units 18-20; then add Unit 21 to right side of these combined units. Join this bottom section of the flower to the top section, matching seams.

5. For the right side of the fleur-de-lis, begin by joining units 22 and 23. Join units 24 and 25. Join these two combined unit sections together, matching seams. Join units 27 and 28; then add Unit 26 to left side of combine units 27/28 as shown.

Making Unit 21

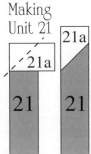

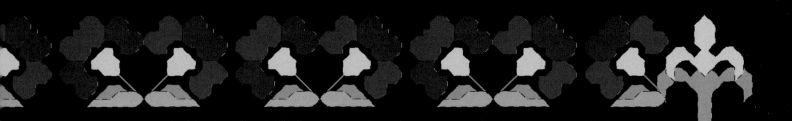

Making Unit 27

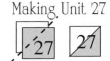

Place 1" squares of fabrics I and IV right sides facing and raw edges matching. Stitch diagonal, trim seam and press.

Join units 24 and 25. Join these two combined unit sections together. Join units 27 and 28; then add mirror image

Join mirror image Unit 29 to right side of combined units 26-28 as shown. Refer to diagram below for constructing mirror image Unit 29. For Block A, join units 30 and 31. For Block B join units 37 and 31. Join these units to bottom of fleur-de-lis. Join these combined units to right side of flower to complete the top section.

6. For the bottom, working from left to right, join units 32 and 23.

Making mirror image Unit 29

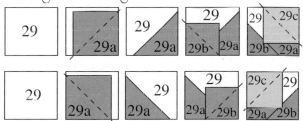

Unit 26 to top of these combined units, and mirror image Unit 29 to the bottom. Join these combined units to right side of fleur-de-lis units. For Block A, join units 33 and 34. For Block B, join units 33 and 39. Add Unit 35 to bottom of these combined units. Refer to diagram at right for making units 36 and 38. The units are identical except for the change in color. Refer to Block B for the color changes. For Block A, join Unit 36 to right side of combined units 33-35. For Block B, join Unit 38 to right side of combined units 33/35/39. Join these combined units to other bottom fleur-de-lis units; then add this combined section to bottom

Making units 36 and 38

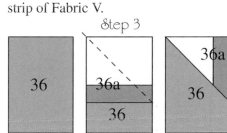

Step 1 Join 1 7/8" x 2 3/8" strip of Fabric I with 1" x 2 3/8" strip of Fabric V.

Step 2 Join 1" x 1 1/2" strips of fabrics V and VII for Unit 36. Use fabrics V and VI for Unit 38.

Step 3

Use 36a as a diagonal corner and place right sides facing on Unit 36. Stitch diagonal. Trim seam and press.

Step 4

Use 36b as a diagonal corner and place right sides facing on Unit 36. Stitch diagonal. Trim seam. Press.

of the blocks. Make two of Block A, and two of Block B.

7. Refer to the photo of the block, and join the blocks together, alternating the A and B blocks to make an 18 1/2" block.

8. Use 6 strands of medium green embroidery floss for the flower stems.

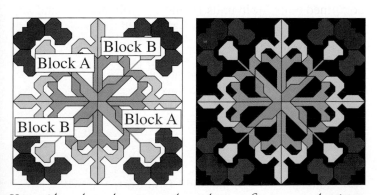

Use the background color of your choice

71

Block finishes to 18" square. Size of block before it
is sewn into the quilt is 18 1/2"

MATERIALS

 Fabric I (background)
Need 12"   1/2 yard

Fabric II (light gold print)
Need 5 1/2"   1/4 yard

Fabric III (dark gold print)
Need 2 1/4"   1/8 yard

Fabric IV (medium green print)
Need 2 1/2"   1/8 yard

Fabric V (light green print)
Need 2 1/2"   1/8 yard

Fabric VI (bright red print)
Need 4 1/2" square   scrap

This pattern is great for a beginner.

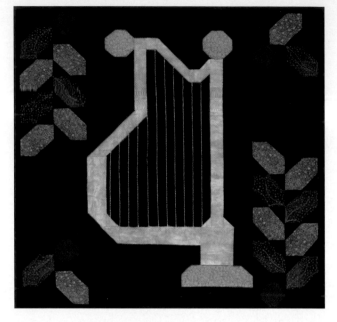

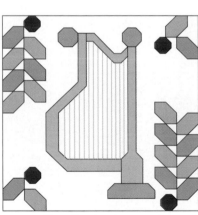

Use the background
color of your choice.

CUTTING

From Fabric I, cut: (background)
• One 5 1/2" wide strip. From this, cut:
  * One - 4 1/2" x 5 1/2" (37)
  * One - 1 5/8" x 5 1/2" (23)
  * One - 2 3/8" x 5 1/4" (29)
  * One - 1 5/8" x 4 7/8" (27)
  * One - 3" x 4 3/4" (7)
  * One - 4 1/2" square (38)
  * One - 4 3/8" x 9 3/8" (19)
  * One - 3" x 4 1/4" (28)
  * One - 3 3/8" x 3 3/4" (3)
  * One - 3 3/8" square (6a)
  * One - 3" square (6b)
  * One - 1 5/8" x 2 3/4" (25)
• One 2 1/2" wide strip. From this, cut:
  * One - 2 1/2" square (9a)
  * One - 1 1/8" x 2 1/2" (10)
  * Four - 1" x 2 1/2" (36)
  * One - 2 3/8" square (9b)
  * One - 1 5/8" x 2 1/4" (2)
  * One - 2" x 2 1/4" (16)
  * One - 1 3/4" x 2 1/4" (18)
  * One - 1 1/4" x 2 1/4" (17)
  * One - 2 1/4" x 9 3/8" (21)
  * One - 1 1/8" x 1 3/4" (13)
  * One - 1 5/8" x 10 1/2" (30)
• Two 1 1/2" wide strip. From these, cut:
  * Thirty-eight - 1 1/2" squares (31a, 32a)
  * Eight - 1 1/2" x 2 1/2" (33)
  * One - 1 1/4" square (8a)
  * Three - 1 1/8" squares (14a, 26a)

Harp

- One 1" wide strip. From this, cut:
  * One - 1" x 3 1/8" (12)
  * Four - 1" x 2" (35)
  * One - 1" x 1 1/4" (5)
  * Twenty-four - 1" squares (1a, 34a)

From Fabric II, cut: (light gold print)
- One 5 1/2" wide strip. From this, cut:
  * One - 1 5/8" x 5 1/2" (22)
  * One - 1 1/4" x 5" (4)
  * One - 1 5/8" x 4 3/4" (8)
  * One - 3 3/8" x 4 1/8" (6)
  * One - 2 1/2" x 3 1/4" (9)
  * One - 2 1/2" x 2 3/4" (24)
  * One - 1 1/4" x 2" (15)
  * One - 1 3/8" x 1 3/4" (14)
  * One - 1 5/8" square (29a)
  * One - 1 1/4" x 9 3/8" (20)
  * One - 1 1/4" square (7a)
  * One - 1 1/8" x 1 1/4" (11)
  * Three - 1 1/8" squares (13a, 19a, 21a)

From Fabric III, cut: (dark gold print)
- One 2 1/4" wide strip. From this, cut:
  * Two - 2 1/4" squares (1)
  * One - 1 7/8" x 4 7/8" (26)

From Fabric IV, cut: (medium green print)
- One 2 1/2" wide strip. From this, cut:
  * Nine - 2 1/2" squares (31)

From Fabric V, cut: (light green print)
- One 2 1/2" wide strip. From this, cut:
  * Ten - 2 1/2" squares (32)

From Fabric VI, cut: (bright red print)
- Four 2" squares (34)

ASSEMBLY

1. Refer to the diagram at right and use diagonal corner technique to make ten of Unit 32, nine of Unit 31, four of Unit 34, and two of Unit 1. Use this technique one of units 6, 7, 8, 9, 13, 14, 19, 21, 26, and 29.

2. To assemble the harp, join units 1 and 2; then add Unit 3 to bottom of these combined units. Join units 4 and 5; then add the to right side of combined 1-3 units. Join Unit 6 to bottom, matching seams. Join units 7 and 8; then add them to the bottom of Unit 6.

3. Join units 10 and 11; then add Unit 9 to right side of these combined units. Join Unit 12 to the top. Join units 13 and 14. Join units 15 and 16; then join these two combined unit sections together as shown. Join units 17, 1, and 18 in a row. Add them to the top of combined units 13-16. Join units 19, 20, and 21; then add them to the bottom of combined units 10-18. Join the two harp sections together.

4. For the harp bottom, join units 22 and

23; then add Unit 24 to right side. Join Unit 25 to right side of Unit 24. Join units 26 and 27; then add Unit 28 to left side of these combined units. Join combined units 22-25 to top of combined units 26-28; then add Unit 29 to left side of these combined units. Join these combined units to harp bottom; then add Unit 30 to the top.

5. For leaves and berries on right side of harp, begin at the top by joining units 34 and 35. Join Unit 36 to berry bottom. Join units 32, 31, 32, and 33 in a row and add this row to bottom of berry section. Join units 33, 31, 32, 31, and 32 in a vertical row. Join this row to left side of berry/leaf row; then add Unit 37 to bottom. For the bottom berry, once again join units 34 and 35; then add Unit 36 to bottom as shown. Join Unit 32 to th bottom. Join units 33, 31, and 33; then add them to the left side of the berry/leaf section. Join this section to bottom of Unit 37 to complete the section. Join this section to the left side of the harp.

6. For the leaf/berry section on the right of the harp, refer to Step 5 and the diagram below for making the berry combined units. Make 2. For the top berry section, join units 33, 32, and 33 in a row. Join Unit 31 to right side of combined berry Unit 36. Join these two rows together; then add Unit 38 to the bottom as shown. Join units 32, 31, 32, 31, and completed berry section in a vertical row. Join units 33, 32, 31, 32, 31, and 33 in a vertical row. Join this row to right side of berry/leaf row; then add to the bottom of Unit 38. Join this section to right side of harp to complete the block.

7. For the strings, we used gold metallic thread stitched with a triple-stitch on the the sewing machine.

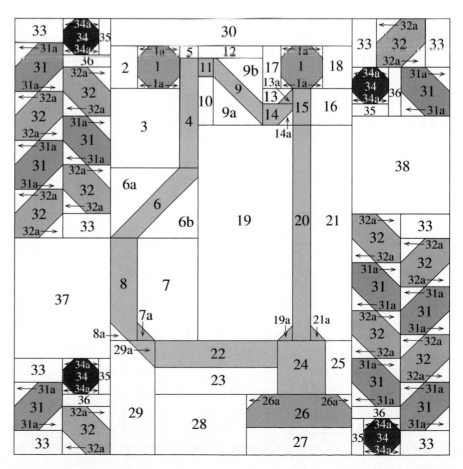

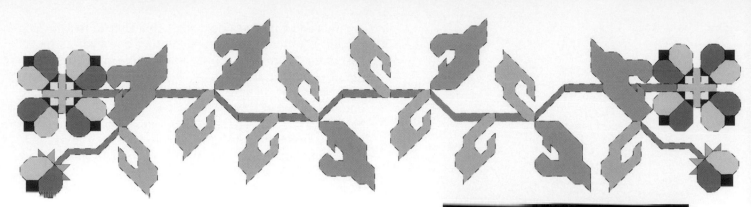

Block finishes to 18" square. Size of block before it is sewn into the quilt is 18 1/2"

MATERIALS

 Fabric I (background)
Need 12 1/2"   1/2 yard

Fabric II (burgundy print)
Need 2 1/8"   1/8 yard

Fabric III (medium rose print)
Need 3 1/2"   1/4 yard

Fabric IV (pink print)
Need 4"   1/4 yard

Fabric V (light gold print)
Need 1"   1/4 yard

Fabric VI (medium gold print)
Need 1"   1/8 yard

Fabric VII (dark green print)
Need 3 1/8"   1/4 yard

Fabric VIII (medium green print)
Need 3 1/2"   1/4 yard

 Fabric IX (light green print)
Need 3 3/4"   1/4 yard

Use the background color
of your choice

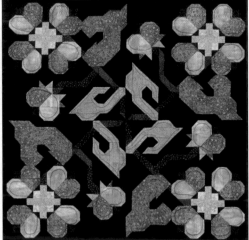

CUTTING

From Fabric I, cut: (background)
- One 2 7/8" wide strip. From this, cut:
  * Four - 1 1/2" x 2 7/8" (12)
  * Four - 2 5/8" squares (34)
  * Four - 2 1/8" x 2 5/8" (46)
  * Four - 1" x 2 5/8" (14)
  * Four - 2 1/4" squares (44)
  * Four - 1" x 1 7/8" (40)
- One 2 1/4" wide strip. From this, cut:
  * Four - 1 1/2" x 2 1/4" (21)
  * Four - 1 1/2" x 2 1/8" (35)
  * Four - 1 7/8" x 2" (16)
  * Twelve - 1" x 2" (8)
  * Four - 1 1/8" x 1 7/8" (36)
- One 1 3/4" wide strip. From this, cut:
  * Eight - 1" x 1 3/4" (33, 38)
  * Four - 1 5/8" squares (45a)
  * Four - 1" x 1 5/8" (30)
  * Four - 1 1/4" x 1 1/2" (28)
  * Sixteen - 1" x 1 1/2" (10a, 20, 25, 39)
- One 1 1/2" wide strip. From this, cut:
  * Sixteen - 1 1/2" squares (13, 31b, 45b, 46b)
  * Sixteen - 7/8" x 1 1/2" (7)
  * Four - 1" x 1 1/8" (18a)
- One 1 1/4" wide strip. From this, cut:
  * Eight - 1 1/4" squares (31a, 42a)
  * Four - 1 1/8" squares (42b)
  * Four - 1" x 3 3/4" (43a)

Apple Blossom Time

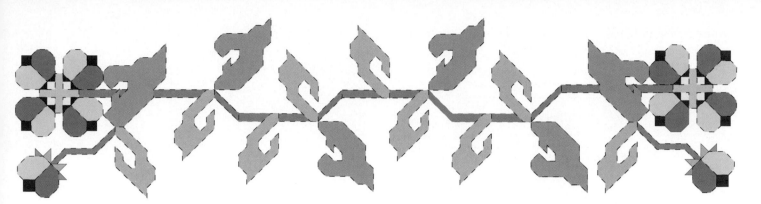

* Four - 1" x 3" (33b)
- Two 1" wide strips. From these, cut:
    * Fifty-six - 1" squares (1b, 4b, 15a, 17b, 24a, 36b, 41a, 43b)
    * Twenty - 7/8" x 1 1/8" (5, 23)
- One 7/8" wide strip. From this, cut:
    * Forty - 7/8" squares (1c, 4a, 17c, 24b)

From Fabric II, cut: (burgundy print)
- One 1 1/8" wide strip. From this, cut:
    * Twenty- 1 1/8" squares (6, 22)
- One 1" wide strip. From this, cut:
    * Thirty-two - 1" squares (1d, 2a)

From Fabric III, cut: (medium rose print)
- One 2" wide strip. From this, cut:
    * Four - 2" x 2 1/2" (17)
    * Sixteen - 1 1/2" x 2" (4)
- One 1 1/2" wide strip. From this, cut:
    * Sixteen - 1 1/2" squares (1a)
    * Sixteen - 1" x 1 1/2" (2)

From Fabric IV, cut: (pink print)
- One 2 1/2" wide strip. From this, cut:
    * Sixteen - 2" x 2 1/2" (1)
    * Four - 1 1/2" x 2" (24)
- One 1 1/2" wide strip. From this, cut:
    * Four - 1 1/2" squares (17a)
    * Four - 1" x 1 1/2" (19)

From Fabric V, cut: (light gold print)
- One 1" wide strip. From this, cut:
    * Sixteen - 1" squares (3)

From Fabric VI, cut: (medium gold print)
- One 1" wide strip. From this, cut:
    * Eight - 1" x 1 1/2" (9)
    * Four - 1" x 3" (11)

From Fabric VII, cut: (dark green print)
- One 2 1/8" wide strip. From this, cut:
    * Four - 2 1/8" squares (46a)
    * Four - 1 7/8" x 2 1/8" (45)
    * Four - 1" x 2" (32a)
    * Four - 1" x 1 1/2" (10)
    * Four - 1" x 1 3/8" (18)
    * Eight - 1 1/8" squares (42b, 45c)
    * Four - 1" x 1 1/8" (30a)
- One 1" wide strip. From this, cut:
    * Four - 1" x 2 5/8" (15)
    * Four - 1" squares (33c)

From Fabric VIII, cut: (medium green print)
- One 3 1/2" wide strip. From this, cut:

* Eight - 1 7/8" x 3 1/2" (41, 42)
* Four - 1" x 2 5/8" (43)
* Four - 1 1/8" x 2 1/4" (36a)
* Four - 1 1/2" x 1 3/4" (37)
* Four - 1" x 1 1/4" (39a)
* Sixteen - 1" squares (13a, 20b, 38a)

From Fabric IX, cut: (light green print)
- One 1 3/4" wide strip. From this, cut:
    * Four - 1 3/4" x 2" (31)
    * Four - 1 1/4" x 3 3/8" (29)
    * Four - 1 1/4" x 2 3/8" (27)
    * Four - 1" x 2 3/8" (33a)
- Two 1" wide strips. From these, cut:
    * Four - 1" x 3 3/8" (26)
    * Four - 1" x 1 1/2" (32)
    * Thirty-two - 1" squares (13b, 17d, 19a, 20a, 28a, 30b)

ASSEMBLY

1. Refer to block diagram on page 76. These instructions are for all four of the 9 1/2" blocks that comprise the main block when sewn together. Use diagonal corner technique to make sixteen of units 1, 2, and 4. Use this technique to make four each of units 13, 15, 17, 19, 20, 24, 28, 31, 38, 41, and 42. Refer to page 76 for illustration on how to make Unit 42.

2. Use diagonal end technique to make four each of units 10, 18, 30, 32, 33, 36, 39, and 43.

Making Unit 10
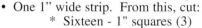

3. To assemble the block, begin with the flower. All four petal sections are assembled the same. Follow these instructions for one petal. Join units 2 and 3; then join Unit 1 to left side of the 2/3 combination. Join units 5 and 6; then add Unit 7 to left side of these combined units. Join Unit 4 to right side of the 5-7 units; then join this section to the top of the flower petal. Make 4. For left side of flower, join units 8 and 9. Referring to block diagram for correct placement, join flower petals to top and bottom of combined 8/9 units. For the center, join units 8, 11, and 8 in a row. Join this row to right side of the combined flower petals. Join units 9 and 10; then add remaining flower petals to top and bottom of

Making Unit 18

combined units 9/10. Join these combined flower petal units to right side of other flower petal combined units to complete the flower.

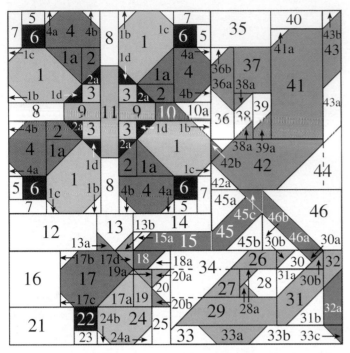

Make 4. When this block is complete, it should measure 9 1/2" square.

4. Join units 12 and 13. Join units 14 and 15; then join the 12/13 combined units to left side of combined 14/15 units. Join these combined units to flower bottom.

5. For large right side leaf, join units 38 and 39; then add Unit 37 to top of these combined units. Join unit 36 to left side, matching seams; then join Unit 35 to the top. Join units 40 and 41; then add them to right side of combined units 35-39.

Join Unit 42 to the bottom of the leaf combined units. Join Unit 43 to right side of the combined units; then join diagonal corner Unit 44 to bottom as shown. Join units 45 and 46, carefully matching seams.

Making Unit 39

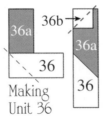

Making Unit 36

Making Unit A32

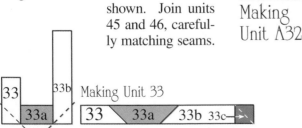

Making Unit 33

Making Unit 30

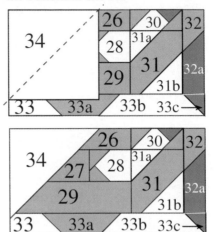

Join units 27 and 28. Join Unit 26 to top of 27/28; then add Unit 29 to the bottom. Join units 30 and 31; then add Unit 32 to right side. Join the combined 26-29 units to left side of the 30/31 combined units, matching seams. Add Unit 33 to the bottom as shown.

Join diagonal corner Unit 34 as shown. If you are using a light background fabric, do not trim the seam, as the darker color of the leaf can show through.
If you are using a dark background, trim the seam.

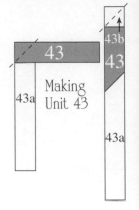

Making Unit 43

Add them to bottom of other combined leaf units. Join the large leaf to right side of the flower units to complete the top part of the block.

6. For the bud section, join units 19 and 20. Add Unit 18 to top of combined units 19/20. Join units 16 and 17; then add them to left side of combined units 18-20. Join units 22 and 23; then add Unit 24 to right side of combined units, and Unit 21 to left side. Join unit 25 to right side of Unit 24. Join these combined units to bottom of combined units 16-20. Refer to the diagram and instructions above, and make combined units 26-34 as shown. Add this section to right side of bud section; then join the bottom bud section to the bottom of the flower section to complete the block. Make four. Refer to the diagram and photo of the complete block, and rotate the blocks as shown when you sew them together.

Making Unit 42

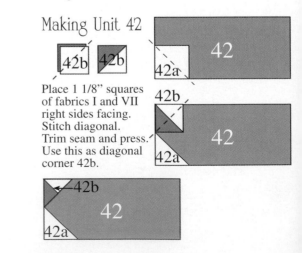

Place 1 1/8" squares of fabrics I and VII right sides facing. Stitch diagonal. Trim seam and press. Use this as diagonal corner 42b.

Block finishes to 18" square. Size of block before it is sewn into the quilt is 18 1/2"

MATERIALS

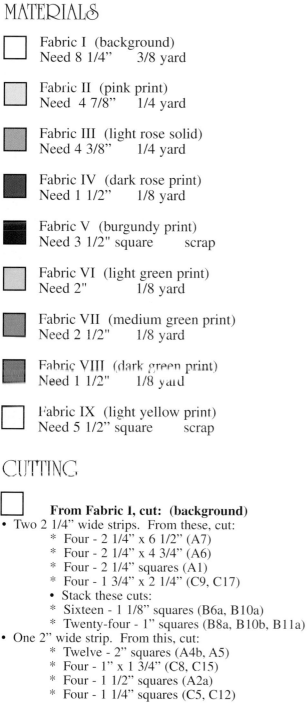

Fabric I (background)
Need 8 1/4"   3/8 yard

Fabric II (pink print)
Need 4 7/8"   1/4 yard

Fabric III (light rose solid)
Need 4 3/8"   1/4 yard

Fabric IV (dark rose print)
Need 1 1/2"   1/8 yard

Fabric V (burgundy print)
Need 3 1/2" square   scrap

Fabric VI (light green print)
Need 2"   1/8 yard

Fabric VII (medium green print)
Need 2 1/2"   1/8 yard

Fabric VIII (dark green print)
Need 1 1/2"   1/8 yard

Fabric IX (light yellow print)
Need 5 1/2" square   scrap

CUTTING

From Fabric I, cut: (background)
• Two 2 1/4" wide strips. From these, cut:
  * Four - 2 1/4" x 6 1/2" (A7)
  * Four - 2 1/4" x 4 3/4" (A6)
  * Four - 2 1/4" squares (A1)
  * Four - 1 3/4" x 2 1/4" (C9, C17)
  • Stack these cuts:
  * Sixteen - 1 1/8" squares (B6a, B10a)
  * Twenty-four - 1" squares (B8a, B10b, B11a)
• One 2" wide strip. From this, cut:
  * Twelve - 2" squares (A4b, A5)
  * Four - 1" x 1 3/4" (C8, C15)
  * Four - 1 1/2" squares (A2a)
  * Four - 1 1/4" squares (C5, C12)

• One 1 3/4" wide strip. From this, cut:
  * Sixteen - 1 5/8" x 1 3/4" (B9)
  * Four - 1 1/2" x 2 1/2" (A3a)

From Fabric II, cut: (pink print)
• One 2 1/8" wide strip. From this, cut:
  * Eight - 2 1/8" x 2 1/2" (B10)
  * Eight - 1 5/8" x 1 3/4" (B4)
  * Two - 1" x 1 3/4" (C13)
  * Two - 1 1/2" x 3" (C3)
• One 1 5/8" wide strip. From this, cut:
  * Eight - 1 1/4" x 1 5/8" (B11)
  * Sixteen - 1 1/8" x 1 3/8" (B3, B7)
• One 1 1/8" wide strip. From this, cut:
  * Sixteen - 1 1/8" squares (B1a, B8b)
  * Two - 1" squares (C16a)

From Fabric III, cut: (lt. rose solid)
• One 1 7/8" wide strip. From this, cut:
  * Eight - 1 3/8" x 1 7/8" (B2)
  * Two - 1" x 1 3/4" (C6)
  * Eight - 1 5/8" x 2 1/2" (B8)
  * Four - 1 1/2" squares (C2a, C3a)
• One 1 3/8" wide strip. From this, cut:
  * Eight - 1 3/8" x 3 1/8" (B6)

Spring in Baltimore

* Eight - 1 1/4" x 1 5/8" (B5)
* Two - 1" x 1 1/4" (C11)
• One 1 1/8" wide strip. From this, cut:
* Sixteen - 1 1/8" squares (B1b, B4a)
* Six - 1" squares (C10a, C13a, C14a)

 From Fabric IV, cut: (dark rose print)
• One 1 1/2" wide strip. From this, cut:
* Two - 1 1/2" x 3" (C2)
* Four - 1 1/2" squares (C1, C3a)
* Two - 1" x 1 1/4" (C4)
* Four - 1" squares (C6a, C7a)

 From Fabric V, cut: (burgundy print)
• Four 1 1/2" squares (C1, C2a)

From Fabric VI, cut: (light green print)
• One 2" wide strip. From this, cut:
* Eight - 2" x 3 1/4" (A4)
* Twelve - 1" squares (B4b, B5b)

From Fabric VII, cut: (medium green print)
• One 1 1/2" wide strip. From this, cut:
* Eight - 1 1/2" x 2 1/4" (A2, A3)
* Four - 1 1/4" x 1 3/4" (C7, C14)
* Four - 1 1/4" squares (C2b)
• One 1" wide strip. From this, cut:
* Twelve - 1" squares (B5a, B8d, B10c, C8a, C15a)

From Fabric VIII, cut: (dark green print)
• One 1 1/2" wide strip. From this, cut:
* Eight - 1 1/2" squares (A4a)
* Four - 1 1/4" x 1 3/4" (C10, C16)
* Four - 1 1/4" squares (C3b)
* Eight - 1" squares (B8c, B10d, C9a, C17a)

From Fabric IX, cut: (light yellow print)
• Four 2 1/2" squares (B1)

ASSEMBLY

1. The completed block is comprised of three smaller blocks. Instructions are given for each block, beginning with Block A shown at left.

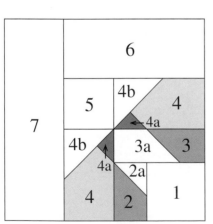

Block A Make 4 When completed block should measure 6 1/2".

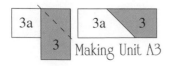

Making Unit A3

2. Use diagonal corner technique to make a total of eight mirror image Unit 4's and four Unit 2's. When making mirror image Unit 4, refer to Block A diagram for correct placement of mirror image units. Join the diagonal corners in alphabetical order. Use diagonal end technique to make four of Unit 3 shown at left.

3. To assemble Block A, join units 1 and 2; then add Unit 3 to top of these combined units. Join Unit 4 to left side of the 1-3 combined

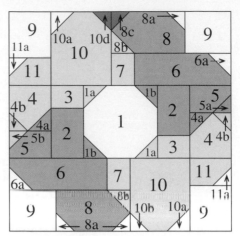

Block B. Make 2. When completed block should measure 6 1/2 "

(8c and 10d). The other two shown at right are made with Fabric VII diagonal corners. Make two of each block. The instructions for unit construction are for all four of Block B units. Use diagonal corner technique to make eight of Unit 4. For Unit 5, you will make eight, however refer to block diagram for color change in units 5a and 5b. Make eight of units 6, 8, 10, and 11, referring to diagrams above for the color change in units 8c, 8d, 10c, and 10d. Use diagonal corner technique to make four of Unit 1.

5. To assemble the block, join units 2 and 3 as shown. Check block diagram for correct placement and join these combined units to opposite sides of Unit 1. Join units 4 and 5, again referring to diagram for correct color placement. Join the combined 4/5 units to opposite sides of combined units 2/3 to complete the center row. The top and bottom rows are assembled the same. Be sure to check block illustration for the color changes. For the top and bottom rows, join Unit 9 and 11; then add Unit 10 to right side. Join units 8 and 9. Join units 6 and 7; then join these two combined unit sections together as shown. Add them to right side of Unit 10. Join these two sections to top and bottom of center row to complete Block B. Make a total of four.

units. Join remaining Unit 4 and 5. Join them to the top of the other combined units, matching corners. Join Unit 6 to the top; then add Unit 7 to left side to complete the block. Make 4.

4. There is a color change in Block B. (Refer to the smaller diagram below). You will make two of Block B with Fabric VIII diagonal corners

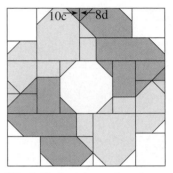

Block B showing color change on units 8d and 10c from Fabric VII. Make 2.

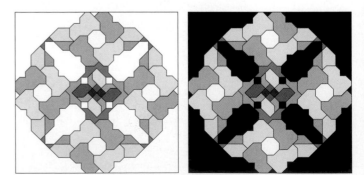

Use the background color of your choice.

78

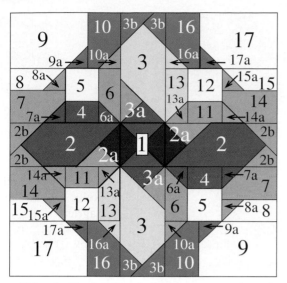

Block C. Make 1 When completed
block should measure 6 1/2 "

to left side of Unit 3 as shown. For the right side units, join units 11 and 12; then add Unit 13 to left side of these combined units. Join units 14 and 15. Join these combined units to right side of combined units 11/12. Join units 16 and 17. Add these combined units to top of combined units 11-14. Join this combined section to right side of Unit 3 as shown. Make two and join them to top and bottom of center row to complete Block C.

8. Refer to the diagram of the entire block below. For the center row, join Block B to opposite sides of Block C as shown, matching seams. Check correct placement of colors. For the top and bottom rows, join Block A to to opposite sides of Block B, matching seams. Join the three rows together to complete the block.

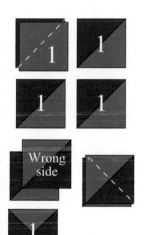

Making Unit C1

Place 1 1/2" squares of fabrics IV and V, right sides facing with raw edges matching. Stitch th diagonal, trim seam and press for C1. Make 2. Place the two triangle-squares right sides facing with darkest fabrics butting up to each other and raw edges matching. Stitch diagonally in opposite direction as shown. Open up, trim seam and press.

6. For Block C, refer to diagram above and use diagonal corner technique to make two of units 2, 3, 6, 7, 8, 9, 10, 13, 14, 15, 16, and 17. Refer to diagram below for making units 2 and 3. These units are the same except for color changes. Refer to the block diagram for color changes. Refer to the diagram and instructions at left for making Unit 1.

7. To assemble the block, begin by joining Unit 2 to opposite sides of Unit 1 to complete the center row. Top and bottom rows are the same. The instructions are for both rows. Join units 4 and 5; then add Unit 6 to right side of combined units 4/5. Join units 7 and 8; then add them to left side of combined 4-6 units. Join units 9 and 10; then add them to the top of combined of combined units 4-8. Join this combined unit section

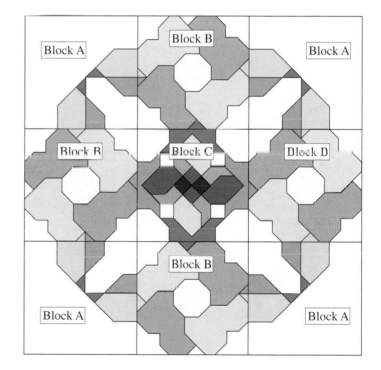

Making units C2 and C3. Unit 3 is made the same way except for color changes.

Place 1 1/2" squares of fabrics III and V, right sides facing with raw edges matching. Stitch th diagonal, trim seam and press for C2a.
Place 1 1/2" squares of fabrics III and IV, right sides facing with raw edges matching. Stitch the diagonal, trim seam and press for C3a.

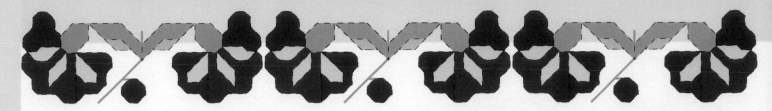

Block finishes to 18" square. Size of block before it is sewn into the quilt is 18 1/2"

MATERIALS

 Fabric I (background)
Need 11 3/8"   1/2 yard

Fabric II (dark red print)
Need 3 7/8"   1/4 yard

Fabric III (bright red print)
Need 5 3/8"   1/4 yard

Fabric IV (medium green print)
Need 2 3/4"   1/8 yard

Fabric V (light green print)
Need 1 3/8"   1/8 yard

Fabric VI (medium gold print)
Need 2 7/8"   1/8 yard

Cutting instructions shown in red indicate the quantity of units are combined and cut in two or more different places to conserve fabric.

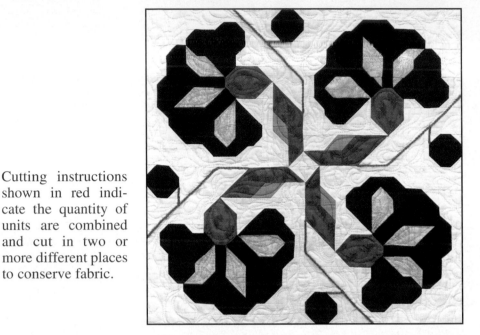

CUTTING

 From Fabric I, cut: (background)
• One 3 7/8" wide strip. From this, cut:
    * Four - 1 7/8" x 3 7/8" (27)
    * Four - 1 3/4" x 3 3/4" (6)
    * Four - 3 1/8" squares (26)
    * Four - 2 1/8" x 2 5/8" (9)
    * Four - 1 1/8" x 2 5/8" (5)
• One 2 1/2" wide strip. From this, cut:
    * Four - 1 3/8" x 2 1/2" (23)
    * Four - 2" x 2 3/8" (28)
    * Four - 1 1/4" x 2 1/4" (33)
    * Four - 1" x 2 1/4" (8)
    * Four - 1 3/4" x 2 1/8" (12)
    * Four - 2" squares (20b)
    * Four - 1" x 1 1/8" (31)
• One 1 3/4" wide strip. From this, cut:
    * Four - 1 3/4" x 2" (21)

    * Four - 1 1/8" x 1 3/4" (19)
    * Eight - 1 1/2" squares (4a, 14a)
    * Four - 1 3/8" squares (24a)
    * One - 1 1/8" x 9 1/2" (13)
• Two 1 1/8" wide strips. From these, cut:
    * Three - 1 1/8" x 9 1/2" (add to13)
    * Four - 1 1/8" x 4 3/8" (22)
    * Twenty - 1 1/8" squares (7a, 29a)
• One 1" wide strip. From this, cut:
    * Twenty-four - 1" squares (1b, 11b, 20a, 32a)

 From Fabric II, cut: (dark red print)
• One 2 5/8" wide strip. From this, cut:
    * Four - 2 5/8" x 3 1/8" (4)
    * Four - 2 1/4" x 2 5/8" (1)
    * Four - 1 5/8" x 2 1/4" (7)
    * Four - 1 3/4" squares (18a)
    * Four - 1 1/8" x 1 5/8" (3)
    * Four - 1" squares (2a)
• One 1 1/4" wide strip. From this, cut:
    * Four - 1 1/4" squares (10b)
    * Sixteen - 1 1/8" squares (5a, 14b, 15, 16)

From Fabric III, cut: (bright red print)
• One 2 3/8" wide strip. From this, cut:
    * Four - 2 3/8" squares (29)
    * Four - 2 1/4" x 2 3/8" (32)
    * Four - 2" x 2 1/8" (11)

Folk Flowers

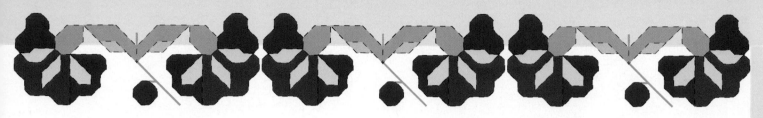

* Four - 2" x 3 1/8" (20)
* Four - 1" squares (10a)
• One 1 7/8" wide strip. From this, cut:
   * Four - 1 7/8" squares (4b)
   * Four - 1 3/4" squares (18c)
   * Four - 1 1/8" x 1 3/4" (30)
   * Four - 1 1/2" squares (18b)
• One 1 1/8" wide strip. From this, cut:
   * Sixteen - 1 1/8" squares (6a, 14c, 17, 21a)

From Fabric IV, cut: (medium green print)
• One 2 3/4" wide strip. From this, cut:
   * Four - 1 3/8" x 2 3/4" (24)
   * Four - 2 3/8" x 3 1/4" (14)
   * Four - 2 1/4" x 4" (25)

From Fabric V, cut: (light green print)
• One 1 3/8" wide strip. From this, cut:
   * Four - 1 3/8" x 1 5/8" (23a)
   * Four - 1 3/8" squares (25a)

From Fabric VI, cut: (medium gold print)
• One 1 3/4" wide strip. From this, cut:
   * Four - 1 3/4" x 3 3/4" (18)
   * Four - 1 5/8" x 2 1/8" (10)
   * Eight - 1 5/8" squares (1a, 2)
• One 1 1/8" wide strip. From this, cut:
   * Twelve - 1 1/8" squares (11a, 16, 17)

ASSEMBLY

1. Refer to Block A diagram below. Using diagonal corner technique, make one of units 1, 2, 4, 5, 6, 7, 10, 11, 14, 18, 20, 21, 24, and 25. Use diagonal end technique to make one of Unit 23. Refer to the diagram at left and make triangle-square units 16 and 17.

2. To assemble Block A, begin by joining units 2 and 3; then add Unit 1 to the top of these combined units, matching seams. Join units 4 and 5; then join them to left side of combined units 1-3. Join Unit 6 to left side of combined units 4/5. Join units 7 and 8; then add Unit 9 to right side of these combined units. Join units 10, 11, and 12 in a row as shown. Join this row to bottom of combined units 7-9. Join all of these combined units to right side of other combined units; then join Unit 13 across the top.

3. For bottom of flower, join units 18 and 19. Join units 20 and 21. Join these two combined units sections together as shown; then join Unit 22 across the bottom. Join units 16, 15, and 17; then add Unit 14 to the bottom of these

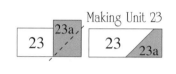

Making Unit 23

combined units. Join these combined units to right side of combined units 18-22. Join units 23 and 24; then add Unit 25 to right side. Join these combined units to bottom of other combined units; then join diagonal corner, Unit 26 to bottom corner as shown. Join units 30 and 31. Join units 32 and 33. Join these two combined unit sections together as shown. Join units 28 and 29; then add Unit 27 to left side of these combined units. Join these units to the bottom of combined units 30-33; then add this entire section to right side of combined units 14-26 to complete the bottom section. Join the top section to the bottom section, matching seams to complete Block A. Make 4.

4. Join the four A blocks together as illustrated below. Use six strands of medium green embroidery floss and chain stitch the stems as shown.

Making units 16 and 17.

Place 1 1/8" squares of fabrics II and VI right sides together. Stitch diagonal down the center, trim seam and press.

Place 1 1/8" squares of fabrics III and VI right sides together. Stitch diagonal down the center, trim seam and press.

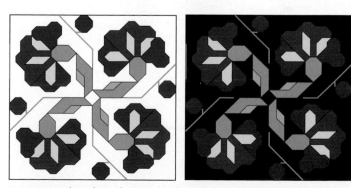

Block A. Make 4. When block is complete, it should measure 9 1/2" square

Use the background color of your choice.

Wreath with Bow

Block finishes to 18" square. Size of block before it
is sewn into the quilt is 18 1/2"

MATERIALS

☐ Fabric I (background)
Need 11 3/8"   1/2 yard

▨ Fabric II (medium green print)
Need 4 3/4"   1/4 yard

▨ Fabric III (light green print)
Need 6 1/2"   1/4 yard

■ Fabric IV (bright red print)
Need 1 7/8"   1/8 yard

■ Fabric V (burgundy print)
Need 1 7/8"   1/8 yard

▨ Fabric VI (light gold print)
Need 2"   1/8 yard

Use the background color
of your choice.

CUTTING

☐ **From Fabric I, cut, (background)**
• One 5 1/8" wide strip. From this, cut:
  * One - 5 1/8" x 5 3/4" (25)
  * Four - 1 1/8" x 4 1/8" (32)
  * Two - 1" X 4 1/8" (38)
  * Two - 2 1/2" x 3 5/8" (16)
  * Two - 2" x 3 5/8" (18)
  * Four - 1 1/2" x 3 1/4" (33)
  * Two - 1 3/8" x 3 1/4" (24)
  * Two - 1 1/4" x 3 1/4" (28)
  * Two - 1 1/8" x 3 1/4" (22)
  * Two - 1 3/8" x 3 1/8" (14)
  * Four - 1 1/4" x 2" (31) Stack this cut.
  * Two - 1" x 2" (19) Stack this cut:
  • From scrap, cut:
  * Eight - 1 1/2" squares (35a)
  * Four - 1 1/8" squares (10b, 12)
• One 2 5/8" wide strip. From this, cut:
  * Two - 2 5/8" x 6" (1)
  * Two - 2 3/8" x 2 1/2" (26)
  * One - 2 1/4" x 2 1/2" (13)
  * Four - 1 7/8" x 2" (30)
  * Two - 1 3/4" x 2" (23)
  * One - 1 5/8" x 2" (21)
  * Two - 1 7/8" squares (3a)
  * Four - 1 5/8" squares (2a, 17a)
• One 1 3/8" wide strip. From this, cut:
  * Twenty - 1 3/8" squares (2b, 3b, 8a, 15a, 27a, 34a)

* Two - 1 1/4" x 6 1/4" (36)
• One 1 1/4" wide strip. From this, cut:
    * Eight - 1 1/4" squares (29a, 34b)
• One 1" wide strip. From this, cut:
    * Thirty-four - 1" squares (4a, 20a)

From Fabric II, cut: (med. green print)
• One 3 3/8" wide strip. From this, cut:
    * Four - 3 3/8" squares (35)
    * Four - 3 1/4" squares (27)
    * Four - 3 1/8" squares (15, 29)
• One 1 3/8" wide strip. From this, cut:
    * Two - 1 3/8" x 1 7/8" (8)
    * Four - 1 3/8" squares (7a, 9a)

From Fabric III, cut: (lt. green print)
• One 3 3/8" wide strip. From this, cut:
    * Four - 3 3/8" squares (35)
    * Four - 3 1/4" squares (27)
    * Two - 3 1/8" x 3 1/4" (34)
• One 3 1/8" wide strip. From this, cut:
    * Six - 3 1/8" squares (15, 29, 37)
    * Two - 1 5/8" squares (13a, 13b)
    * Two - 1 1/8" x 1 5/8" (11)
    * Two - 1 1/2" squares (7b)

From Fabric IV, cut: (bright red print)
• One 1 7/8" wide strip. From this, cut:
    * Two - 1 7/8" x 2 3/8" (3)
    * Two - 1 7/8" x 2 1/4" (7)
    * Two - 1 3/8" x 1 7/8" (9)
    * Two - 1 5/8" x 3 5/8" (17)
    * Two - 1 5/8" x 2 1/4" (10)
    * Two - 1 1/4" x 2" (5)
    * Two - 1 1/4" squares (4b)
    * Two - 1 1/8" squares (15b)

From Fabric V, cut, (burgundy print)
• One 1 7/8" wide strip. From this, cut:
    * Two - 1 7/8" x 2 1/8" (2)
    * Two - 1 5/8" squares (10a)
    * One - 1 1/4" x 1 1/2" (6)
    * Two - 1 1/4" x 2" (4)
    * Two - 1" squares (3c)

From Fabric VI, cut: (light gold print)
• One 2" wide strip. From this, cut:
    * Eight - 2" squares (20)

ASSEMBLY

1. Use diagonal corner technique to make units 27, 29, and 35. This will be a total of ten. Refer to diagram on page 84 for making the triangle-squares; then adding the diagonal corners. Use diagonal corner technique to make eight of Unit 20, and two each of units 34 and 37 . Refer frequently to the block diagram above for correct placement of mir-

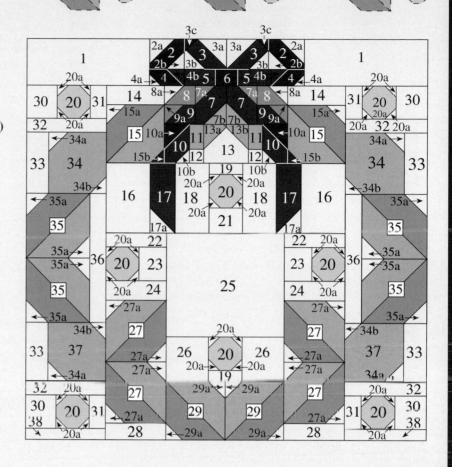

ror image units. Using diagonal corner technique, make two of mirror image units 2, 3, 4, 7, 8, 9, 10, 15, and 17. Make one of Unit 13, joining the diagonal corners in alphabetical order. The corners will overlap 1/4".

2. To assemble the wreath, beginning with top row, join mirror image units 2, 3, 3, and 2 in a row. Join units 4, 5, 6, 5, and 4 in a row. Join this row to bottom of 2/3 row, matching seams. Join Unit 1 to opposite sides of the bow to complete the top row.

3. For the wreath center section, join units 14 and 15. Join units 8 and 9. Join mirror image units 7 as shown; then join mirror image units 8 and 9 to opposite sides of the joined Unit 7's. Join units 11 and 12; then add mirror image Unit 10 to outside end of these combined units. Join these combined mirror image units to opposite sides of Unit 13. Join the combined 7-9 units to the top of the combined 10-13 units, matching seams. Join combined units 14/15 to opposite sides of bow tie units as shown. Join units 19, 20, and 21; then add Unit 18 to opposite sides of these combined units. Join units 16 and 17 as shown; then add them to opposite sides of Unit 18. Join these combined units to bottom of combined bow tie units. Join units 20 and 23, referring to diagram for correct placement as the combined units are mirror images. Join Unit 22 to the top, and Unit 24 to the bottom of these combined units. Join Unit 27's together as shown; then join Unit 28 to bottom of the combined 27 units. Join these combined units to bottom of combined units 20-24. Join units 19 and 20; then join Unit 26 to opposite sides of the combined 19/20 units. Join Unit 25 to top. Join two Unit 29's together as shown; then add them to the bottom of the 19-25 units. Join combined units 20-28 to opposite sides of combined units 19-29. Join these combined units to the bottom of the bow tie section to complete the center section of the wreath.

4. For the wreath sides, refer frequently to block diagram as the combined units will be mirror images. Begin at top by joining units 30, 20 and 31 in a row; then add Unit 32 to bottom. Join units 33 and 34; then add to bottom of berry section. Join two of Unit 35, checking block diagram for correct placement of the leaves. Add Unit 36 to inside edge of the combined 35 units; then join to bottom of other combined units. Join units 33 and 37; then add Unit 32 to the top of these combined units. Join units 30, 20, and 31; then add Unit 38 to bottom of these combined units as shown. Join these combined units to bottom of combined leaf units to complete the row. Join the two rows to opposite sides of center portion of wreath, matching seams where necessary.

5. Join the top bow section to the top of the wreath, matching seams where necessary.

Making units 15, 27, 29, and 35

Unit 15 mirror image

Place 3 1/8" squares of Fabrics II and III right sides together with raw edges matching for units 15 and 29. Stitch diagonal as shown. Trim seam to 1/4" and press open. Refer to block illustration for unit numbers, and join remaining diagonal corners.

For Unit 27, place 3 1/4" squares of Fabrics II and III right sides together, and complete as directed above.

For Unit 35, place 3 3/8" squares of Fabrics II and III right sides together, and complete as directed for units 15 and 29.

Bow & Swag Quilt Border

Borders, before they are sewn into quilt should measure 10 1/4" wide. Quilt finishes to: 81 1/2" x 101 1/2"

MATERIALS

☐	Fabric I (medium gold print)	Need 82 1/8"" 2 1/2 yards
■	Fabric II (dark red print)	Need 30" 1 yard
☐	Fabric III (dark gold print)	Need 9" 3/8 yard
☐	Fabric IV (light green print)	Need 8 3/8" 3/8 yard
☐	Fabric V (yellow print)	Need 15 7/8" 5/8 yard
■	Fabric VI (navy print)	Need 8 7/8" 3/8 yard
■	Fabric VII (medium blue print)	Need 19 3/8" 5/8 yard
■	Fabric VIII (Kona Cotton black)	Need 67 1/2" 2 yards
	Backing	7 1/4 yards

Cutting instructions shown in red indicate the quantity of units are combined and cut in two or more different places to conserve fabric.

CUTTING

From Fabric I, cut: (medium gold print)
- One 5" wide strip. From this, cut:
  - * Four - 5" squares (E1)
  - * Four - 7/8" x 4 1/4" (E9)
  - • Stack these cuts:
  - * Four - 1 1/4" x 2 5/8" (E3a)
  - * Twelve - 1 1/4" x 1 7/8" (B13, C13, E2a)
  - * Twenty - 1 1/8" x 1 1/4" (A9, B9, C9)
  - * Twenty - 1" squares (D4b)
- One 4 1/4" wide strip. From this, cut:
  - * Ten - 3 7/8" x 4 1/4" (D9)
- Two 3 5/8" wide strips. From these, cut:
  - * Four - 3 5/8" x 10 1/4" (E13)
  - * Four - 3 5/8" x 7 1/8" (E12)
  - • Stack these cuts:
  - * Eight - 1 3/4" squares (E4)
  - * Eight - 1 5/8" x 1 3/4" (F2, G2)
- Two 2 1/2" wide strips. From these, cut:

- * Eight - 2 1/2" x 7 3/8" (F6, G6)
- * Thirty-eight - 1 1/4" squares (A11a, A12a, B11a, B15a, B16a, C11a, C15a, C16a, D1b, D2b, D8a, D7b, F5a, G5a)
- Seven 2 3/8" wide strips. From these, cut:
  - * Eight - 2 3/8" x 16 1/2" (B22, C22)
  - * Six - 2 3/8" x 14 1/2" (A17)
  - * Ten - 2 3/8" x 2 3/4" (D6)
  - • Stack this cut:
  - * Sixteen - 1 1/8" x 3 1/4" (B18, C18)
- Eleven 2 1/4" wide strips. From these, cut:
  - * Eight - 2 1/4" x 16 1/2" (B21, C21)
  - * Six - 2 1/4" x 14 1/2" (A16)
  - * Eight - 2 1/4" x 6 1/2" (B14, C14)
  - * Eight - 2 1/4" x 5 3/4" (B10, C10)
  - * Twelve - 2 1/4" x 5 1/8" (A10)
  - * Twenty - 2 1/4" squares (D5a)
  - * Twelve - 1 1/8" x 2 5/8" (A14) Stack this cut.
- Two 1 7/8" wide strips. From these, cut:
  - * Eight - 1 7/8" x 3 3/8" (E7, E8)
  - * Eight - 1 7/8" squares (B20, C20)

* Twenty - 1 1/8" x 1 7/8" (A15, B19, C19)
* Four - 7/8" x 2 7/8" (E5) Stack this cut.
* Nine - 1 3/8" squares (D1a, F4a, G4a)
- Three 1 5/8" wide strips. From this and scrap, cut:
    * Sixty - 1 5/8" squares (D2a, D5b, D10a)
    * Nineteen - 1 3/8" squares (add to 1 3/8" sq. above)
- Four 1 1/4" wide strips. From these, cut:
    * 114 - 1 1/4" squares (add to 1 1/4" squares above)
    * Twenty - 1 1/8" squares (A2a, A4c, A12b, A13a, B2a, B4c, B16b, B17a, C2a, C4c, C16b, C17a, F5b, G5b)
- Five 1 1/8" wide strips. From these, cut:
    * Ten - 1 1/8" x 6 1/2" (D11)
    * 128 - 1 1/8" squares (add to 1 1/8" squares above)

From Fabric II, cut: (dark red print)
- Three 2 3/4" wide strips. From these, cut:
    * Eight - 2 3/4" x 4 1/4" (B11, C11)
    * Eight - 2 3/4" x 3 1/2" (B7, C7)
    * Twenty-eight - 1 1/2" x 2 3/4" (A6, B6, C6)
    * Twelve - 1 1/8" x 2 3/4" (A8)
- One 2 1/4" wide strip. From this, cut:
    * Twelve - 2 1/4" x 3 1/2" (A7)
- Four 1 7/8" wide strips. From these, cut:
    * Fourteen - 1 7/8" x 4" (A11, B15, C15)
    * Twenty-eight - 1 7/8" x 3" (A12, B16, C16)
    * Eight - 1 7/8" squares (B14a, C14a)
- Six 1 1/4" wide strips. From these, cut:
    * Twenty - 1 1/4" x 4 1/8" (D8)
    * Sixteen - 1 1/4" x 3 1/4" (B17, C17)
    * Sixteen - 1 1/4" x 2 7/8" (B8, B12, C8, C12)
    * Twelve - 1 1/4" x 2 5/8" (A13)
- Four 1 1/8" wide strips. From these, cut:
    * 132 - 1 1/8" sq. (A3a, A4b, A5a, A10a, B3a, B4b, B5a, B10a, C3a, C4b, C5a, C10a)

From Fabric III, cut: (dark gold print)
- Four 2 1/4" wide strips. From these, cut:
    * Fifty-six - 2 1/4" squares (A1, B1, C1)

From Fabric IV, cut: (light green print)
- Two 2 1/2" wide strips. From these, cut:
    * Twenty-eight - 2 1/2" x 2 3/4" (A5, B5, C5)
- Three 1 1/8" wide strips. From these, cut:
    * Eighty-four - 1 1/8" squares (A4a, A6a, B4a, B6a, C4a, C6a)

From Fabric V, cut: (yellow print)
- Five 1 3/8" wide strips. From these, cut:
    * 126 - 1 3/8" squares (A1a, B1a, C1a, 14 for applique flower centers)
- Eight 1 1/8" wide strips. From this and scrap, cut:
    * Fifty-six - 1 1/8" x 2 7/8" (A4, B4, C4)
    * Fifty-six - 1 1/8" x 2 1/4" (A2, A3, B2, B3, C2, C3)

From Fabric VI, cut: (navy print)
- One 2 1/2" wide strip. From this, cut:
    * Four - 2 1/2" squares (E11)
    * Twenty - 1 1/4" x 2" (D4a) Stack this cut.
    * Twenty - 1 1/8" squares (D1c) Stack this cut.
- One 1 7/8" wide strip. From this, cut:
    * Twenty - 1 7/8" x 2" (D2)
- One 1 5/8" wide strip. From this, cut:
    * Twenty - 1 5/8" squares (D7a)
- One 1 1/2" wide strip. From this, cut:
    * Sixteen - 1 1/2" squares (E6a, E7a, E8a, E10a)
    * Ten - 1 1/4" x 1 1/2" (D3)
- One 1 3/8" wide strip. From this, cut:
    * Eight - 1 3/8" x 1 3/4" (F4, G4)
    * Eight - 1 1/4" x 3 3/8" (F5, G5)

From Fabric VII, cut: (medium blue print)
- Two 2 3/4" wide strips. From these, cut:
    * Eight - 2 3/4" squares (E1a)
    * Twenty - 2 1/4" x 2 3/4" (D5)
    * Eight - 1 3/8" x 1 3/4" (F1, G1) Stack this cut.
- One 1 7/8" wide strip. From this, cut:
    * Twenty - 1 7/8" x 2" (D1)
- One 1 3/4" wide strip. From this, cut:
    * Sixteen - 1 3/4" squares (E11a, F3, G3)
    * Four - 1 1/2" x 2 7/8" (E6)
- Four 1 5/8" wide strips. From these, cut:
    * Twenty - 1 5/8" x 3 7/8" (D10)
    * Twenty - 1 5/8" x 2 3/8" (D7)
    * Four - 1 1/2" x 4 1/4" (E10)
    * Five - 1 1/4" x 4 3/8" (E2, E3)
- Three 1 1/4" wide strips. From these, cut:
    * Three - 1 1/4" x 4 3/8" (add to E2, E3 above)
    * Twenty - 1 1/4" x 2 1/4" (D4)
    * Twenty-four - 1 1/4" squares (D8b, E11b)

From Fabric VIII, cut: (Kona Cotton black)
- Twenty-seven 2 1/2" wide strips. Nine for straight-grain binding. From remainder, cut:
    * Sixteen - 2 1/2" x 18 1/2" (Q1)
    * Ten - 2 1/2" x 31 1/2" (Q2) Piece two together to equal 62 1/2" length.

BLOCKS A, B, AND C ASSEMBLY

1. For blocks A, B, and C, units 1-6 are the same. So that diagonal corners for these units can be chain pieced, we are giving you the total of 1-6 units; then the units will be broken up for each individual block. Use diagonal corner technique to make fifty-six of Unit 1. Make fifty-six of mirror image Unit 4. Make twenty-eight of mirror image units 2, 3, 5, and 6.

2. For Block A, use diagonal corner technique to make two each of mirror image units 10, and 12. Make two of Unit 13, and one of Unit 11.

3. For Block B, use diagonal corner technique to make two of mirror image 16. Make two of Unit 17. Make one of units 10, 11, 14, and 15. As Block C is a mirror image of Block B, use diagonal corner technique to make the same units, referring to block diagrams for correct placement of mirror image units.

4. To assemble the flower and leaf for all three blocks, begin by joining four Unit 1's together as shown. Join mirror image Unit 2's, 3's and 4's together as shown. Join combined Unit 2's to top of combined Unit 1's; then add combined Unit 3's to bottom. Referring to block diagrams for correct placement of color, join the combined Unit 4's to opposite sides of the flower. Join mirror image units 5 and 6 for blocks A, B, and C.

5. For Block A, join Unit 7 to opposite sides of the 5/6 combined units. Join units 8 and 9; then add them to opposite sides of combined units 5-7. Join mirror image Unit 10 to top of combined leaf units; then add to opposite sides of the flower. Join Unit 16 across the top. For the bottom row, join units 13 and 14; then add Unit 15 to side of these combined units as shown. Join units 12, 11, and 12 in a row; then add the combined 13-15 units to opposite sides, matching seams where necessary. Join this row to bottom of flower section; then add Unit 17 across the bottom to

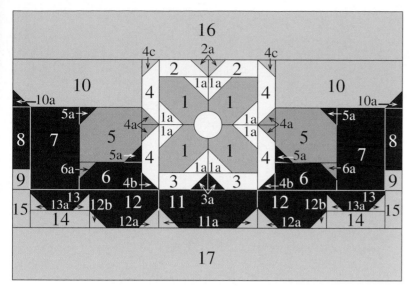

Block A. Make 6. When completed block should measure 10 1/4" x 14 1/2"

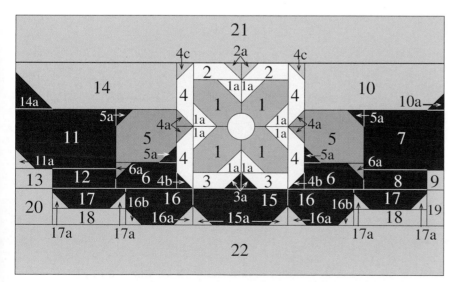

Block B. Make 4. When completed block should measure 10 1/4" x 16 1/2"

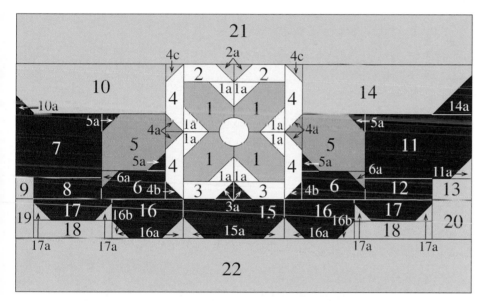

Block C. Make 4. When completed block should measure 10 1/4" x 16 1/2"

complete Block A. Make 6.

6. The assembly for B and C blocks is the same. The only difference is that they are mirror images, so check diagrams frequently for correct placement of units. These instructions are for assembling both blocks. Begin by joining units 8 and 9; then add Unit 7 to top of these combined units. Join these units to side of combined units 5/6; then add Unit 10 across the top. Join units 12 and 13; then join Unit 11 across the top. Join these combined units to side of combined 5/6 units; then add Unit 14 across the top. Join these two combined unit sections to opposite sides of flower, checking diagrams for correct placement of mirror image units. Add Unit 21 across the top of this flower section.

7. For the bottom row join units 17 and 18; then add Unit 19 to outside edge of these combined units. Join another set of units 17 and 18; then add Unit 20 to outside edge as shown. Join units 16, 15 and 16; then join the two combined swag units to opposite sides of the 16/15/16 row. Join this row to bottom of flower section, matching seams where necessary. Join Unit 22 across the bottom to complete blocks B and C. Make 4 of each block.

BLOCK D ASSEMBLY

1. Refer to diagram below for Block D. Use diagonal corner technique to make two each of mirror image units 1, 2, 5, 7, 8, and 10. Use diagonal end technique to make two of mirror image Unit 4, shown on page 88.

2. To assemble the block, begin by joining

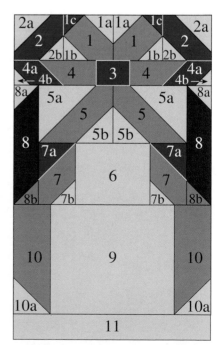

Block D. Make 10. When completed block should measure 6 1/2" x 10 1/4"

Making mirror image Unit D4

mirror image Unit 1's as shown in block diagram. Join mirror image Unit 2's to opposite sides of joined Unit 1's. Join mirror image Unit 4, Unit 3, and remaining Unit 4 in a row. Join this row to bottom of combined 1/2 units. Join mirror image Unit 5's as shown. Join mirror image Unit 7, Unit 6, and remaining Unit 7 as shown; then join these combined units to combined Unit 5's. Join Unit 8 to opposite sides of these combined units; then add them to bottom of bow top, matching seams. Refer to diagram and join mirror image Unit 10, Unit 9, and Unit 10 in a row; then add Unit 11 across the bottom. Join these units to bottom of other combined bow units, matching seams. Make 10 of Block D.

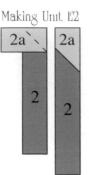

Making Unit E2

BLOCK E ASSEMBLY

1. To make Block E, refer to block diagram and using diagonal corner technique, make one of units 1, 6, 7, 8, and 10. Use diagonal end technique to make one of units 2 and 3.

2. To assemble the block, refer to block diagram, and begin by joining unit 2 to left side of Unit 1. Join Unit 3 across top of combined 1/2 units; then add diagonal corner Unit 4 as shown. Join units 5 and 6; then join Unit 7 to right side of these combined units. Join these units to top of combined 1-4 units. Join units 9 and 10; then add Unit 8 to bottom of these combined units. Join these units to left side of other combined units. Join Unit 12 to the bottom; then join Unit 13 to right side. For the bow, refer to diagram at the bottom of the page. Make Unit 11; then follow drawings and instructions for making the E11 corner. Make 4 of Block E.

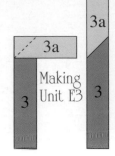

Making Unit E3

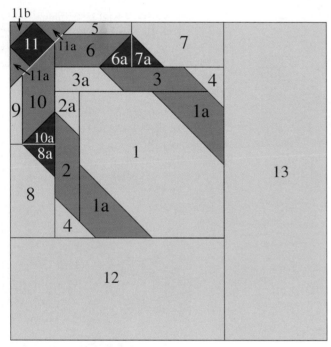

Block E. Make 4. When completed block should measure 10 1/4" square

ASSEMBLING BLOCKS F & G

1. Blocks F and G are mirror images. These instructions are for both blocks. Use diagonal corner technique to make two mirror image units 4 and 5.

2. To assemble the blocks, begin by joining units 1 and 2; then add diagonal corner, Unit 3 as shown at right. Join mirror image Unit 4 to the bottom of these combined units; then add mirror image Unit 5 to side as shown. Join Unit 6 to bottom of bow units to complete the blocks. Make 4 of each block.

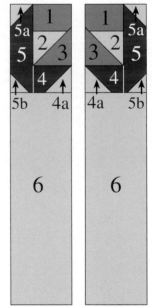

Block F   Block G
Make 4 of each block. When completed, each block should measure 2 1/2" x 10 1/4"

Making Unit E11 Corner

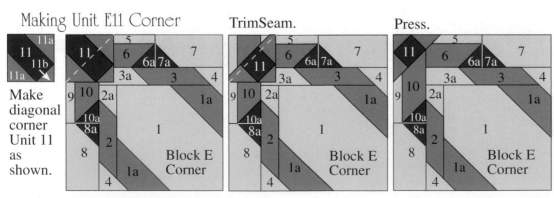

Make diagonal corner Unit 11 as shown.

TrimSeam.

Press.

Use Unit 11 as diagonal corner. Place right sides facing and raw edges matching as shown. Stitch diagonal.

The quilt blocks in this collection were designed to be interchangeable. Our quilts are an example of what can be done with the blocks and borders. Select the blocks of your choice for each quilt.

89

1. To assemble the quilt top, refer to the quilt top diagram on page 89. Make four rows of three blocks per row. Join the rows using Unit Q1 between the blocks and at opposite ends of the blocks as shown. Join the rows by using previously piece Unit Q2 between the rows and at the top and bottom of the rows to complete the top of the quilt.

2. To assemble the border sides, join blocks G, C, D, A, D, A, D, B, and F in a row. Make two. Join rows to opposite sides of quilt top.

3. To assemble the top and bottom borders of the quilt, join blocks E, F, B, D, A, D, C, G, and E. Join these borders to top and bottom of quilt top, matching corner seams.

4. Refer to page 7 for making straight-grain, french-fold binding. Join the nine 2 1/2" wide strips of Fabric VIII, and bind your quilt.

Rose Quilt Border

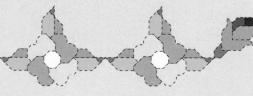

Borders, before they are sewn into the quilt should measure 10 3/4" wide.
Quilt finishes to: 82 1/2" x 102 1/2".

MATERIALS

☐ Fabric I (muslin)
Need 133"   3 7/8 yards

☐ Fabric II (pink print)
Need 12 3/4"   1/2 yard

☐ Fabric III (med. rose solid)
Need 16 1/4"   5/8 yard

☐ Fabric IV (dark rose print)
Need 4 1/4"   1/4 yard

☐ Fabric V (burgundy batik)
Need 28"   1 yard

☐ Fabric VI (light green print)
Need 9 1/2"   3/8 yard

☐ Fabric VII (med. green print)
Need 15 5/8"   1/2 yard

☐ Fabric VIII (dark green print)
Need 7 7/8"   3/8 yard

☐ Fabric IX (light yellow print)
Need 2 1/2"   1/8 yard

Backing   7 3/8 yards

Cutting instructions shown in red indicate the quantity of units are combined and cut in two or more different places to conserve fabric.

CUTTING

☐ **From Fabric I, cut: (muslin)**
• One 10 3/4" wide strip. From this, cut:
     * Four - 3 1/4" x 10 3/4" (Q5)
     * Two - 1 3/4" x 10 3/4" (Q4)
     * Four - 1 5/8" x 10 3/4" (Q3)
     * Four - 1 1/4" x 10 3/4" (D41)
     • Stack the following cuts:
     * Four - 1 1/4" x 5 1/4" (D31)
     * Twenty-eight - 1 1/2" x 2 1/4" (A14)

     * Fifty - 1" squares (A8a, A10b, A11a)
• Three 4 5/8" wide strips. From these, cut:
     * Twenty - 4 1/2" x 4 5/8" (B13, C13)
     * Four - 3" x 4 5/8" (D17)
     * Four - 1 3/8" x 4 1/2" (D30)
     * Thirty-four - 1" squares (add to 1" squares)
• Six 3 3/4" wide strips. From these, cut:
     * Twenty-eight - 3 3/4" x 5 1/2" (A22)
     * Twenty-eight - 2 1/4" x 3 3/4" (A18)
     * Twenty-four - 1 1/4" x 3 3/4" (B12, C12, D18)
     * Four - 1 3/8" x 2" (D14) Stack this cut.
• Six 2 3/4" wide strips. From these, cut:

* Twenty-four - 2 3/4" x 5 1/4" (B14, C14, D12)
* Twenty-eight - 2 3/4" x 3 1/4" (A13)
* Fourteen - 1 1/2" x 2 3/4" (A21a)
* Four - 1 3/8" x 5 1/4" (D40) Stack this cut.
• Eighteen 2 1/2" wide strips. From these, cut:
   * Ten - 2 1/2" x 31 1/2" (Q2) Piece two together
     to = five 62 1/2" lengths.
   * Sixteen - 2 1/2" x 18 1/2" (Q1)
   * Four - 2" x 4 3/8" (D39)
   * Forty-two - 2" squares (A17, A20)
   * Thirty-two - 1 1/2" x 2" (B10, C10, D11, D16, D26)
• Three 1 5/8" wide strips. From these, cut:
   * Fifty-six - 1 5/8" x 1 3/4" (A9)
   • Five 1 1/2" wide strips. From these, cut:
   * Fourteen - 1 1/2" x 13" (A23)
   * Twenty-two - 1 1/8" squares (A6a, A10a, A12a, B1a,
     B2a, B3a, B5a, B9a, C1a, C2a, C3a, C5a, B7a, C7a,
     C9a, D2a, D3a, D4a, D6a, D8a, D10a, D20b, D21a,
     D22a, D23a, D27a, D28a, D32b, D33a, D35a, D36a,
     D38a)
• Three 1 3/8" wide strips. From these, cut:
   * Twenty-eight - 1 3/8" x 3 3/8" (B8, C8, D9, D25)
   * Eight - 1 3/8" squares (D13a)
   * Eighteen - 1 1/8" squares (add to 1 1/8"squares)
• Seven 1 1/8" wide strips. From these, cut:
   * Thirty-two - 1 1/8" x 1 1/2" (B4, C4, D5, D24, D37)
   * 204 - 1 1/8" squares (add to 1 1/8" squares above)

From Fabric II, cut: (pink print)
• Two 2 1/2" wide strips. From these, cut:
   * Twenty-eight - 2 1/8" x 2 1/2" (A10, A12)
   * Twenty-eight - 1 1/4" x 1 5/8" (A11)
• Two 1 5/8" wide strips. From these, cut:
   * Twenty-eight - 1 5/8" x 1 3/4" (A4)
• Four 1 1/8" wide strips. From these, cut:
   * Fifty-six - 1 1/8" x 1 3/8" (A3, A7)
   * Fifty-six - 1 1/8" squares (A1a, A8b)

From Fabric III, cut: (medium rose solid)
• Three 2 1/8 " wide strips. From these, cut:
   * Twenty-eight - 2 1/8" x 3 1/8" (B1, C1, D20, D32)
   * Four - 2 1/8" squares (D1)
   * Four - 1 1/2" x 2 1/8" (D6)
   * Ten - 1 5/8" x 2 1/2" (A8)
• Two 1 5/8" wide strips. From these, cut:
   * Eighteen - 1 5/8" x 2 1/2" (add to A8 above)
   * Twenty-eight - 1 1/4" x 1 5/8" (A5)
• Four 1 3/8" wide strips. From these, cut:
   * Twenty-eight - 1 3/8" x 3 1/8" (A6)
   * Twenty-eight - 1 3/8" x 1 7/8" (A2)
   * Twenty-four - 1 1/8" squares (A1b, A4a)
• One 1 1/8" wide strip. From this, cut:
   * Thirty-two - 1 1/8" squares (add to 1 1/8" squares)

From Fabric IV, cut: (dark rose print)
• Two 1 1/2" wide strips. From these, cut:
   * Twelve - 1 1/2" x 2 1/8" (D2, D28, D33)
   * Twenty - 1 1/2" x 2" (B5, C5)
• One 1 1/4" wide strip. From this, cut:
   * Thirty-two - 1 1/4" squares (B1b, C1b, D1a, D20a, D32a)

From Fabric V, cut: (burgundy batik)
• Ten 2 1/2" wide strips for straight-grain binding.
• Two - 1 1/2" wide strips. From these, cut:
   * Twenty - 1 1/2" x 1 5/8" (B6, C6)
   * Twelve - 1 1/2" squares (D7, D29, D34)

From Fabric VI, cut: (light green print)
• Two 3 3/4" wide strips. From these, cut:
   * Forty-two - 2" x 3 3/4" (A16, A19)
• Two 1" wide strips. From these, cut:
   * Seventy - 1" squares (A4b, A5a, A8c, A12b)

From Fabric VII, cut: (medium green print)
• Four 1 3/4" wide strips. From these and scrap, cut:
   * Twenty-eight - 1 3/4" x 3 3/8" (B7, C7, D8, D22)
   * Four - 1 3/4" x 2 3/4" (D36)
   * Twenty-eight - 1 3/4" x 2 1/8" (B2, C2, D3, D21)
• Five 1 1/2" wide strips. From these, cut:
   * Fourteen - 1 1/2" x 2 1/2" (A21)
   * Fifty-six - 1 1/2" squares (A13a, A15)
   * Sixty - 1 1/8" x 1 1/2" (B3, B9, C3, C9, D4, D10,
     D23,D27, D38)
   * Four - 1 1/8" x 3 1/8" (D35)
   * Four - 1 1/8" x 2" (D15)
• One 1 1/8" wide strip. From this, cut:
   * Four - 1 1/8" squares (D16a)
   * Fourteen - 1" squares (A5b)

From Fabric VIII, cut: (dark green print)
• One 2" wide strip. From this, cut:
   * Four - 2" x 2 1/8" (D13)
   * Nineteen - 1 3/4" squares (A16a, A19a)
• One 1 3/4" wide strip. From this, cut:
   * Twenty-three - 1 3/4" squares (add to 1 3/4" squares)
• Three 1 3/8" wide strips. From these, cut:
   * Four - 1 3/8" x 2 1/8" (D30a)
   * Fifty-two - 1 3/8" squares (B8a, B13a, C8a, C13a,
     D9a, D17a, D25a)
   * Twenty-four - 1 1/4" x 1 3/8" (B11, C11, D19)

From Fabric IX, cut: (light yellow print)
• One 2 1/2" wide strip. From this, cut:
   * Fourteen - 2 1/2" squares (A1)

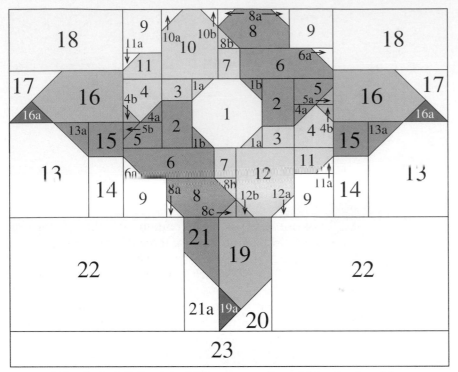

flower bottom. Join this section to bottom of flower, matching seams.

5. The flower sides are made the same, however they are mirror images. Refer to diagram below left for making combined units 16/17 and combined units 19/20. Join Unit 18 to top of combined units 16/17. Join units 14/15; then add Unit 13 to side of these combined units. Referring to block diagram for correct placement, join the side sections to opposite sides of the flower.

6. For the bottom section of Block A, join units 22, 21, combined units 19/20 and Unit 22; then add Unit 23 across the bottom. Join this section to the bottom of the flower, matching leaf seams to flower bottom to complete the block. Make 14.

Block A Make 14. When completed block should measure 10 3/4 " X 13"

BLOCK A ASSEMBLY

1. To make the units for Block A, use diagonal corner technique to make two mirror image units 13 and combined units 16/17. Make two of units 4, 5, 6, 8, and 11 (refer to diagram for diagonal corner color changes). Make one of units 1, 10, 12, and combined units 19/20. Use diagonal end technique to make one of Unit 21.

2. To assemble the block, join units 2 and 3. Refer to block diagram above for correct placement and join these combined units to opposite sides of Unit 1. Join units 4 and 5, again referring to diagram for correct placement of units. Add combined 4/5 units to opposite sides of flower center combined units.

Making Unit A21

3. For flower top, join units 7 and 6. Join units 8 and 9. Join these two combined unit sections together as shown; then add Unit 10 to left side. Join units 9 and 11; then add them to left side of Unit 10. Join these combined units to flower center, matching seams.

4. For flower bottom, join units 6 and 7. Join units 9 and 8; then join these two combined unit sections together. Join Unit 12 to right side of the combined units. Join units 11 and 9 as shown. Add them to right side of Unit 12 to complete the

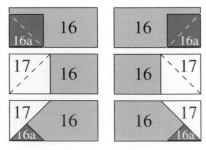

Making combined mirror image units A16/17 and A19/20.

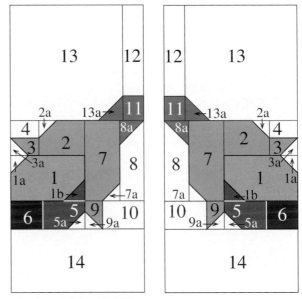

Block B Make 10. When completed block should measure 5 1/4 " X 10 3/4"

Block C Make 10. When completed block should measure 5 1/4 " X 10 3/4"

BLOCKS B & C ASSEMBLY

1. Blocks B and C are the same, except that they are mirror images. Instructions given are for Block B. Refer to Block C diagram for correct position of mirror image units.

2. Use diagonal corner technique to make one of units 1, 2, 3, 5, 7, 8, 9, and 13.,

3. To assemble the block, begin by joining units 3 and 4; then add Unit 2 to right side of these combined units. Join Unit 1 to bottom; then add Unit 7 to right side. Join Unit 8 to right side of Unit 7. Join units 6, 5, 9, and 10 in a row; then add Unit 14 to bottom of the row. Join this row to bottom of bud, matching Unit 9 seam. Join units 11 and 12; then add Unit 13 to top. Join these combined units to top of bud to complete the block. Make 10 of each block.

BLOCK D ASSEMBLY

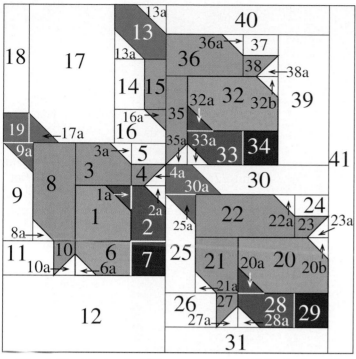

Block D. Make 4. When completed block should measure 10 3/4" sqaure

then add Unit 13 to top. Join these combined units to top of bud to complete the block. Make 10 of each block.

BLOCK D ASSEMBLY

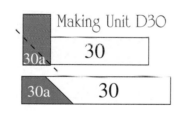

Making Unit D30

1. Use diagonal corner technique to make one of units 1, 2, 3, 4, 6, 8, 9, 10, 13, 16, 17, 20, 21, 22, 23, 25, 27, 28, 32, 33, 35, 36, and 38. Use diagonal end technique to make one of Unit 30, shown at right.

2. To assemble the block, join units 1 and 2. Join units 4 and 5; then add Unit 3 to left side of these combined units. Join combined units 1/2 to bottom of combine units 3-5; then add Unit 8 to left side. Join Unit 9 to left side of Unit 8. Join unit 11, 10, 6, and 7; then add Unit 12 to bottom of these combined units. Join these units to bottom of other bud units. Join units 18 and 19; then add Unit 17 to right side of the 18/19 combined units. Join units 14 and 15; then add Unit 13 to top of the 14/15 combined units and Unit 16 to the bottom, matching seams. Add combined units 17-19 to left side of combined units 13-16; then add these units to bud combined units as shown to complete the left side of the block.

3. For the right side, beginning at the top part of the section, join units 37 and 38; then add Unit 36 to left side of these combined units. Join units 33 and 34; then add Unit 32 to top of the 33/34 combined units. Join Unit 35 to the left side. Join combined units 36-38 to the top; then add Unit 39 to the right side. Join Unit 40 to the top to complete the bud.

4. For bottom bud, join units 20 and 21. Join units 23 and 24; then add Unit 22 to left side of combined units 23/24. Join these combined units to the top of combined units 20/21. Join Unit 25 to the left side of the combined units; then add Unit 30 to the top. Join units 26, 27, 28 and 29 in a row; then add Unit 31 across the bottom. Join this row to bottom of bud. Join the top bud to the bottom bud; then join Unit 41 to right side. Join the two sections of the block together to complete Block D. Make 4.

QUILT ASSEMBLY

1. To assemble the quilt top, refer to the quilt top diagram on page 96. Make four rows of three blocks per row. Join the rows using Unit Q1 between the blocks and at opposite ends of the blocks as shown. Join the rows by using previously piece Unit Q2 between the rows and at the top and bottom of the rows to complete the top of the quilt.

2. To assemble the border sides, beginning with the left side border at the top, join blocks A, C, Unit Q3, Block B, Block A, Block C, Unit Q4, Block B, Block A, Block C, Unit Q3, Block B, and Block A. Join this row to right side of quilt top.

3. For the right side border, join Block A, Block B, Unit Q3, Block C, Block A, Block B, Unit Q4, Block C, Block A, Block B, Unit Q3, Block C, and Block A. Join this border row to right side of quilt top.

4. For top border, join Block D, Block A, Block B, Unit Q5, Block C, Block A, Block B, Unit Q5, Block C, Block A, and Block D.

5. For bottom border, join Block D, Block A, Block C, Unit Q5, Block B, Block A, Block C, Unit Q5, Block B, Block A, and Block D. Join this row to bottom of quilt top.

6. Refer to page 7 for making straight-grain, french-fold binding. Join the ten 2 1/2" wide strips of Fabric V, and bind your quilt.

Refer to diagram above for embroidery placement. Use six strands of medium green embroidery floss and chain stitch the scallops.

Love Birds Wall Quilt

Love Birds Wall Quilt

Wall quilt finishes to: 36" square.

MATERIALS FOR BORDER ONLY

Fabric I (muslin)
Need 13"   1/2 yard

Fabric II (light green print)
Need 9"   3/8 yard

Fabric III (light gold print)
Need 3"   1/8 yard

Fabric IV (rust print)
Need 4 1/2"   1/4 yard

Fabric V (dark gold print)
Need 4"   1/4 yard

Fabric VI (navy print)
Need 21"   3/4 yard

Fabric VII (medium blue print)
Need 8"   3/8 yard

Fabric VIII (light blue print)
Need 7"   1/4 yard

Backing   1 1/4 yards

Cutting instructions shown in red indicate the quantity of units are combined and cut in two or more different places to conserve fabric.

CUTTING

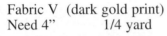

From Fabric I, cut: (muslin)
- Two 1 1/2" wide strips. From these, cut:
    * Thirty-six - 1 1/2" squares (A6)
    * Ten - 1" x 3" (Q12)
- Ten 1" wide strips. From these, cut:
    * Ten - 1" x 3" (add to Q12)
    * 392 - 1" squares (A1, A4, A5a, A7a, A8, B1, B4, B12, C1, C4, C12, F2)

From Fabric II, cut: (light green print)
- Two 2" wide strips. From these, cut:
    * Four - 2" x 20" (Q5)
    * Four - 1" x 2" (B10, C10)
- Two 1 1/2" wide strips. From these, cut:
    * Eight - 1 1/2" x 5 1/2" (Q4)
    * Eight - 1 1/2" x 3" (Q3)
    * Four - 1" x 1 1/2" (D1, E1)
- Two 1" wide strips. From these, cut:
    * Four - 1" x 3" (B11, C11)
    * Fifty-two - 1" squares (B5a, B7, B8a, C5a, C7, C8a, D2a, D3a, E2a, E3a, F3a)

From Fabric III, cut: (light gold print)
- Three 1" wide strips. From these, cut:
    * Twelve - 1" x 2" (F3)
    * Ninety-two - 1" squares (Q11, A8, B7, B9, C7, C9, F1)

From Fabric IV, cut: (rust print)
- Two 2 1/4" wide strips. From these, cut:
    * Two - 2 1/4" x 22" (Q2)
    * Two - 2 1/4" x 18 1/2" (Q1)

From Fabric V, cut: (dark gold print)
- Four 2" wide strips. From these, cut:
    * Two - 2" x 36" (Q14)
    * Two - 2" x 33" (Q13)

From Fabric VI, cut: (navy print)
- Two 3" wide strips. From these, cut:
    * Seventy-six - 1" x 3" (A7, B8, C8)
    * Four - 1" x 2" (B6, C6)
    * Four - 1" x 1 1/2" (D2, E2)
- Four 2 1/2" wide strips for straight-grain binding.
- Five 1" wide strips. Three for Strip Set 1. From remainder, cut:
    * Eighty - 1" squares (A3a, B3a, C3a)

From Fabric VII, cut: (medium blue print)
- Two 1 1/2" wide strips. From these, cut:
    * Eighty - 1" x 1 1/2" (A3, B3, C3)
- Five 1" wide strips. Three for Strip Set 1. From remainder, cut:
    * Eighty - 1" squares (A2, B2, C2)

From Fabric VIII, cut: (light blue print)
- Seven 1" wide strips. Three for Strip Set 1. From remainder, cut:
    * 160 - 1" squares (A2, A3b, B2, B3b, C2, C3b)

STRIP SET ASSEMBLY

1. The directions for this project are for the borders. To make the 18" center block, refer to pages 33-36 for yardage requirements, colors, cutting, and assembly of the center block.

2. For this border project, many of the combined units are strip pieced with diagonal corners added onto the strip sets after they have been pieced and cut into segments. Follow the instructions on page 5 for strip piecing, and below for making the required strip sets. Refer to the segment diagrams below and add the diagonal corners as directed. These segments will be used in the blocks shown below.

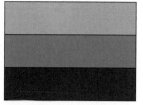

Strip Set 1. Make 3. Cut into 80 - 1 1/2" segments.

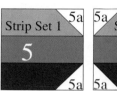

For Block A. Make 36.

For Block A. Make 36.

For Block B, make 2.

For Block C, make 2.

For Block D, make 2.

For Block E, make 2.

BLOCKS A, B, C, D, E, and F ASSEMBLY

1. To assemble Block A units, use diagonal corner technique and make a total of seventy-two mirror image units 3 and 7. Refer to diagram of triangle-squares below, and make seventy-two of Unit 2, and thirty-six of Unit 8 for Block A. For Block B units, use diagonal corner technique and make four of mirror image Unit 3. Make two of Unit 8. Make four of triangle-square Unit 2, and two of triangle-square Unit 7. For Block C units, make four of mirror image Unit 3, and two of Unit 8 as shown. Make four of triangle-square Unit 2, and two of triangle-square Unit 7. For blocks D and E units, use diagonal corner technique to make a total of four mirror image Unit 2. For block F, use diagonal corner technique to make twelve of Unit 3.

2. To assemble Block A, begin by making the checkerboard center. Refer to Block A diagram for correct placement of the units, and join units 1 and 2. Make two and join them together as shown. Join one mirror image Unit 3 to left side of the 1/2 combined units. Join remaining mirror image Unit 3 and Unit 4. Add them to bottom of the checkerboard center section. Join Strip Set 1, Unit 5 to top of center section. Join remaining Strip Set 1, Unit 5 to Unit 6. Add these to side of center section as shown. Join mirror image Unit 7 to bottom. Join remaining mirror image Unit 7 to Unit 8; then add them to left side of other combined units to complete Block A. Make 36.

Block A. Make 36. When complete, block should measure 3 1/2" square.

3. To assemble Block B units, make checkerboard center as you did for Block A. joining units 1-4. Join Strip Set Unit 5 to left side of center section. Join units 6 and 10. Join these combined units to right side of center section. Join units 8 and 11. Join units 7 and 9. Join units 9

Making triangle-square units 2, 7, and 8.

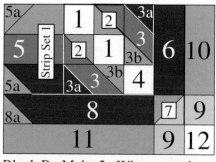

Place 1" squares of fabrics VII and VIII right sides facing and raw edges matching for Unit 2. For Unit 7, place 1" squares of fabrics II and III together. For Unit 8, place 1" squares of fabrics I and III together. Stitch a diagonal down the center. Trim seam, open and press.

Block B. Make 2. When complete, block should measure 3" x 4"

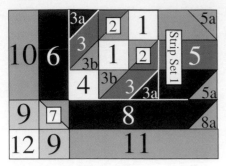

Block C. Make 2. When complete, block should measure 3" x 4"

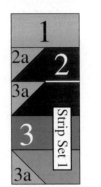

Block D. Make 2. When complete, block should measure 1 1/2" x 3".

Block E. Make 2. When complete, block should measure 1 1/2" x 3".

Block F. Make 12. When complete, block should measure 1 1/2" x 2".

and 12. Refer to diagram on page 99 and join the 7/9 and 9/12 units together; then add combined units 8/11 to left side of the combined 7-12 units. Join this row to bottom of other combined units to complete the block. Make two.

4. Refer to the diagram at left for Block C. Assemble this block as in Step 3 above. The only difference is that Block C is a mirror image of Block B, so refer to block diagram frequently for correct position of units. Make two.

5. Blocks D and E are assembled the same, except they are mirror images. Assembly is for Block D. Refer to block diagrams for correct position of mirror image units. To assemble, join units 1, 2, and Strip Set 1, Unit 3 in a row. Make two of each block.

6. To assemble Block F, join units 1, 2, and 1 in a row; then join Unit 3 to bottom to complete the block. Make twelve.

QUILT TOP ASSEMBLY

1. To assemble the quilt top, begin with the Love Bird block, and join Unit Q1 to top and bottom of the block; then add Unit Q2 to opposite sides as shown in quilt diagram. To assemble the top green border, join Unit Q3, Block F, Unit Q4, Block F, Unit Q4, Block F, and Unit Q3 in a horizontal row. Join Unit Q5 to bottom of the row. Make four. Set two aside. Join Block E to left side of combined border blocks and units; then add Block D to right side. Make two. Join one to the top of the quilt, and one to the bottom.

2. For the side green borders, use the remaining horizontal block and unit rows. and join Block B to top of short side, and Block C to the bottom. Make two and join to opposite sides of the quilt top. Refer to quilt diagram for correct placement.

3. For all flower borders, refer to block diagram and join two Block A's together. Make 16 of these sets. Join all units Q11 and Q12. Refer to top border for correct placement. Join Q11/ Q12 units between the Block A sets and at opposite ends of the row. Make four of these rows. Join one to top, and one to bottom of quilt top as shown. For side borders, add one Block A to opposite ends of previously made rows. Join these rows to opposite sides of quilt top, matching all seams where necessary. Join Unit Q13 to top and bottom of quilt top; then add Unit Q14 to opposite sides to complete the quilt top.

4. Refer to page 7 for making straight-grain, french fold binding. Join the four 2 1/2" wide strips of Fabric VI together, and bind the quilt.

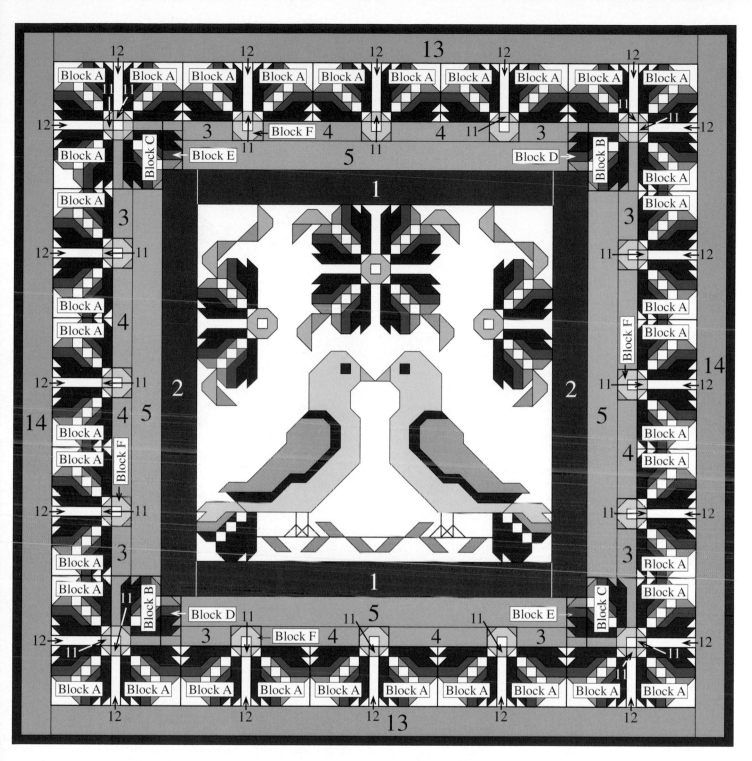

QUILT TOP DIAGRAM

Apple Blossom Time Quilt

Quilt finishes to: 89" x 106"

MATERIALS

Fabric I (ivory with pink print)
Need 140"   4 1/8 yards

Fabric II (Kona Cotton solid black)
Need 109 1/2" 3 1/4 yards

Fabric III (dark green print)
Need 25 1/4"   7/8 yard

Fabric IV (medium green print)
Need 52 1/2"   1 5/8 yards

Fabric V (light green print)
Need 61 1/4"   1 7/8 yards

Fabric VI (medium gold print)
Need 40"   1 1/4 yards

Fabric VII (yellow print)
Need 3"   1/4 yard

Fabric VIII (dark barn red print)
Need 8 1/4"   3/8 yard

Fabric IX (dark salmon print)
Need 21 1/2"   3/4 yard

Fabric X (light peach print)
Need 17 1/2"   5/8 yard

Backing   7 1/2 yards

Cutting instructions shown in red indicate the quantity of units are combined and cut in two or more different places to conserve fabric.

CUTTING

From Fabric I, cut: (ivory with pink print)
- Four 9 1/2" wide strips. From these, cut:
  * Fourteen - 5 1/2" x 9 1/2" (H5, H13, H21, H29, J5, J13, J21)
  * Twelve - 3 1/2" x 9 1/2" (H9, H20, H25, H36, J9, J20)
  * Sixteen - 1 1/2" x 9 1/2" (H11, H17, H27, H33, H37, J11, J17, J23)
  * Stack these cuts:

- * Twenty-eight - 1 1/2" x 2 3/4" (D6, E6)
  * Twenty-six - 1 1/2" x 2 1/2" (F5, F6, F8a, G5, G6,G8a)
- Two 7 1/2" wide strips. From these, cut:
  * Four - 7 1/2" x 8 3/4" (H4, J4)
  * Sixteen - 1 1/2" x 7 1/2" (F11, G11)
  * Six - 2 1/2" x 9 1/2" (H14, H30, J14) Stack this cut.
- Two 6 1/2" wide strips. From these, cut:
  * Two - 6 1/2" x 12 1/2" (J26)
  * Six - 3 1/2" x 6 1/2" (H18, H34, J18)
  * Sixteen - 1 1/2" x 6 1/2" (F10a, G10a)
  * Stack these cuts:
  * Two - 1 1/2" x 12 1/2" (H39)
  * Twenty - 1 1/2" squares (F1a, F8b, G1a, G8b)
- Three 5 1/2" wide strips. From these, cut:
  * Fourteen - 4 1/2" x 5 1/2" (H6, H12, H22, H28, J6, J12, J22)
  * Six - 3 1/2" x 5 1/2" (H8, H24, J8)
  * Fourteen - 1 1/2" x 5 1/2" (H7, H15, H23, H31, J7, J15, J25)
  * Stack this cut:
  * Twenty-two - 1 1/2" x 2 1/2" (add to 1 1/2" x 2 1/2" above)
- One 4 3/4" wide strip. From this, cut:
  * Twenty-eight - 1 1/2" x 4 3/4" (D6b, E6b)
- Four 4 1/2" wide strips. From these, cut:
  * Twenty-eight - 4 1/2" squares (D1, E1)
  * Eight - 4 1/4" squares (H3a, J3a)
  * Twelve - 1 1/2" squares (add to 1 1/2" sq. above) Stack this cut.
- One 4 1/4" wide strip. From this, cut:
  * Four - 3 3/4" x 4 1/4" (H1, J1)
  * Twenty-six - 2" squares (D3, E3) Stack this cut.
- Seven 3 1/2" wide strips. From these, cut:
  * Forty - 3 1/2" squares (F7a, G7a, H10a, H19a, H26a, H35a, J10a, J19a)
  * Twenty-eight - 2 1/2" x 3 1/2" (D5a, E5a)
  * Thirty-two - 1 1/2" x 3 1/2" (F2, F9, G2, G9)
  * Two - 2" squares (add to 2" squares above)
- Two 3" wide strips. From these, cut:
  * Twenty-eight - 3" squares (D5b, E5b)

From Fabric II, cut: (Kona cotton solid black)
- One 4 3/4" wide strip. From this, cut:
  * Four - 4 3/4" squares (A34)
  * Four - 3 3/4" x 4 3/4" (A46)
  * Four - 1 1/2" x 4 3/4" (A14)
- One 4 1/2" wide strip. From this, cut:
  * Two - 4 1/2" x 8 1/2" (C1)
  * Four - 3 1/2" x 4 1/4" (B38)
  * Four - 2 1/2" x 4" (A21)
- One 4" wide strip. From this, cut:

* Four - 4" squares (A44)
* Four - 3" x 4" (B16)
* Four - 2 1/2" x 3 3/4" (A35)
• Three 3 1/2" wide strips. From these, cut:
* Four - 3 1/2" x 5" (B49)
* Eight - 3 1/2" squares (B31a, C4a)
* Four - 3 1/4" x 3 1/2" (A16)
* Four - 1 3/4" x 3 1/2" (B14)
* Twenty-four - 1 1/2" x 3 1/2" (A8, B8)
* Four - 1 3/4" x 3 1/4" (A36)
* Four - 1 1/2" x 3 1/4" (A40)
* Four - 1 1/2" x 2 1/4" (B27)
• Four 3" wide strips. From these, cut:
* Two - 3" x 13 1/2" (C24)
* Four - 3" x 10 1/2" (C23)
* Four - 3" x 10" (Q1)
* Four - 3" squares (B31b)
* Four - 2 1/2" x 3" (B17)
* Ten - 1 1/2" x 3" (A33, A38, C8)
* Four - 2 3/4" squares (A45a)
* Four - 1 1/2" x 2 3/4" (A30)
• Sixteen 2 1/2" wide strips. Ten for straight-grain binding
From remaining six, cut:
* Two - 2 1/2" x 18 1/2" (C9)
* Four - 2 1/2" x 6" (B19)
* Four - 2 1/2" x 5 1/4" (A12)
* Twenty - 2 1/2" squares (A13, A31b, A45b, A46b, C13)
* Four - 2" x 2 1/2" (A28)
* Thirty-six - 1 1/2" x 2 1/2" (A10a, A20, A25, A39, B50, C6a, C11, C12, C21)
* Thirty-six - 1 1/4" x 2 1/2" (A7, B7, C19)
* Four - 2 1/4" squares (B20a)
• Five 2" wide strips. From these, cut:
* Four - 2" x 6 1/4" (B26)
* Four - 2" x 5 3/4" (B23)
* Four - 2" x 5 1/2" (C15)
* Four - 2" x 2 1/4" (B29)
* Twenty-eight - 2" squares (A31a, A42a, B26b, B35a, C3, C4b, C14a)
* Four - 1 3/4" x 2" (B25a)
* Sixteen - 1 3/4" squares (A42b, B15c, B20b, B24)
• Two 1 3/4" wide strips. From these, cut:
* Four - 1 3/4" x 3 3/4" (B21)
* Eight - 1 1/2" x 1 3/4" (A18a, B36)
* Forty - 1 1/4" x 1 3/4" (A5, A23, B5, C17)
• Eleven 1 1/2" wide strips. From these, cut:
* Two - 1 1/2" x 36 1/2" (Q2)
* Four - 1 1/2" x 12 1/2" (B13)
* Four - 1 1/2" x 11 1/2" (B12)
* Four - 1 1/2" x 8" (C22)
* Four - 1 1/2" x 7" (A43a)
* Eight - 1 1/2" x 5 1/2" (A33b, C7)
* 124 - 1 1/2" squares (A1b, A4b, A15a, A17b, A24a, A36b, A41a, A43b, B1b, B4b, B25b, B35b, B43a, B44, C7b, C10b, C14b, C20a)
• Three 1 1/4" wide strips. From these, cut:
* Ninety-two - 1 1/4" squares (A1c, A4a, A17c, A24b, B1c, B4a, B15b, B28a, B43b, C10c, C20b)

From Fabric III, cut: (dark green print)
• One 4 1/2" wide strip. From this, cut:

* Twelve - 3 1/2" x 4 1/2" (H10, H19, H26, H35, J10, J19)
• One 4 1/4" wide strip. From this, cut:
* Four - 4 1/4" x 5 1/4" (H3, J3)
* Four - 3 3/4" squares (A46a)
* Four - 1 1/4" x 3 3/4" (B22)
• One 3 1/4" wide strip. From this, cut:
* Four - 3 1/4" x 3 3/4" (A45)
* Four - 2" x 3" (B26a)
* Four - 1 3/4" x 2 1/2" (B25)
* Eight - 1 1/2" x 2 1/2" (A10, B41)
• One 2 1/2" wide strip. From this, cut:
* Eight - 2 1/2" squares (B20, C14)
* Four - 1 1/2" x 2 1/4" (A18)
* Four - 2" squares (C23a)
* Four - 1 1/2" x 1 3/4" (A30a)
• One 1 3/4" wide strip. From this, cut:
* Eight - 1 3/4" squares (A42b, A45c)
* Twelve - 1 1/2" x 2" (B47, C6, C16)
• Six 1 1/2" wide strips. From these, cut:
* Four - 1 1/2" x 4 3/4" (A15)
* Four - 1 1/2" x 3 3/4" (H2, J2)
* Thirty-six - 1 1/2" x 3 1/2" (A32a, B10, D5a, E5a)
* Forty-six - 1 1/2" squares (A33c, B42, D7, E7, H16, H32, H38, J16, J24)

From Fabric IV, cut: (medium green print)
• One 4 1/4" wide strip. From this, cut:
* Four - 4 1/4" squares (B40)
* Four - 1 3/4" x 4" (A36a)
* Four - 3 3/4" x 4 1/2" (B46)
• Seven 3 1/2" wide strips. From this, cut:
* Sixteen - 3 1/2" x 5 1/2" (F7, G7)
* Fifty-two - 2 1/2" x 3 1/2" (B43, F1, F3, F4, G1, G3, G4)
* Four - 2" x 3 1/2" (B48)
* Thirty-two - 1 1/2" x 3 1/2" (F8, F10, G8, G10)
* Four - 3" squares (B35)
• Two 3 1/4" wide strips. From these, cut:
* Eight - 3 1/4" x 6 1/2" (A41, A42)
* Four - 2 1/2" x 3" (A37)
  • Stack these cuts:
* Four - 1 1/2" x 4 3/4" (A43)
* Four - 1 1/2" x 3 3/4" (B52)
* Four - 1 1/2" x 2" (A39a)
• One 2 1/4" wide strip. From this, cut:
* Four - 2 1/4" squares (B51a)
* Four - 1 3/4" x 2" (B37)
* Seventeen - 1 1/2" squares (A13a, A20b, A38a, B17a, B19a, B41a, B42, B49a, C12a, F5a, F6a, F11a, G5a, G6a, G11a)
• Ten 1 1/2" wide strips. From these, cut:
* Two - 1 1/2" x 38 1/2" (Q3)
* Four - 1 1/2" x 29" (Q4) Piece together to = two 57 1/2" lengths.
* Twenty-four - 1 1/2" x 2 1/2" (B45, C13a, F9a, G9a)
* Eighty-seven - 1 1/2" squares (add to 1 1/2" sq. above)

From Fabric V, cut: (light green print)
• Seven 4 1/2" wide strips. From these, cut:
* Thirty-two - 4 1/2" squares (C1a, D1, E1)
* Thirty-two - 4" x 4 1/2" (B31, D5, E5)
* Four - 2" x 4 1/4" (A27)

- One 4" wide strip. From this, cut:
  * Twenty-eight - 1 1/2" x 4" (D6a, E6a)
- One 3 1/2" wide strip. From this, cut:
  * Four - 3 1/2" x 4" (C4)
  * Four - 3" x 3 1/2" (A31)
  * Four - 2" x 3 1/2" (B28)
- One 2 3/4" wide strip. From this, cut:
  * Four - 2 3/4" squares (B57a)
  * Four - 2 1/2" squares (C13)
  * Four - 1 1/2" x 2 1/2" (A32)
  * Four - 2" x 2 1/4" (B30)
- Four 2" wide strips. From these, cut:
  * Four - 2" x 6 1/4" (A29)
  * Thirty-two - 2" squares (C2, D4, E4)
  * Thirty-two - 1 1/2" x 2" (B32, D2, E2)
  * Four - 1 1/2" x 6 1/4" (A26)
- Six 1 1/2" wide strips. From these, cut:
  * Eight - 1 1/2" x 4 1/4" (A33a, C7a)
  * Eight - 1 1/2" x 3" (B27a, C6b)
  * 108 - 1 1/2" squares (A13b, A17d, A19a, A20a, A28a, A30b, B15d, B17b, B18a, B19b, B29a, B31c, B34a, B58a, C5, C6c, C10d, C12b, D5c, E5c)
- Two 1 1/4" wide strips. From these, cut:
  * Sixty-four - 1 1/4" squares (C3a, D3a, E3a)

From Fabric VI, cut: (medium gold print)
- Six 3" wide strips. From these, cut:
  * Two - 3" x 40 1/2" (Q5)
  * Four - 3" x 31 1/2" (Q6) Piece together to = two 62 1/2" lengths.
  * Four - 2 3/4" x 5 3/4" (B34)
  * Four - 2 3/4" x 4 1/4" (B39)
- Six 2 3/4" wide strips. From these, cut:
  * Four - 2 3/4" x 22 1/2" (B60)
  * Four - 2 3/4" x 20 1/4" (B59)
  * Four - 2 3/4" x 11 1/2" (B57)
  * Four - 2 3/4" squares (B58)
  * Eight - 2 1/2" x 2 3/4" (B51, B53)
- One 2 1/2" wide strip. From this, cut:
  * Sixteen - 1 1/2" x 2 1/2" (A9, B9)
  * Four - 2" squares (B48a)
  * Four - 1 3/4" x 2" (B33)
- Two 1 1/2" wide strip. From this, cut:
  * Eight - 1 1/2" x 5 1/2" (A11, B11)
  * Four - 1 1/2" squares (B56a)
  * Four - 1 1/4" x 2" (B54)
  * Four - 1 1/4" squares (B56B)

From Fabric VII, cut: (yellow print)
- Two 1 1/2" wide strips. From these, cut:
  * Thirty-two - 1 1/2" squares (A3, B3)

From Fabric VIII, cut: (dark barn red print)
- One 2" wide strip. From this, cut:
  * Four - 2" squares (B55)
  * Nineteen - 1 3/4" squares (A6, A22, B6, C18)
- One 1 3/4" wide strip. From this, cut:
  * Twenty-one - 1 3/4" squares (add to 1 3/4" sq. above)
- Three 1 1/2" wide strips. From these, cut:
  * Sixty-four - 1 1/2" squares (A1d, A2a, B1d, B2a)

From Fabric IX, cut: (dark salmon print)
- Four 3 1/2" wide strips. From these, cut:
  * Four - 3 1/2" x 4 1/2" (A17)
  * Four - 2 3/4" x 3 1/2" (B56)
  * Thirty-six - 2 1/2" x 3 1/2" (A4, B4, C20)
  * Thirty - 1 1/2" x 2 1/2" (A2, B2, B18, C13a)
- Three 2 1/2" wide strips. From these, cut:
  * Forty - 2 1/2" squares (A1a, B1a, B15a, C10a)
  * Ten - 1 1/2" x 2 1/2" (add to 1 1/2" x 2 1/2" above)

From Fabric X, cut: (light peach print)
- Five 3 1/2" wide strips. From these, cut:
  * Four - 3 1/2" x 4 3/4" (B15)
  * Thirty-six - 3 1/2" x 4 1/2" (A1, B1, C10)
  * Four - 2 1/2" x 3 1/2" (A24)
  * Four - 2 1/2" squares (A17a)
  * Four - 1 1/2" x 2 1/2" (A19)

BLOCKS A AND B ASSEMBLY

1. The illustration below is for Block A. This block forms the center of the quilt. The block is identical to the Apple Blossom block on pages 74-76, with the exception of the

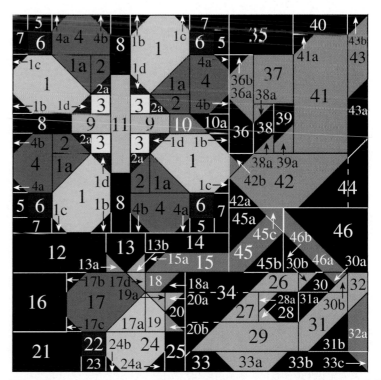

Block A. Make 4. When completed, block should measure 18 1/2" square.

size and color. For this quilt, the background color is black, and we doubled the size of the "A" block. Follow the cutting instructions given for this quilt and the measurements of the block above. Follow the *assembly instructions* beginning on page 75 to assemble Block A. Make four of the block as directed; then join them together to form the center of the quilt, as shown in the quilt diagram, and set aside.

2. To assemble Block B, refer to the block diagram below and use diagonal corner technique to make four of units 1, 2, and 4. Use this technique to make one of units 15, 17, 18, 19, 20, 25, 28, 29, 31, 34, 35, 41, 43, 48, 49, 51, 56, 57, and 58.

Use diagonal end technique to make one each of units 25, 26, and 27. Refer to diagram of Unit B42 below, and make

Making Unit B25

combined units 21/22, matching seams. Join Unit 23 to the right side of combined units 20-22. Join units 24 and 25; then add them to the bottom of combined units 20-23 as shown. Join the combined 18/19 units to the left side of the 20-25 units; then join the bud combined units to the top, matchig seams.

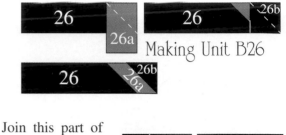

Making Unit B26

Join this part of the bud section to left side of the flower section.

6. For bottom leaf section and

Making Unit B27

frame, begin by joining units 29 and 30; then add Unit 28 to the side of these combined units. Join Unit 27 to the top; then join Unit 31 to right side as shown. Join Unit 26 across the top, matching seams. Join units 32 and 33; then add Unit 34 to right side. Join units 36 and 37; then add Unit 35 to left side of these combined units. Join units 38 and 39; then add diagonal corner Unit 40 to top of the 38/39 combined units as shown. Join combined 35-37 units to the top of 38-40 combined units. Join these units to the right side of combined 26-34 units as shown.

7. Join units 41 and 42. Join units 44 and 45; then add Unit 43 to top of these combined units.

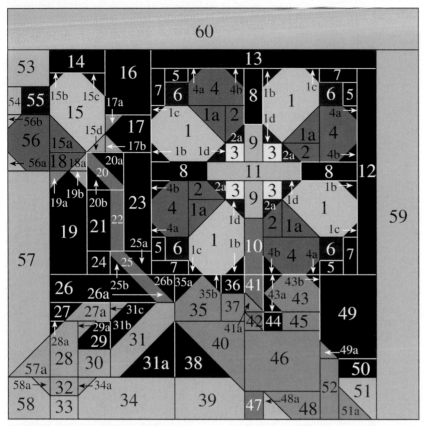

Block B. Make 4. When completed, block should measure 22 1/2"

the triangle-square as directed.

3. To assemble Block B, as all four petal sections of the flower are the same, refer to the top right petal to make this section. Join units 2 and 3; then add Unit 1 to top of the 2/3 combined units, matching seams. Join units 5 and 6; then add Unit 7 to the top of the 5/6 combined units, and Unit 4 to the bottom. Join these combined units to the right side of combined units 1-3 to complete the section. Make four.

4. To complete the large flower join units 8 and 9; then add a flower petal section to opposite sides of the 8/9 combined units, rotating the petals as shown. Join units 9 and 10; then add the two remaining petals to opposite sides of the 9/10 combined units, again rotating the petals as shown. Join units 8, 11, and 8 for flower center section. Join the two combined petal sections to top and bottom of the center section. Join Unit 12 to the right side of the flower; then add Unit 13 to the top.

5. For the bud section, join units 14 and 15. Join units 16 and 17; then join these two combined unit sections together as shown in the block diagram above. Join units 18 and 19. Join units 21 and 22; then add Unit 20 to the top of

Making Unit B42

Place 1 1/2" squares of fabrics III and IV right sides facing and raw edges matching. Stitch a diagonal down the center. Open out, trim seam, and press.

Add combined units 41 and 42 to left side; then join Unit 46 to the bottom of these combined units. Join units 47 and 48; then add them to the bottom of Unit 46. Join units 50 and 51; then join Unit 52 to left side of these combined units. Add Unit 49 to the top. Join these combined units to right side of other leaf and border combined units, matching seams to complete the bottom leaf section. Join this section to the bottom of the flower section, matchig seam; then add border Unit 59 to right side of the block.

8. To complete the bud and border left side, join units 54 and 55; then join Unit 53 to the top of these combined units and Unit 56 to the bottom. Join units 57 and 58; then add these combined units to bottom of Unit 56 to complete the bud and border left side. Join this to left side of block, matching the leaf seams; then join Unit 60 across the top to complete the block. Make four for quilt corners.

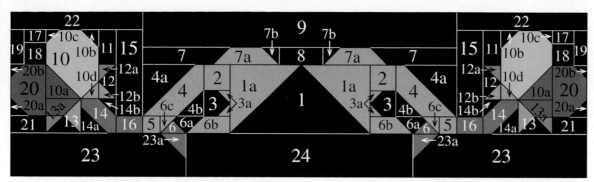

Block C. Make 2. When completed, block should measure 10" x 33 1/2"

BLOCK C ASSEMBLY

1. For Block C, use diagonal corner technique to make two of mirror image units 4, 10, 12, 14, 20, and 23. Use this technique to make two of unit 3, and one of Unit 1.

2. Use diagonal end technique to make two mirror image units 6 and 7. Refer to diagram below for making Unit

Making mirror image Unit C13

For mirror image Unit B13, place 2 1/2" squares of fabrics II and V right sides facing and raw edges matching. Stitch a diagonal down the center. Trim seam and press.

For mirror image Unit B13a, join 1 1/2" x 2 1/2" strips of fabrics IV and IX.

Place Unit 13 on top of Unit 13a, right sides facing and raw edges matching. Stitch a diagonal down center as shown below. Open out as shown. Trim seam and press. Refer to illustration on right for mirror image placement.

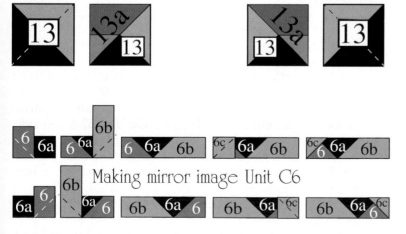

Making mirror image Unit C6

C13. Follow diagrams and instructions. Make two mirror image triangle-squares.

3. To assemble the block, refer frequently to the block diagram for correct placement of mirror image units. To begin, join units 2 and 3; then join mirror image Unit 4 to

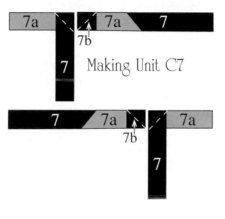

Making Unit C7

side of these combined units. Join Unit 5 and mirror image Unit 6 as shown; then add these combined units to the bottom of combined 2-4 units. Make two. Join the mirror image combined units to opposite sides of Unit 1. Join mirror image Unit 7, Unit 8, and remaining mirror image Unit 7 in a horizontal row; then add this row to the top of combined leaf units. Join Unit 9 across the top.

4. For the mirror image buds, join units 15 and 16. Join units 11 and 12; then add Unit 10 to the side of these combined units. Join units 13 and 14; then add them to the bottom of the 10-12 combined units. Join units 15 and 16 to the side as shown. Join units 17 and 18; then add Unit 19 to the side of the 17/18 combined units. Join Unit 20 to the bottom; then add Unit 21 to the bottom of Unit 20. Join these combined units to outside edge of the other combined bud units. Join Unit 22 across the top of the bud units. Join the mirror image buds to opposite ends of the leaf units as shown. Join mirror image Unit 23, Unit 24, and remaining mirror image Unit 23 in a horizontal row. Add to the bottom of the bud/leaf combination, matching seams to complete the block. Make two.

BLOCKS D & E ASSEMBLY

1. Refer to block diagrams on page 108. The two blocks are the same except that they are mirror images. Assembly instructions are given for Block D. Refer frequently to the block diagrams for correct placement of the mirror image units.

2. Use diagonal corner technique to make one each of units 3 and mirror image Unit 5. Use diagonal end technique to make one of mirror image Unit 6. Refer to

Making units D1, and E1.

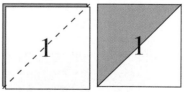

Place 4 1/2" squares of fabrics I and V right sides facing and raw edges matching. Stitch a diagonal seam down the center. Trim seam, and press.

107

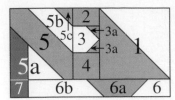

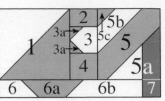

Block D. Make 14 When block is completed, it should measure 5 1/2"" x 9 1/2"

Block E. Make 14 When block is completed, it should measure 5 1/2" x 9 1/2"

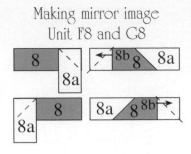

Making mirror image Unit F8 and G8

2. Use diagonal corner technique to make one of units 1, 5, 6, and 7. Use diagonal end technique to make one of units 8, 9, and 10 as shown in diagrams below.

3. To assemble the block, begin by joining units 2 and 3; then add Unit 1 to bottom of combined units. Join units 6, 5, and 4 in a vertical row;

the diagram on page 107 for making triangle-square Unit 1.

3. To assemble the leaves, begin by joining units 2, 3 and 4 in a vertical row. Join Unit 1 to the right side of this row. Refer to

Making mirror image Unit D5 and E5

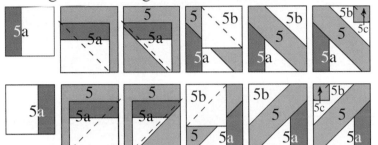

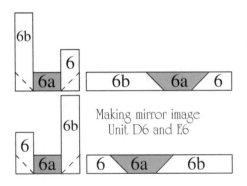

Making mirror image Unit D6 and E6

the diagram above for making mirror image Unit 5. Join this unit to combined units 1-4 as shown. Join mirror image Unit 6 and Unit 7. Add this row to bottom of leaf, matching the stem seam to complete the blocks. Make fourteen of each block.

then add them to left side of combined units 1-3. Join Unit 7 to side of these combined units as shown. Join units 8 and 9; then add them to the top of the leaf, matching seams. Join Unit 10 to the bottom; then add Unit 11 to right side of

Making mirror image Unit F9 and G9

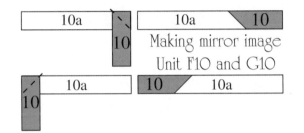

Making mirror image Unit F10 and G10

the combined leaf units to complete the block. Make ten of Block F, and six of Block G.

BLOCKS H AND J ASSEMBLY

1. Blocks H and J comprise the leaf borders of the quilt and are a combination of blocks D, E, F, and G. Refer to the diagrams of each border block on the following page.

2. For Block H, use diagonal corner technique to make one of units 3, 10, 19, 26, and 35.

3. To assemble this border block, begin by joining units 1 and 2; then join Unit 3 to bottom of the 1/2 combined units. Join Block F as shown to left side, and Unit 4 to right side. Join Unit 5, Block D, and Unit 6 in a row. Join this row to the bottom of the Block F row. Join units 7, Block E, and Unit 8. Join units 9 and 10. Join the 9/10 combined units to the bottom of combined Block E section, matching stem seam. Join Unit 11 to top of Block G as shown. Add these combined units to right side of the Block E combined units; then join this section to bottom of the combined Block F and Block D section.

4. Join Unit 12, Block E, and Unit 13; then add these combined Block E units to bottom of other combined units. Join Unit 14 to top of Block F as shown. Join Unit 15 to right side of Block D. Join units 16 and 17; then add the 16/17 combined units to the bottom of the Block D units matching stem seam. Join Unit 18 to left side of the Block D combined units. Join units 19 and 20; then add these combined units to bottom of the combined Block D units.

BLOCKS F AND G ASSEMBLY

1. Refer to block diagrams below. The two blocks are the same except that they are mirror images. Assembly instructions are given for Block F. Refer frequently to the block diagrams for correct placement of the mirror image units.

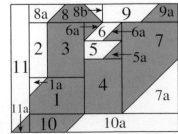

Block F. Make 10. When block is completed, it should measure 7 1/2" x 9 1/2"

Block G. Make 6. When block is completed, it should measure 7 1/2" x 9 1/2"

108

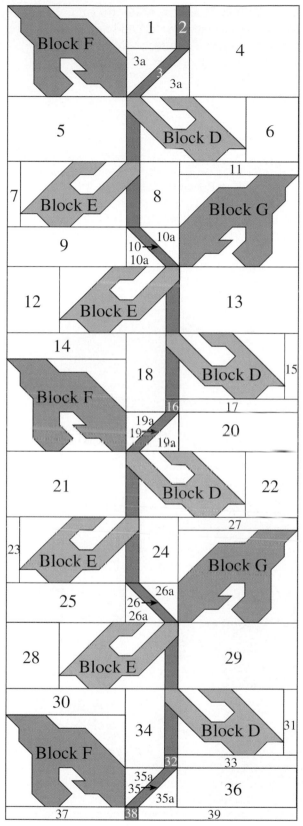

Block H. Make 2. Side leaf borders. When completed, this section should measure 22 1/2"x 62 1/2"

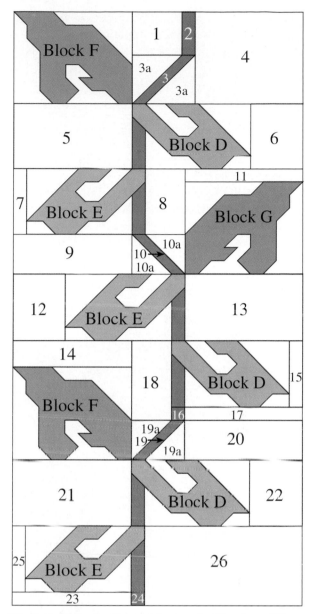

Block J. Make 2. Top and bottom leaf borders. When completed, this section should measure 22 1/2" x 45 1/2"

Join combined Unit 14 and Block F to left side of the combined Block D units. Join this section to bottom of other combined leaf section, matching stem seam. Join unit 21, Block D, and Unit 22. Add this row to bottom of other combined leaf section.

5. Join units 23, Block E, and Unit 24. Join units 25 and

26. Add these combined units to bottom of the Block F combined units, once again matching stem seam. Join Unit 27 and Block G. Add this combination to right side of combined Block E section; then join to bottom of other leaf section, matching stem seam. Join Unit 28, Block E, and Unit 29 in a row. Join this row to bottom of other leaves. Join Unit 30 and Block F. Join Unit 31 to right side of Block D. Join units 32 and 33; then add them to bottom of Block D/Unit 31 combination, matching stem seam. Join Unit 34 to left side of these combined units. Join units 35 and 36. Add them to the bottom of the Block combination, once again matching stem seam. Join combined Unit 30/Block F to left side of the Block D combination. Join units 37, 38, and 39 and add them to bottom of this final leaf block combination. Join this section to bottom of other leaves to complete the Block H border. Make two.

6. To make Block J border, use diagonal corner technique to make one each of units 3, 10, and 19. To assemble this leaf border, follow assembly instructions in steps 3 and 4 for Block H, as Block J border is the same until the final section. To complete the final section, join Unit 25 and Block E. Join units 23 and 24. Add these combined units to bottom of Unit 25/Block E combination, matching stem seams. Join Unit 26 to right side; then add this final Block E leaf combination to the bottom of the other combined leaf section to complete the Block J border. Make two.

QUILT TOP ASSEMBLY

1. Refer to the diagram on the following page to assemble the quilt top. Join Unit Q2 to opposite sides of the previously joined Block A's. Join Unit Q1 to opposite sides of Block C. Join the Block C sections to top and bottom of center section, referring to diagram for correct positioning of Block C. Join Unit Q3 to top and bottom of center section. Join Unit Q4 to opposite long sides of center section. Join Unit Q5 to top and bottom of center section; then add pieced border Unit Q6 to opposite sides. Refer to quilt diagram for correct placement of borders and corners. Join Block J border to top and bottom of quilt top. Make sure that leaves and stem are placed exactly as the diagram shows. The corner blocks are rotated as they are joined, so that the border stem goes over one side of the corner and goes under the other side of the corner. Join the corners to short ends of Block H borders; then add them to opposite sides of the quilt, matching the stems and the corners.

2. Refer to page 7 for making straight-grain, french fold binding. Join the ten 2 1/2" wide strips of Fabric II for the binding, and bind your quilt.

Block J

Block G

Block D

Block D

Block F

Block E

Block E

Block F

Block F

Block E

Block B

Block B

5   3

4

1   Block C   1

6   2

When completed, this center section should measure 45 1/2" x 62 1/2"

Block F

Block D

Block E

Block D

Block A

Block A

Block G

Block E

Block H

Block F

Block A

Block A

Block F

Block E

Block D

Block D

Block H

Block E

Block E

Block G

Block G

Block D

Block F

Block E

1   Block C   1

Block E

Block D

Block F

6   2   4

5   3

Block B

Block J

Block B

Block E

Block F

Block E

Block F

Block D

Block E

Block D

Block D

Block G

111

Well Dearie, this sure beats the way I had to make them!

Visit Zelda at: http://www.zeldawisdom.com